SCOTS

THE LANGUAGE OF THE PEOPLE

CREDITS

Carl MacDougall and Black & White Publishing
would like to thank the following:

W. L. Lorimer Memorial Trust for use of 'John 2: 1–9'
by William Laughton Lorimer

The Trustees of the National Library of Scotland
for use of 'The Halted Moment' by William Soutar

John McLellan for use of 'The Ringlets' by Robert McLellan

The Saltire Society for use of 'Lesson' by Robert Garioch

Felicity Henderson for the use of 'The Freedom Come-All-Ye'
by Hamish Henderson

Sheila Douglas for use of 'The King o the Black Art' by John Stewart

Faber & Faber for use of 'The Blue Jacket' by Marion Angus

Carcanet Press for the use of 'Wheesht Wheesht' by Hugh MacDiarmid
and 'The Chaffinch Map of Scotland' by Edwin Morgan

Adam McNaughtan for use of 'The Scottish Song' by Adam McNaughtan

Tom Leonard for use of 'The Voyeur' by Tom Leonard from *Intimate
Voices: Poems 1965–1983*, Etruscan Books 2003

Bloodaxe Books for use of 'Den of the Old Men' by Kathleen Jamie
from *Mr & Mrs Scotland are Dead: Selected Poems 1980–1994*, Bloodaxe
Books, 2002

SCOTS

THE LANGUAGE OF THE PEOPLE

CARL MACDOUGALL

BLACK & WHITE PUBLISHING

First published 2006
by Black & White Publishing Ltd
99 Giles Street, Edinburgh, EH6 6BZ

ISBN 13 978 1 84502 084 2
ISBN 10 1 84502 084 7

Based on the television series
produced for BBC Scotland by

hopscotch films

Design by Tilley&Tilley

Typeset by RefineCatch Limited, Bungay, Suffolk

Printed and bound by
Creative Print and Design Group Ltd

: CONTENTS

CONTENTS CONTINUED

: ACKNOWLEDGEMENTS

In making *SCOTS: The Language of the People*, I am delighted to acknowledge the helpful advice and commitment of executive producers John Archer and Ewan Angus (for the BBC), producer Beatrix Alexander, assistant producer Graeme Burnet and series researcher Fiona Gay. My warmest thanks are due for the helpful care and concern of my companions on the road, director Paul Murton, the film crew of Neville Kidd, Douglas Kerr and Francis MacNeil and those who managed the production back in the office, Fiona Clark and Claire Mackenzie.

PREFACE

A LANGUAGE IS A DIALECT WITH AN ARMY AND A NAVY.
Max Weinreich, *YIVO Bletter*, January–February 1945

SCOTS: The Language of the People is a four part television series, made by Hopscotch Films for BBC Scotland. It stemmed from the premise that Scots is a language and that an understanding of this language is crucial to an understanding of the people of Scotland.

Scots was the language of the Scottish court, the government and judiciary. It was the vehicle used by urbane and educated men to write sophisticated, philosophical literature but more importantly it carried the voice of the ordinary Scot and when others deserted the language this was where it was preserved, in speech and in song; though, by the twentieth century, distinctions began to appear. The first edition of the *Scottish National Dictionary* described Glasgow speech as 'hopelessly corrupt'.

The Reformation of 1560 and the fact that the Bible was not translated into Scots saw the beginning of the marginalisation. The Union of the Crowns in 1603 and the removal of the court further reduced Scots' status, to the extent that, when the parliaments were united in 1707, Scots no longer had a place in official discourse and it became a predominantly oral language.

The advent of the Edinburgh Enlightenment saw the educated classes' struggle to rid themselves of 'Scotticisms' and even the Scots poetry revival initiated by Ramsay and Fergusson and championed by Burns did little to question the assumption that Scots had become the language of the heart but not of the head. Dictionaries of Scotticisms were published, Scottish MPs at Westminster took elocution lessons and Scots was seen as corrupt, uncouth and underdeveloped.

The project to produce a unified British culture and identity was well underway and the role of language was crucial: 'In garb, in manners, in government, we are the same; and if the same language were spoken on both sides of the Tweed… no striking mark of distinction would remain between the sons of England and Caledonia,' Sir John Sinclair commented in his *Observations on the Scottish Dialect* written in 1782. Four years later Burns produced his Kilmarnock edition of *Poems Chiefly in the Scottish Dialect* with an English introduction, the language he used for his correspondence. By this time English was seen as the language of the intellect, an idea that was reinforced during the nineteenth century and is still around today when Scots at worst is used for humour, song and lyric poetry and at best tilts towards a literary language. Fiction writers may have used Scots dialogue but, until Lewis Grassic Gibbon unified thought, narrative and speech, the body of the text was in English. And, despite the efforts of Hugh MacDiarmid and the writers who followed his lead, successive generations of schoolteachers told their charges to 'speak properly'. They did not obliterate the language but they certainly reduced its status, ensuring there was a language for the playground and another for the classroom. This has given us what at best can be described as an ambivalent attitude towards our language.

At the heart of the matter is national self-belief. We all know Scots but rarely speak it and respond most directly to when it's sung rather than spoken, giving Edwin Muir's assertion that English is a language of the intellect and Scots a language of the heart a new and distinctive relevance which has never been more apposite. Perhaps we'll speak Scots when we hear it being used as the language of authority, when we believe in it as a means of national self-expression.

But, in the five years since devolution, the issue of a Scottish national identity has been increasingly debated and, where there is a question of national identity, the issue of language can never be far away. This was the case with Catalonia, is at the heart of the Basque and Irish insurrections, ran through the divisions in the former Yugoslavia and propels the European Union to provide aid to sustain and develop minority languages. Gaelic already benefits from this and the signs are its language base is increasing, especially in the playground. Scots could similarly benefit if a reasonable case was made.

This anthology, covers more than 800 years from the anonymous thirteenth-century makars to Edwin Morgan, Tom Leonard, Adam McNaughtan and Kathleen Jamie. Our greatest writers, William Dunbar, Robert Burns, James Hogg, Sir Walter Scott, Robert Louis Stevenson and Hugh MacDiarmid, are here. Extracts from the great epic poems on Bruce and Wallace, the works of Gavin Douglas, Robert Henryson and Sir David Lyndsay sit with anonymous ballad makers and unknown writers whose work appeared in nineteenth-century newspapers and magazines. The great prose pieces are included, from the sixteenth-century curiosities to stories by John Galt, Lewis Grassic Gibbon and Robert McLellan. Our finest poets and songwriters such as Allan Ramsay, Hamish Henderson and Carolina Oliphant, rub shoulders with Marion Angus and Robert Fergusson, Robert Tannahill, Neil Munro, Robert Garioch and William Soutar.

This is a small selection, an introduction which hopes to show how the language developed and survived and how its present state is healthier than ever. It is the birthright of every Scot and a wonderful legacy which has created and maintained our identity in the face of indifference and whose survival depends on its use.

: For Paul

ANON.

Scots was scarcely recorded prior to the fourteenth century and anthologies began with this fragment because it was thought to be the earliest piece of Scottish poetry and may well be among the oldest in recognisable Scots. Material from before this time was written in Latin, Welsh, Gaelic, Old English, Old French and Norse and was not readily available in translation. Recent publications have sought to restore 800 years of Scotland's literary heritage.

'Scotland after Alexander' is included in Andrew of Wyntoun's *Origynale Chronykil of Scotland*, transcribed in 1424. It was sung after the death of Alexander III, who was killed in 1286 when he was thrown from his horse near Kinghorn in Fife. His death resulted in Edward I's troops occupying every castle from Roxburgh to Elgin and removing the Stone of Scone.

:SCOTLAND AFTER ALEXANDER

Qwhen Alexander our kynge was dede,
    That Scotlande lede in lauche[1] and le,[2]
Away was sons[3] of alle and brede,
    Off wyne and wax, of gamyn[4] and gle.[5]
Our golde was changit in to lede.
    Christ, borne in virgynyte,
Succoure Scotlande, and ramede,[6]
    That stade[7] is in perplexite.

[1] law   [2] protection   [3] abundance, plenty   [4] sport
[5] enjoyment   [6] remedy, cure   [7] stood

JOHN BARBOUR   ⋮

John Barbour (c.1320–95) first appears in records in 1357 as Aberdeen's archdeacon. He is known to have studied in Oxford and Paris and was an auditor for King Robert II's household when he wrote *The Bruce*.

The epic is in twenty parts, culminating in the Battle of Bannockburn, and is thought to have been written around 1375. It is assumed that a gift of £10 Barbour received in 1377 was in recognition of his poem and that an awareness of his patron led to its uncomplicated heroic approach; but his details and character studies give a portrait of the people and their times that would otherwise be lost, as well as a vivid account of the two-day battle.

'The Bruce' is the earliest surviving long poem in Scots and is also quoted in Wyntoun's *Chronykil*.

: THE BRUCE

Freedom

A! Fredome is a noble thing!
Fredome maiss[1] man to have liking:
Fredome all solace to man givis:
He livis at ease that freely livis!
A noble heart may have nane ease,
Na ellis nocht[2] that may him please,
Gif fredome failye; for free liking
Is yearnit[3] owre all other thing.
Na he, that ay has livit free,
May nocht knaw weill the propertie,
The anger, na the wrechit doom,
That is couplit to foul thralldom.
Bot gif he had assayit[4] it,
Than all perquer[5] he suld it wit;
And suld think fredome mair to prize
Than all the gold in warld that is.

[1] makes   [2] not anything else   [3] desired   [4] tried
[5] by heart

BLIND HARRY ⋮

Harry's epic was written more than 150 years after Wallace's death and appears to have been printed around 1508 by Scotland's first printers, Chepman & Myllar, from their premises in the Cowgate, Edinburgh. At least six editions appeared in the seventeenth century but the version that found its way into most Scottish homes was William Hamilton of Gilbertfield's adaptation into contemporary Scots, published in 1722. This was the version Robert Burns, Lord Byron, John Keats and William Wordsworth admired.

For all that it has lively, vivid battle scenes and recounts political and social details, its origins and continuing popularity speak for the patriotism of the times, immortalising Wallace as a common man and martyr. The appeal is patriotic rather than literary or historical.

Of Blind Harry (1450–93) we know next to nothing. He appears to have been from the Lothians and, according to the accounts of the Lord High Treasurer, was among the harpers and singers who received gifts from James IV. Dunbar, in his 'Lament for the Makaris', enters him in the middle of his roughly chronological list of deceased poets.

: THE WALLACE

A DESCRIPTION OF WALLACE

Wallace stature of greatness, and of hicht,
Was jugit thus, be discretioun of richt,
That saw him baith dissembill[1] and in weid;[2]
Nine quarteris large he was in lenth indeed;
Thrid part lenth in shouldris braid was he,
Richt seemly, strang, and lusty for to see;
His limbis great, with stalwart pace and sound,
His browis hard, his armes great and round;
His handis made richt like till a pawmer,[3]
Of manlike mak, with nailes great and clear;
Proportionit lang and fair was his visage;
Richt sad of speech, and able in courage;
Braid breist and heich, with sturdy crag and great;
His lippis round, his nose was square and great;
Bowand broun hairit, on browis and breeis licht,
Clear aspre[4] een, like diamondis bricht.
Under the chin, on the left side, was seen,
Be hurt, a wain; his colour was sanguine.
Woundis he had in mony divers place,
Bot fair and well keepit was his face.
Of riches he keepit no proper thing;
Gave as he wan, like Alexander the king.
In time of peace, meek as a maid was he;
Whar weir approachit the right Ector was he.
To Scottis men a great credence he gave;
Bot knawin enemies they couth him nocht dissave.

---

[1] naked   [2] dressed   [3] palm tree   [4] sharp

ROBERT HENRYSON   :

It seems reasonable to assume that the Robertus Henrisone found in the Glasgow University records for 1462 is the man William Dunbar refers to in the 'Lament for the Makars'. Dunbar associates Henryson with Fife and the earliest extant edition of Henryson's rendering of Aesop's *Fables* (*The Morall Fabillis of Esope the Phrygian*, published in 1570) describes Henryson as a 'Scholemaister of Dunfermeling'.

The school was linked to the neighbouring Benedictine Abbey and this has given rise to the speculation that Henryson (c.1425–c.1505) worked as their legal representative, since a notary of the same name was active in Dunfermline in 1478. His poetry certainly supports the image of him as both a teacher and a lawyer. His versions of the *Fables* have a powerful moral resolve and a detailed grasp of legal mechanisms. Henryson's major poems, besides the *Fables*, include his masterpiece, 'The Testament of Cresseid', where he adds a darker, more abrupt sequel to Chaucer's 'Troilus and Criseyde'.

: THE ABBEY WALK

Alone as I went up and doun,
In ane abbey was fair to see,
Thinkand what consolations
Was best into adversitie,
On case[1] I kest on side mine ee,
And saw this written upon a wall:
'Of what estate, man, that thou be,
Obey, and thank thy God of [2] all.

'Thy kingdom and thy great empire,
Thy royalty, nor rich array,
Sall nocht endure at thy desire,
But as the wind will wend away;
Thy gold and all thy gudis gay,
When fortune list will fra thee fall;
Sen thou sic samples sees ilk day,
Obey, and thank thy God of all.

'Job was maist rich in Writ we find,
Tobie[3] maist full of cheritie:
Job wox puir, and Tobie blind,
Baith temptit with adversitie.
Sen blindness was infirmitie,
And poverty was natural,
Therefore richt patiently baith he and he[4]
Obeyit and thankit God of all.

---

[1] by chance   [2] for   [3] Tobit   [4] the one and the other

'Though thou be blind, or have ane halt,
Or in thy face deformit ill,
Sa it come nocht, through thy default,
Na man suld thee repreif by skill[5]
Blame nocht thy Lord, sa is his will;
Spurn nocht thy foot aganis the wall;
But with meek heart and prayer still
Obey, and thank thy God of all.

'God of his justice mon correct,
And of his mercy pity haif;
He is ane Judge to nane suspect.
To punish sinful man and saif.
Though thou be lord attour the laif [6]
And efterward made bound and thrall,
Ane puir beggar, with scrip and staff,
Obey, and thank thy God of all.

'This changing and great variance
Of erdly[7] statis up and doun
Is nocht but casualty and chance,
As some men sayis, without reasoun,
But by the great provisioun
Of God above that rule thee sall;
Therefore ever thou mak thee boun[8]
To obey, and thank thy God of all.

[5] with reason   [6] above the rest   [7] earthly   [8] ready

'In wealth be meek, heich[9] nocht thy self;
Be glad in woeful povertie;
Thy power and thy warldis pelf
Is nocht but very Vanitie.
Remember Him that deit on tree,
For thy sake tastit the bitter gall;
Wha heis law hairtis and lawis hie[10]
Obey and thank thy God of all.

[9] exalt   [10] who raises the low and humbles the high

WILLIAM DUNBAR   :

'The Flyting of Dunbar and Kennedy' appears to offer some information about William Dunbar's background, character and appearance but it is difficult to know what truth lies beneath the insults. If we are to believe Maister Kennedy, Dunbar was, among other things, a filthy dwarf with dietary problems. What Dunbar called Kennedy marks him as the originator of a tradition still very much alive in Scottish writing – the ability to move between registers and styles in a voice that is distinctively Scottish and uses the full range of language for literary effect.

A flyting was a versified quarrel which poets often extemporised and, though the tone is fractious, there must have been a sense of playing to the gallery. In his best known poem, 'The Lament for the Makars', Dunbar writes:

> Gud Maister Walter Kennedy
> In poynt of deid lyis verily –
> Gret routh it wer that so suld be;
> *Timor mortis conturbat me.*

Not much is known about William Dunbar (c.1460–c.1513). It is assumed he was from the Lothians and spent many years in Edinburgh. He may have been a Franciscan monk and court poet to James IV. He took a master's degree at St Andrews in 1479 and by 1504 had taken priest's orders. Between 1500 and 1513 he was a member of James IV's household. The last mention of Dunbar is the court records for May 1513, a few months before the Battle of Flodden.

Dunbar is the most versatile and talented of the late medieval poets. He could write on almost any subject and experimented with many genres. The brevity and compression of his verse can disguise an outrageous humorous streak and dark melancholy. Despite the lapse of five centuries, the force of his personality comes through to move, shock and entertain. It is not surprising that, when Hugh MacDiarmid sought a new poetic model that was tough, witty and unsentimental, he recommended Dunbar rather than Burns.

:MEDITATION IN WINTER

In to thir dark and drublie[1] dayis,
When sable all the heavens arrayis,
    With misty vapouris, cloudis and skyis,[2]
    Nature all courage me denies
Of sangis ballattis and of playis.

When that the nicht does lengthen houris,
With wind, with hail, with heavy shouris,
    My dule spreit dois lurk for schoir,[3]
    My heart for languor dois forloir,[4]
For lack of simmer with his flouris.

I wake, I turn, sleep may I nocht,
I vexit am with heavy thocht;
    This warld all owre I cast about,
    And aye the mair I am in dout,
The mair that I remeid have socht.

I am assayit on every side,
Despair sayis aye, 'In time provide,
    And get some thing whereon to leif,[5]
    Or with great trouble and mischief,
Thou sall into this court abide.

Then Patience says, 'Be nocht aghast:
Hald Hope and Truth within thee fast;
    And lat Fortune wirk furth her rage,
    Whan that no reasoun may assuage,
Till that her glass be run and past.

---

[1] dripping   [2] shadows   [3] hide for fear
[4] is utterly lost   [5] live

And Prudence in my ear sayis aye,
'Why wald thou hald that will away?[6]
    Or crave that thou may have mo space,
    Thou tending to ane other place,
A journey going every day?'

And than sayis Age, 'My friend, come near,
And be nocht strange, I thee requeir:
    Come, brother, by the hand me tak,
    Remember thou has compt to mak
Of all thy time thou spendit here.'

Syne Deid castis up his yettis wide,
Saying, 'Thir open sall ye abide;
    Albeit that thou were never sa stout,
    Under this lintel sall thou lout:[7]
There is nane other way beside.'

For fear of this all day I droop;
No gold in kist, nor wine in cup
    No ladeis beauty, nor lovis bliss
    May lat me to remember[8] this:
How glad that ever I dine or sup.

Yet, when the nicht beginnis to short,
It dois my spreit some pairt confort,
    Of thocht oppressit with the shouris.
    Come, lusty summer! with thy flouris;
That I may live in some disport.

---

[6] why would you keep what will disappear?   [7] stoop
[8] prevent my remembering

: *Then Patience says, 'Be nocht aghast:*
Hald Hope and Truth within thee fast;

GAVIN DOUGLAS

Gavin Douglas (c.1476–1522) graduated from St Andrews University in 1494. His father was Archibald Douglas, fifth Earl of Angus, and, like others from his background, he may have studied in Paris.

He was appointed provost of the Collegiate Church of St Giles, Edinburgh, in 1503 and became Bishop of Dunkeld in 1516. His political wranglings and obvious preferences for family members brought him into conflict with the regent, the Duke of Albany. He eventually fled to England and died in London.

Douglas is best known for his translation of Virgil's *Aeneid*, the first complete translation of a classical text in Britain, begun early in 1512 and finished on 22 July 1513, less than two months before Flodden.

His best work is in the prologues he wrote to preface each book. His depictions of a frosty December or a May morning include exact, often sumptuous descriptions of the natural world and convey something of an energetic, contrary and confrontational personality. He discusses the problems of translation, confessing that, where Scots is scant or inexact, he adapted Latin and French, while defending his use of Scots as a medium of learning, insisting his language is Scots, rather than the 'Inglis' used by other writers.

: AN EVENING AND MORNING IN JUNE

(i)

The licht begouth to quenschyng out and fail,
The day to dirken, decline, and devail;[1]
The gummis[2] risis, doun fallis the donk rime,[3]
Baith here and there skuggis[4] and shadows dim;
Up goes the bak with her peelit leddren flicht,[5]
The larkis descendis from the skyis hicht,
Singand her compline sang eftir her guise,
To tak her rest, at matin hour to rise:
Out owre the swyre[6] swimmis the soppis of mist,
The nicht furthspread her cloak with sable lyst;[7]
That all the beauty of the fructuous field
Was with the earthis umbrage[8] clean owreheild:[9]
Baith man and beast, firth, flood, and woodis wild
Involvit in the shadows war insylde:[10]
Still war the fowlis fleis[11] in the air
All store[12] and cattle sesit[13] in their lair;
All creature where so them likis best
Bownis[14] to tak the halesome nichtis rest,
Eftir the dayis labour and the heat:
Close waren[15] all and at their soft quiet,
But steerage[16] or removing, he or she,
Outhir beast, bird, fish, fowl by land or sea.

---

[1] sink [2] vapours [3] mist [4] shades
[5] bat flying with wings of peeled leather
[6] valley [7] border [8] shadow
[9] covered over [10] enfolded [11] birds that fly [12] stock
[13] tethered [14] prepares [15] were [16] movement

And shortly every thing that doth repair
In firth or field, flood, forest, earth or air,
Or in the scroggis,[17] or in the buskis ronk,[18]
Lakis, maressis,[19] or their poolis donk,[20]
Astablit[21] lyggis still to sleep and restis
Be[22] the small birdis sittand on their nestis,
The little midges and the urisome fleis,[23]
As weel the wild as the tame bestial,
And every other thingis great and small,—
Out tak[24] the merry nichtingale Philomene,
That on the thorn sat singand fro the spleen.
Whais mirthful nottis langand[25] for to hear,
Until ane garth under ane green laurere[26]
I walk anon, and in a siege[27] doun sat
Now musing upon this, and now on that.
I see the Pole, and eek the Ursas bricht
And hornyt Lucine castand bot dim licht,
Because the summer skyës shane so clear . . . .

(ii)

Yonder doun dwynis[28] the even sky away,
And up springis the bricht dawning of the day
In till ane other place, not fer in sunder,
That to behald was plesance, and half wonder.
Furth quenching gan the sternes ane be ane
That now is left bot Lucifer alane.
And furthermore, to blazon this new day,
Wha micht discryve the birdis blissful lay?
Belyve[29] on wing the busy lark upsprang
To salus the blythe morrow with her sang;
Soon owre the fieldis shinis the licht clere,
Welcome to pilgrim baith and labourere.

[17] thickets   [18] rank   [19] marshes   [20] dank
[21] settled   [22] from   [23] troublesome flies
[24] except   [25] longing   [26] laurel   [27] seat
[28] sinks   [29] straightway

Tyte[30] on his hindis[31] gaif the grieve ane cry,
'Awake! On foot! Go till our husbandry!'
And the herd callis furth upon his page
To drive the cattle to their pasturage;
The hindis wife clepis[32] up Katherine and Jill;
'Yea, dame,' said they, God wat, with ane good will.
The dewy green powderit with daisies gay
Shew on the sward ane colour dapple gray;
The misty vapours springand up full sweet
Maist comfortable to glaid all mannis sprete;
Thereto thir birdis singis in their shawis[33]
As menstralis playis 'The jolly day now dawis'.
                    (Prologue to the Thirteenth Book of *The Aeneid*, II. 163–86.)

[30] quickly   [31] hinds   [32] calls   [33] copses

THE BANNATYNE MANUSCRIPT

'Bannatyne's Manuscript is in a folio form, containing upwards of eight hundred pages, very neatly and closely written and designed, as has been supposed, to be sent to the press,' wrote Sir Walter Scott in a memoir printed by the Bannatyne Club in 1829. 'The labour of compiling so rich a collection was undertaken by the author during the time of pestilence, in the year 1568, when the dread of infection compelled men to forsake their usual employments . . .

'In this dreadful period, when hundreds, finding themselves surrounded by danger and death, renounced all care save that of selfish precaution for their own safety, and all thoughts save apprehensions of infection, George Bannatyne had the courageous energy to form and execute the plan of saving the literature of a whole nation; and, undisturbed by the universal mourning for the dead, and general fears of the living, to devote himself to the task of collecting and recording the triumphs of human genius;–thus, amid the wreck of all that was mortal, employing himself in preserving the lays by which immortality is at once given to others, and obtained for the writer himself.'

George Bannatyne (1545–1608) was born in Newtyle, Forfar. He was an Edinburgh merchant who is thought to have compiled his manuscript in Forfar in 1568, when plague ravaged the capital. The Bannatyne Manuscript is the chief repository of Middle Scots poetry, especially for the texts of Robert Henryson, William Dunbar, David Lyndsay and Alexander Scott. Allan Ramsay printed some in *Ever Green* in 1724 and Lord Hailes also used Bannatyne's collection in his *Ancient Scottish Poems*, which was published in 1770.

The Bannatyne Club was formed in Edinburgh in 1823 to publish historical and literary material from Scottish sources.

:TWO POEMS

How the first heilandman of God was maid of ane horss turd in Argylle, as is said

God and Sanct Petir was gangand be the way[1]
Heiche up in Ardgyle quhair thair gait[2] lay;
Sanct Petir said to God in a sport word,
'Can ye not mak a heilandman of this horss turd?'
God turnd owre the horss turd with his pykit staff,[3]
And up start a heilandman blak as ony draff.[4]
Quod god to the heilandman, 'Quhair wilt thow now?'
'I will doun in the lawland, Lord, and thair steill a kow.'
'And thow steill a cow, carle,[5] thair thay will hang thee.'
'Quattrack,[6] Lord, of that? For anis mon I die.'
God than he lewch and owre the dyk lap,[7]
And owt of his scheith his gully owtgatt.[8]
Sanct Petir socht this gully fast up and doun,
Yit cowld not find it in all that braid[9] roun.
'Now,' quo God, 'Heir a marvell. How can this be,
That I sowld want my gully, and we heir bot three?'
'Humff!' quo the heilandman, and turnd him abowt,
And at his plaid nuk the gully fell owt.
'Fy!' quo Sanct Petir, 'Thow will nevir do weill,
And thow bot new maid, sa sone gais to steill!'
'Umff!' quo the heilandman, and swere be yon kirk,
'Sa lang as I may geir gett to steill, will I nevir wirk.'

[1] along the way   [2] road   [3] spiked walking stick   [4] dregs
[5] fellow   [6] what matter   [7] wall jumped
[8] knife popped out   [9] area

The Bewteis of the Fute-ball

Brissit brawnis and broken banis,
Strife, discord, and waistis wanis,[1]
Crookit in eild,[2] syne halt withal–
Thir are the bewteis of the fute-ball.

[1] children   [2] old age

: *Sanct Petir said to God in a sport word,*
'Can ye not mak a heilandman of this
horss turd?'

SIR DAVID LYNDSAY

For centuries, Sir David Lyndsay (c.1486–1555) was the most popular early Scottish poet. His attacks on the corrupt Roman Catholic church led to him being seen as a Protestant defender.

For all that we know more of Lyndsay's life than of any other medieval makar, a number of details – such as the year of his birth and his mother's name – are unknown. He came from a landowning Fife family and was closely associated with the Scottish court. He fell out of favour for a time and ended his life as an ambassador but his earliest work, *The Dreme*, has an affectionate account of Lyndsay entertaining the infant James V.

We know he was born in the last years of King James III's reign and was a personal servant, later being Lord Lyon King of Arms to James IV, James V and Mary of Guise. As a herald, he went on diplomatic missions to Denmark, France and England and he was involved in ceremonial duties including court entertainments and pageants. He organised and took a speaking part in the ceremony at St Andrews welcoming Mary of Guise to Scotland.

Lyndsay's earlier, shorter poems are intimately concerned with the court and, while his work retains the concept of divine benevolence, his satires attack greedy courtiers and knowing churchmen. Addressing royalty, his tone can be both candid and confidential.

His undoubted masterpiece is *Ane Satyre of the Thrie Estaitis*, the most important surviving drama of early Scottish literature, which appears to have existed in at least two forms – a version for indoor performance at court and a much longer version designed for public performance at Castle Hill, Cupar, in 1552 and at Edinburgh in 1554.

:ANE SUPPLICATION IN CONTEMPTIOUN OF SYDE TAILLIS

Schir, though your grace has put great order
Baith in the Hieland and the Border,
Yet make I supplicatioun
Till have some reformatioun
Of ane small fault whilk is nocht treason,
Though it be contrary to reason.
Because the matter been so vile
It may nocht have an ornate style:
Wharefore I pray your excellence
To hear me with great patience:
Of stinkand weedis[1] maculate
No man may make a rose chaplet.
Soverane, I mean of thir syde taillis
Whilk through the dust and dubbis[2] traillis
Three quarteris lang behind their heelis,
Express agane all Commoun weillis.
Though bishopis in their pontificalis
Have men for to bear up their tailis
For dignity of their office,
Richt so ane queen or ane Emprice,
Howbeit they use sic gravity
Conformand to their majesty;
Though their robe royalis be upborne,
I think it is ane very scorn
That every lady of the land
Suld have her tail so syde trailand,
Howbeit they bene of hie estate,
The Queen they suld nocht counterfait.
Wharever they go it may be seen

[1] dirty clothes   [2] muddy puddles

How kirk and causay[3] they soup clean.
The imagis into the kirk
May think of their syde taillis irk,
For when the wedder bene most fair,
The dust flies highest in the air
And all their faces dois begarie.
Gif they culd speak, they wald them warie.
To see I think ane pleasant sicht
Of Italy the ladyis bricht,
In their clothing maist triumphand
Above all other Christian land.
Yet when they travel through the townes
Men seis their feet beneath their gownis,
Four inch abune their proper heelis,
Circulate about as round as wheelis,
Whare through there dois na poulder[4] rise
There fair white limbis to supprise.
Bot I have most into despite
Puir claggokis clad in raploch white[5]
Whilk has scant twa merkis for their fees
Will have twa ellis beneath their knees.
Kittok[6] that clekkit was yestreen,
The morn will counterfeit the Queen.
Ane muirland Meg that milkis the yowis
Claggit[7] with clay abune the howis,[8]
In barn nor byre she will nocht bide
Without her kirtle tail be syde.
In boroughis wanton burgess wivis
Wha may have sidest taillis strivis,
Weill borderit with velvet fine:
Bot following them it is ane pyne;
In summer when the streetis dryis
They raise the dust abune the skyis:
None may go near them at their ease
Without they cover mouth and neis,

---

[3] street   [4] dust   [5] poor girls dressed in coarse cotton
[6] a familiar disrespectful name for a girl or whore   [7] mired   [8] houghs

I think maist pain after ane rain
To see them tuckit up again;
Then when they step furth through the street
Thare faldingis flappis about their feet,
Their laithlie lining furthward flypit
Whilk has the muck and midding wypit.

Bot wald your grace my counsel tak
Ane proclamation ye suld mak,
Baith through the land and borrowstounis
To shaw their face and cut their gownis.
Nane suld fra that exemptit be
Except the Queenis Majesty.

SIR RICHARD MAITLAND   ⋮

Sir Richard Maitland of Lethington (1496–1586) lost his sight in 1560, when he was in his sixty-fourth year. He was a Lord of Session and Lord Privy Seal and resigned from the bench in 1584, after more than seventy years. On Maitland's retirement, James VI sent a letter to the Court of Session, saying that Sir Richard 'hes deulie and faithfully servit our grandshir, gude sir, gude dame, mother, and ourself, being oftentymes employit in public charges, quhereof he deutifullie and honestlie acquit himself, and being ane of your ordinar number this mony yeiris has diligentlie, with all sincerity and integrity, servit therein, and now being of werry great age, and aitho' in spirit and judgment able anon to serve as appertenes, by the great age, and being unwell, is sa debilitat that he is not able to make sic continual residens as he wald give, and being movit in conscience that by his absence for lack of number, justice may be retardit and parties frustrat, has willingly demittit his office'.

A knight with the surname Matulent who came to England with William the Conqueror later changed his name to Maitland, though the first of the family recorded in Scotland was a Thomas de Matulent, who flourished in the reign of William the Lion. His grandson, Sir Richard Maitland, owned the barony of Thirlestane and other Berwickshire estates, which the family still retain, and was the main benefactor of Dryburgh Abbey, having donated several valuable lands for 'the welfare of his soul, and that of his wife, and the souls of his predecessors and successors'. It is assumed he is the hero of the ballad 'Auld Maitland'.

Sir Richard Maitland's father, William, fell at Flodden. Sir Richard took to poetry when he lost his sight and he died in his ninetieth year. His wife, to whom he had been married for sixty years, died on the day of his funeral.

Given the hope that he 'sall them see hing on a tree', it seems Sir Richard did not write this poem with a sense of detachment.

:AGAINS THE THIEVIS OF LIDDISDALE

Of Liddisdale the common thievis
Sa pertlie stealis now and reivis,
    That nane may keep
    Horse, nolt,[1] nor sheep,
Nor yit dar sleep for their mischiefis.

They plainlie through the countrie ridis;
I trow the meikle devil them guidis;
    Where they onset
    Ay in their gate
There is na yett[2] nor door them bidis.

They leif richt nocht; wherever they gae
There can na thing be hid them frae;
    For, gif men wald
    Their houses hald,
Then wax they bauld to burn and slay.

Thae thievis have nearhand herreit haill
Ettrick Forest and Lauderdale;
    Now are they gane
    In Lothiane,
And sparis nane that they will wale.

Thae landis are with stouth[3] sa socht,
To extreme povertie are brocht;
    Thae wicked shrewis
    Has laid the plowis,
That nane or few is that are left oucht.

[1] cattle   [2] gate   [3] stealing

By common taking of black-mail,
They that had flesh and bread and ale,
   Now are sa wraikit,
   Made pure and naikit,
Fain to be slaikit with water-kail.

Thae thievis that stealis and tursis[4] hame,
Ilk ane of them has ane to-name:[5]
   Will of the Lawis,
   Hab of the Shawis;
To mak bare wa'is, they think na shame.

They spuilye puir men of their packis;
They leave them nocht on bed nor backis;
   Baith hen and cock,
   With reel and rock,[6]
The Lairdis Jock, all with him takis.

They leave not spindle, spoon, nor spit,
Bed, bowster, blanket, serk, nor sheet:
   John of the Park
   Ripes kist[7] and ark;
For all sic wark he is richt meet.

He is weil kend, John of the Side;
A greater thief did never ride:
   He never tires
   For to break byres;
Owre muir and mires owre gude ane guide.

There is ane, callit Clement's Hob,
Fa ilk puir wife reivis her wob,[8]
   And all the lave,
   Whatever they have:
The devil resave therefor his gob!

---

[4] carry   [5] nickname   [6] distaff   [7] chest
[8] web

To see sa great stouth wha wald trow it,
Bot gif some great man it allowit?
    Richt sair I rue,
    Though it be true,
There is sa few that dar avow it.

Of some great men they have sic gate,
That ready are them to debate
    And will up-wear[9]
    Their stolen gear,
That nane dar steir them, air nor late.

What causes thievis us our-gang[10]
Bot want of justice us amang?
    Nane takis care
    Though all forfare:[11]
Na man will spare now to do wrang.

Of stouth thoch now they come gude speed
That neither of men nor God has dreid,
    Yet, or I die,
    Some sall them see
Hing on a tree whill they be deid.

[9] defend   [10] oppress   [11] perish

ROBERT WEDDERBURN   :

Next to Knox's *Historie of the Reformatioun, The Gude and Godlie Ballatis* is credited with spreading early Reformation doctrines. Also known as *The Dundee Book,* its pieces were collected and composed by Robert Wedderburn (1510–57), a priest, and his brothers James, a merchant, and John, also a priest. All had studied at St Andrews and were for a time exiled for their Reformed sympathies.

Besides a metrical translation of the Psalms, the book contained a number of 'Spirituall Sangis' and 'Plesand Ballatis' whose object was to convey instruction in points of faith, stimulate devotion and highlight the iniquities of the Roman Catholic church. Their knowing, thinly disguised worldliness may also have ensured their popularity. No. 20 begins 'Johne, cum kis me now' and the line 'The Lord thy God I am' opens the second verse. 'Quho is at my windo?' asks no. 17 and 'My Lufe murnis for me, for me' is the first line of no. 19.

But the true message isn't far away. Less loving and gentle is no. 29, which begins, 'The Paip, that pagane full of pryde.' And in no. 23 the metaphor of the hunt and the identity of hunter and hunted are clearly stated in the fourth verse.

:THE GUDE AND GODLIE BALLATIS

With huntis up, with huntis up,
    It is now perfite day,
Jesus, our King, is gane in hunting,
    Quha lykis to speid thay may.

Ane cursit fox lay hid in rox
    This lang and mony ane day,
Devoring scheip, quhill he micht creip,
    Nane micht him schaip[1] away.

It did him gude to laip[2] the blude
    Of young and tender lammis;
Nane culd he mis, for all was his,
    The young anis with thair dammis.

The hunter is Christ, that huntis in haist,
    The hundis ar Peter and Paull,
The Paip is the fox, Rome is the rox,
    That rubbis us on the gall.

That cruell beist, he never ceist,
    Be his usurpit power,
Under dispens to get our pence,
    Our saulis to devoir.

[1] scare   [2] lap

Quha culd devyse sic merchandise
    As he had thair to sell,
Onles it war proud Lucifer,
    The greit maister of Hell.

He had to sell the Tantonie bell,[3]
    And pardonis thairin was;
Remissioun of sinnis in auld scheip skinnis,
    Our saulis to bring from grace.

With bullis of leid,[4] quhyte wax and reid,
    And uther quhylis with grene,
Closit in ane box, this usit the fox,
    Sic peltrie[5] was never sene.

With dispensatiounis and obligatiounis,
    According to his law,
He wald dispens, for money from hence,
    With thame he never saw.

To curs and ban the sempill pure[6] man,
    That had nocht to fle the paine;
Bot quhen he had payit all to ane myte,
    He mon be absolvit than.

To sum, God wot, he gave tot quot,[7]
    And uther sum pluralitie;
Bot first with pence he mon dispens,
    Or ellis it will nocht be.

[3] Tantonic bell: the small jingling bell carried by pardoners (from the French 'tintonner')
[4] lead   [5] trash   [6] simple poor   [7] 'toties quoties' – indulgence

Kingis to marie, and sum to tarie,
 Sic is his power and micht,
Quha that hes gold, with him will he hold,
 Thocht it be contrair all richt.

O blissit Peter, the fox is ane lier,
 Thow knawis weill it is nocht sa,
Quhill at the last, he salbe downe cast
 His peltrie, pardonis, and all.

ALEXANDER SCOTT

Although he is considered to be the finest Scottish love poet prior to Burns, little is known of Alexander Scott (c.1525–c.1584). He was a musician at the Chapel Royal, Stirling, and Inchmahome Priory and by 1565 was a canon at Inchaffray in Perthshire.

All his thirty-six known poems are from the Bannatyne Manuscript and are mainly in the tradition of courtly love complaints. He is occasionally overtaken by happiness but more usually favours love's inconsistencies, contradictions, confusions and emotional betrayals. A footnote – 'Quhen his wife left him' – has been added to the manuscript of 'To Love Unluvit' giving rise to the speculation that at least some of his work is based on personal experience.

The earliest use of the word jig in connection with a dance is in Alexander Scott's poem 'Ballad Maid to the Derisioun and Scorne of Wantoun Women'. This has led to the belief that the dance rhythm is Scots in origin, though the poem suggests other connotations:

> Sum luvis, new cum to town,
> With jeigis to make thgame jolly;
> Sum luvis dance up and doun,
> To maiss their melancholy.

Scott seems to have been friendly with Alexander Montgomerie (c.1545–c.1610), though their careers were very different. Montgomerie was a favourite of James VI who kept his Catholic faith, which is thought to have contributed to his fall from grace and eventual banishment. Many of Montgomerie's lyrics were set to music, though his long poem 'The Cherry and the Slae' shifts from a love complaint to the difficulties of having to choose between the old and new religions, when Catholicism is symbolised as a cherry and Presbyterianism as the sloe. He is the last of the poets associated with the Scottish court. The tradition ended when James VI succeeded to the English throne.

:TO LOVE UNLUVIT

To love unlovit is ane pain;
For she that is my sovereign,
 Some wanton man so hie has set her,
That I can get no love again,
 But breks my hairt, and nocht the better.

When that I went with that sweet may,[1]
To dance, to sing, to sport and play,
 And oft times in my armis plet[2] her;
I do now murne both nicht and day,
 And breks my hairt, and nocht the better.

Where I was wont to see her go
Richt trimly passand to and fro,
 With comely smiles when that I met her;
And now I live in pain and woe,
 And breks my hairt, and nocht the better.

Whattan ane glaikit[3] fool am I
To slay myself with melancholy,
 Sen weel I ken I may not get her!
Or what suld be the cause, and why,
 To brek my hairt, and nocht the better?

My hairt, sen thou may not her please,
Adieu, as good love comes as gaes,
 Go choose ane other and forget her;
God give him dolour[4] and disease,
 That breks their hairt, and nocht the better.

[1] maid   [2] embrace   [3] silly   [4] sorrow

ROBERT LINDSAY   :

Sir Gilbert Hay's translations of French and Latin texts comprise our earliest literary prose. And, though Latin was the language of learned discourse, the advent of printing and the Reformation led to an awareness among both Catholic and Protestant writers that the most direct route to the public mind was through their mother tongue.

But John Knox's eye was fixed on readers south of the Border and he adjusted his prose accordingly. His initiative was justified when James VI moved to London and commissioned a Bible translation into English. For the next three centuries, English prose spoke to Protestant Scotland.

James V instructed the Moray archdeacon John Bellenden to translate Hector Boece's *Historia Gentis Scotorum*; the completed text was published in Edinburgh in 1533 and reprinted three times in the next fifteen years. Bellenden's *History and Chronicles of Scotland* was followed in 1549 by *The Complaynt of Scotland*, which has been ascribed to Robert Wedderburn, who helped compile *The Gude and Godlie Ballatis*. Like Gavin Douglas, Wedderburn finds Scots insufficiently supple and adjusts the language to suit his needs.

Robert Lindsay (1532–c.1590) was born at Pitscottie in the parish of Ceres, Fife. His *Historie and Cronikles of Scotland* is the first to use a natural, vernacular style. The *Historie* was completed in the mid 1570s, but was not published till 1782. It is the only work for which Lindsay is remembered and is a continuation of Boece's history, as translated by Bellenden. Everything is grist to Lindsay's mill and he combines a journalistic eye for unusual detail with an ear for scandal.

: THE SIAMESE TWINS

In this meane tyme thair was ane great marvell sene in Scottland. Ane bairne was borne, raknit to be ane man chyld bot frome the waist upe was two fair, fair persouns withr all memberis and protratouris perteinand to twa bodyis, to wit twa heidis weill eyit, weill eirit and weill handit be twa bodyis. The on bak was to the utheris, bot frome the waist done they war bot on personage and could not weill knaw be the ingyne of man quhilk of the twa bodyis the legis and previe memberis proceidit. Nothwithstanding, the kingis majestie gart tak great cure and deliegence upoun the upbringing of thir two bodyis in ane personage, gart nurische them and leir them to pley and singe upoun the instrumentis of musick, quho war become in schort tyme verie ingeneous and cunning in the art of musick, quhairby they could pleay and singe two pairtis, the on the tribill, the uther the tennour; quhilk was very dulse and melodious to heir be the common pepill, quho treatit thame wondrous weill. Allso they could speik sindrie and dyviers langagis, that is to say Latine, Frinche, Italieans, Spanis, Dutch, Dens and Inglische and Earische. Thir two bodyis lang conteinuant to the aige of xxviii yeiris and than the ane depairtit lang befoir the uther, quhilk was dollorous and heavie to the langest levar. For quhilk men requyrit of him and bad him be mirrie, he answerit and said, 'How cane I be merrie that hes my trew marrow as ane deid carreoun upoun my bak, quhilk was wont to singe and pleay with me to commone and talk in lyke maner? Quhene I was sade he wald gif me comfort and I wald do lykewise unto him, bot now I have no thing bot dollour of the beiring of so heavie ane burthine, deid and cald undesollvit on my bak, quhilk takis all eardlie plesour frome me in this present lyfe. Thairfoir I pray to allmightie god to delyver me out of this present lyfe, that we may be laide and dissolvit in the earth quhair fre we come.'

ROBERT SEMPILL   :

'The Life and Death of Habbie Simson, the Piper of Kilbarchan' by Robert Sempill of Beltrees (c.1590–c.1660) first appeared in 1706 in James Watson's *Choice Collection of Comic and Serious Scots Poems Both Ancient and Modern*. Sempill had fought for Charles I in the English Civil War and his publisher had been jailed for Jacobite sympathies.

The date of Watson's publication is significant. His collection was compiled in an atmosphere of confederacy, at a time when Scots were becoming increasingly aware of what it meant to be Scottish.

Watson was conscious of the effects of his collection. He believed the act of writing would provide definitive texts and presents a show-case of Scotland's finest pieces, offering a range of voices that is linguistically and socially inclusive. Scottish writing traditionally emphasised a multiplicity of voices and, had Watson not recognised this, the form may well have been lost.

It is unlikely Sempill's elegy would be remembered had the form not been taken up by other poets. What became known as 'standard Habbie' dominated Scottish vernacular verse for at least 100 years. Allan Ramsay and Robert Fergusson found it was especially suited to satire and social comment and, by the time Burns used it, the form was well established. In his hand it became more varied than before; its use in 'To a Mouse', 'Holy Willie's Prayer' and 'To a Louse', among others, led to the form becoming known as 'Burns Stanza'.

:THE LIFE AND DEATH OF HABBIE SIMSON, THE PIPER OF KILBARCHAN

Kilbarchan now may say alas!
For she hath lost her game and grace,
Both *Trixie* and *The Maiden Trace*;
 But what remead?[1]
For no man can supply his place:
 Hab Simson's dead.

Now who shall play *The Day it Dawis*,
Or *Hunt's Up*, when the cock he craws?
Or who can for our kirk-town cause
 Stand us in stead?
On bagpipes now nobody blaws
 Sen Habbie's dead.

Or wha will cause our shearers shear?
Wha will bend up the brags of weir,[2]
Bring in the bells, or good play-meir[3]
 In time of need?
Hab Simson cou'd, what needs you speir?
 But now he's dead.

So kindly to his neighbours neast[4]
At Beltan and St. Batchan's feast
He blew, and then held up his breast,
 As he were weid:[5]
But now we need not him arrest,
 For Habbie's dead.

---

[1] help [2] play the war-tunes [3] play more [4] nearest [5] feverish

At fairs he play'd before the spear-men
All gaily graithed[6] in their gear men:
Steel bonnets, jacks, and swords so clear then
      Like any bead:[7]
Now wha shall play before such weir-men[8]
      Sen Habbie's dead?

At clark-plays[9] when he wont to come
His Pipe play'd trimly to the drum;
Like bikes[10] of bees he gart it bum,[11]
And tun'd his reed:
Now all our pipers may sing dumb,
      Sen Habbie's dead.

And at horse races many a day,
Before the black, the brown, the gray,
He gart his pipe, when he did play,
      Baith skirl and skreed:
Now all such pastime's quite away
      Sen Habbie's dead.

He counted was a weil'd wight-man,[12]
And fiercely at football he ran:
At every game the gree he wan
      For pith and speed.
The like of Habbie was na than,
      But now he's dead.

And than, besides his valiant acts,
At bridals he won many placks;[13]
He bobbed ay behind fo'k's backs
      And shook his head.
Now we want many merry cracks
      Sen Habbie's dead.

---

[6] kitted-out   [7] ring of folk   [8] warriors

[9] A play composed or acted by clerics or school-men.

[10] hives   [11] made it drone   [12] brave   [13] coins

He was convoyer of the bride,
With Kittock hinging at his side;
About the kirk he thought a pride
    The ring to lead:
But now we may gae but a guide,
    For Habbie's dead.

So well's he keeped his decotum
And all the stots of *Whip-meg-morum*;
He slew a man, and wae's me for him,
    And bure the fead![14]
But yet the man wan hame before him,
    And was not dead.

And whan he play'd, the lasses leugh
To see him teethless, auld, and teugh,
He wan his pipes besides Barcleugh,
    Withouten dread!
Which after wan him gear eneugh;
    But now he's dead.

Ay when he play'd the gaitlings[15]
And when he spake, the carl bledder'd,[16]
On Sabbath days his cap was fedder'd,
    A seemly weid;[17]
In the kirk-yeard his mare stood tedder'd
    Where he lies dead.

Alas! for him my heart is saur,
For of his spring I gat a skair,[18]
At every play, race, feast, and fair,
    But guile or greed;
We need not look for pyping mair,
    Sen Habbie's dead.

[14] put up with the feud   [15] urchins   [16] old man boasted
[17] proper outfit   [18] share

ALLAN RAMSAY

⋮

Allan Ramsay (1685–1758) was born in Leadhills, where his father was a mine superintendent. He moved to Edinburgh and opened a wigmaking business in the Grassmarket in 1710.

In 1712 he helped found the Easy Club, which met in various locations off the High Street, ostensibly to discuss literature and politics. Club members took pseudonyms from literary figures and Ramsay is first included as Isaac Bickerstaff, after a character in Richard Steele's *Tatler*. Following the club's decision to adopt Scottish names, Ramsay changed to Gavin Douglas.

By 1720 he had abandoned wigmaking and, in 1725, the year *The Gentle Shepherd* was first performed, he had moved to premises among the High Street luckenbooths where he opened Britain's first circulating library. This was where William Creech later published the second edition of Burns's poetry. Although the city fathers openly disapproved of Ramsay's library, they failed to shut it down. However, when his New Theatre opened in Carruber's Close in 1736, the premises were closed the following year.

Ramsay did much to initiate the eighteenth-century revival of vernacular poetry. As editor of the *Ever Green*, he was inspired by the Bannatyne manuscripts and anthologised poets such as Dunbar and Henryson. His five-volume *Tea Table Miscellany* resurrected many traditional songs and ballads, though often in a bowdlerised form.

Lucky Spence was a well-known Edinburgh brothel keeper and Ramsay's poem established something of a convention by celebrating the city's prostitutes and the capital's double standards. Robert Garioch commemorated Register Rachel, Cougate Kate and Nae-neb Nellie, and Sandra o the Black Bull is the subject of Elegy XIII of Sydney Goodsir Smith's *Under the Eildon Tree*.

:LUCKY SPENCE'S LAST ADVICE

Three times the carline[1] grain'd[2] and rifted,[3]
Then frae the cod[4] her pow[5] she lifted,
In bawdy policy well gifted,
 When she now faun,[6]
That Death na langer wad be shifted,
 She thus began:

'My loving lasses, I maun leave ye,
But dinna wi' ye'r greeting grieve me,
Nor wi' your draunts and droning deave[7] me,
 But bring's a gill;
For faith, my bairns, ye may believe me,
 'Tis 'gainst my will.

O black-ey'd Bess and mim-mou'd Meg,
O'er good to work or yet to beg;
Lay sunkots[8] up for a sair leg,
 For whan ye fail
Ye'r face will not be worth a feg,[9]
 Nor yet ye'r tail.

---

[1] old woman [2] groaned [3] belched [4] pillow [5] head
[6] found   [7] pester   [8] something [9] fig

When e'er ye meet a fool that's fow,
That ye're a maiden gar him trow,
Seem nice, but stick to him like glew;
    And whan set down,
Drive at the jango till he spew,[10]
    Syne he'll sleep soun.

Whan he's asleep, then dive and catch
His ready cash, his rings or watch;
And gin he likes to light his match
    At your spunk-box,[11]
Ne'er stand to let the fumbling wretch
    E'en take the pox.

Cleek a'ye can be hook or crook,
Ryp ilky poutch frae nook to nook;
Be sure to truff[12] his pocket-book,
    Saxty pounds Scots
Is nae deaf nits:[13] In little bouk
    Lie great bank-notes.[14]

To get a mends of whinging fools,
That's frighted for repenting-stools.[15]
Wha often, whan their metal cools,
    Turn sweer to pay,
Gar the kirk-boxie hale the dools[16]
    Anither day.

---

[10] press liquor on him till he's sick   [11] tinder-box   [12] steal   [13] empty nuts

[14] This puns on a proverb, 'Guid gear in sma bouk' ('Size isn't everything')

[15] frightened of public disgrace

[16] make the Church fine-box win the game

But dawt Red Coats, and let them scoup,
Free for the fou of cutty stoup;
To gee them up, ye need na hope
    E'er to do well:
They'll rive[17] ye'r brats[18] and kick your doup,[19]
    And play the Deel.

There's ae sair cross attends the craft,
That curst Correction-house,[20] where aft
Vild Hangy's taz[21] ye'r riggings saft
    Makes black and blae,
Enough to pit a body daft;
    But what'll ye say.

Nane gathers gear withouten care,
Ilk pleasure has of pain a skare;[22]
Suppose then they should tirl[23] ye bare,
    And gar ye fike,[24]
E'en learn to thole; 'tis very fair
    Ye're nibour like.

Forby, my looves, count upo' losses,
Ye'r milk-white teeth and cheeks like roses,
Whan jet-black hair and brigs of noses,
    Faw down wi' dads[25]
To keep your hearts up 'neath sic crosses,
    Set up for bawds.

Wi' well-crish'd loofs[26] I hae been canty,
Whan e'er the lads wad fain ha'e faun[27] t'ye;
To try the auld game Taunty Raunty,[28]
    Like coofers keen,
They took advice of me your aunty,
    If ye were clean.

---

[17] rip   [18] togs   [19] arse

[20] Edinburgh's Bridewell for 'disorderly females' built in 1748.

[21] vile hangman's whip   [22] share   [23] strip   [24] twitch   [25] in lumps

[26] greased palms   [27] like to have fallen   [28] rumpy pumpy

Then up I took my siller ca'
And whistl'd benn whiles ane, whiles twa;
Roun'd[29] in his lug, that there was a
    Poor country Kate,
As halesom as the well of Spaw,
    But unka blate.[30]

Sae whan e'er company came in,
And were upo' a merry pin,
I slade[31] away wi' little din
    And muckle mense,[32]
Left conscience judge, it was a' ane
    To Lucky Spence.

My bennison[33] come on good doers,
Who spend their cash on bawds and whores
May they ne'er want the wale of cures
    For a sair snout:[34]
Foul fa' the quacks wha that fire smoors,
    And puts nae out.

My malison[35] light ilka day
On them that drink, and dinna pay,
But tak a snack and rin away;
    May't be their hap
Never to want a gonorrhoea,
    Or rotten clap.

[29] whispered   [30] shy   [31] slid   [32] discretion   [33] blessing
[34] syphilis can destroy the nose   [35] curse

Lass gi'e us in anither gill,
A mutchken,[36] Jo, let's tak our fill;
Let Death syne registrate his bill
    Whan I want sense,
I'll slip away with better will,'
    Quo' Lucky Spence.

---

[36] $^1/_4$ pint Scots or $^3/_4$ pint imperial

ROBERT FERGUSSON   :

The popular writers of Fergusson's day wrote in English. John Home's five-act drama *The Douglas* was, according to a member of the first-night audience, at least the equal of Shakespeare; James Macpherson's *Ossian* was immediately accepted as translations of ancient Highland poetry representing an older classical tradition the equal of Greece or Rome; and William Wilkie's *The Epigoniad* was supposed to be the work of a Scottish Homer.

In London, James Thomson combatted an intense anti-Scottish prejudice by producing 'Rule Britannia' for a masque, *Alfred*, to music by Thomas Arne. 'Rule Britannia' was written with a friend from Edinburgh University's Grotesque Club, David Mallett. After Thomson died, Mallett claimed the work as his own.

Mallett was the son of a Crieff innkeeper. His family name was Malloch but, when he arrived in London in 1723, he changed it to something more euphonious. George Gilfillan describes Mallett as 'a bad, mean, insincere, and unprincipled man, whose success was procured by despicable and dastardly arts'. Robert Ford calls him 'dastardly, mean, and unscrupulous as a man . . . no credit to Perthshire and Scotland'. He is credited with writing 'The Birks of Invermay', mentioned in the second last verse of 'Elegy on the Death of Scots Music' and reputedly Robert Fergusson's favourite song but a number of alternative versions exist.

Robert Fergusson (1750–74) died a miserable and lonely death at the age of twenty-four, raving in a straw-littered cell under a cloud of religious mania, locked in the Edinburgh madhouse at Bristo. In the 'Epistle to William Simson', Burns wrote:

> O Fergusson! Thy glorious parts
> Ill-suited law's dry, musty, arts!
> My curse upon your whunstane hearts,
>   Ye E'nbrugh gentry!
> The tythe o' what ye waste at cartes
>   Wad stow'd his pantry!

Burns frequently acknowledged his debt to Fergusson and, not long after arriving in Edinburgh, erected a headstone to the man he called 'by far my elder Brother in the muse'.

Fergusson's death inspired his physician to campaign for psychiatric patients to be treated as ill, rather than being kept prisoner and, in 1807, Andrew Duncan opened the world's first public asylum in Edinburgh.

....

: ELEGY ON THE DEATH OF SCOTS MUSIC

Mark it, Caesario; it is old and plain,
The spinsters and the knitters to the sun,
And the free maids that weave their thread with bond,
Do use to chant it.

Shakespeare's Twelfth Night

On Scotia's plains, in days of yore,
When lads and lasses tartan wore,
Saft Music rang on ilka shore,
    In hamely weed;
But harmony is now no more,
    And *music* dead.

Round her the feather'd choir wad wing,
Sae bonnily she wont to sing,
And sleely wake the sleeping string,
    Their sang to lead,
Sweet as the zephyrs of the spring;
    But now she's dead.

Mourn, ilka nymph and ilka swain,
Ilk sunny hill and dowie glen;
Let weeping streams and Naiads drain
    Their fountain-head;
Let echo swell the dolefu' strain,
    Since music's dead.

Nae lasses now, on simmer days,
Will lilt at bleaching of their claes;
Nae herds on Yarrow's bonny braes,
Or banks of Tweed,
Delight to chant their hameil lays,
Since music's dead.

When the saft vernal breezes ca'
The grey-hair'd Winter's fogs awa,
Naebody then is heard to blaw,
    Near hill or mead,
On chaunter,[1] or on aiten[2] straw,
    Since music's dead.

At gloamin now the bagpipe's dumb,
When weary owsen[3] hameward come;
Sae sweetly as it wont to bum,
    And pibrochs skreed;[4]
We never hear its warlike hum;
    For music's dead.

Macgibbon's[5] gane: Ah! wae's my heart!
The man in music maist expert,
Wha could sweet melody impart,
    And tune the reed,
Wi' sic a slee[6] and pawky art;
    But now he's dead.

---

[1] chanter   [2] oat   [3] oxen   [4] screech
[5] probably William Macgibbon, editor of *Collection of Scots Tunes* (1742–55)
[6] crafty

Ilk carline now may grunt and grane,
Ilk bonny lassie mak great mane,
Since he's awa, I crow there's nane
  Can fill his stead;
The blythest sangster on the plain
  Alake, he's dead!

Now foreign sonnets bear the gree,
And crabbit queer variety
Of sounds fresh sprung frae Italy,
  A bastard breed!
Unlike that saft-tongu'd melody
  Which now lies dead.

Could lav'rocks[7] at the dawning day,
Could linties[8] chirming frae the spray,
Or todling burns that smoothly play
  O'er gowden bed,
Compare wi' *Birks of Invermay*
  But now they're dead.

O Scotland! that could yence afford
To bang the pith of Roman sword,
Winna your sons, wi' joint accord,
  To battle speed?
And fight till Music be restor'd,
  Which now lies dead?

[7] larks [8] linnets

ROBERT BURNS

His struggle to educate himself and maintain his family bolsters our myth of self-reliance; his tortured love life gave rise to the best love songs ever written; his attacks on religious and political humbug and hypocrisy are still apposite; and his political thinking, especially the social and egalitarian principles found in 'A Man's a Man', have endeared him to successive generations of Scots. We love his contradictions and use him as an adaptable national icon, often to espouse causes of which he would heartily, and, in many cases one feels, vehemently disapprove.

Of course, the obverse is also true. It is not so much that Robert Burns (1759–96) has shaped our national identity; rather that our national identity, or lack of it, has shaped our view of Burns – just as it has shaped our view of other writers, painters and musicians, to say nothing of historical figures such as William Wallace and contemporary public icons.

He remains what we have made him – a myth evolved by the popular imagination, a communal poetic creation, a Protean figure. We can shape him to our own likeness. In 1949 Edwin Muir addressed his ability to straddle contradictory aspects of our national character, concluding that, to the respectable, this secondary Burns is a decent man; to the Rabelaisian, he is bawdy; to the sentimentalist, sentimental; to the Socialist, a revolutionary; to the Nationalist, a patriot; to the religious, pious; to the self-made man, self-made; to the drinker, a drinker. He has the power of making any Scotsman, whether generous or canny, sentimental or prosaic, religious or profane, more whole-heartedly himself than he could have been without assistance; and in that way perhaps more human. He greases our wheels – we could not roll on our way so comfortably but for him – and it is impossible to judge impartially a convenient conveyance to which we have grown accustomed.

:HOLY WILLIE'S PRAYER

And send the Godly in a pet to pray.

Pope

Argument.

Holy Willie was a rather oldish batchelor Elder in the parish of Mauchline,[1] and much and justly famed for that polemical chattering which ends in tippling Orthodoxy, and for that Spiritualized Bawdry which refines to Liquorish Devotion. – In a Sessional process with a gentleman in Mauchline, a Mr Gavin Hamilton, Holy Willie, and his priest, father Auld, after full hearing in the Presbytry of Ayr, came off but second best; owing partly to the oratorical powers of Mr Robt Aiken, Mr Hamilton's Counsel; but chiefly to Mr Hamilton's being one of the most irreproachable and truly respectable characters in the country. – On losing his Process, the Muse overheard him at his devotions as follows –

O thou that in the heavens does dwell!
Wha, as it pleases best thysel,
Sends ane to heaven and ten to hell,
   A' for thy glory!
And no for ony gude or ill
   They've done before thee.[2]

---

[1] His name was William Fisher (1739–1809), and he was 48 when the poem was written.

[2] Calvinist doctrine held that only the 'elect' are saved and all others are damned (even newborn babies), regardless of whether they do good deeds on earth or not.

I bless and praise thy matchless might,
When thousands thou has left in night,
That I am here before thy sight,
    For gifts and grace,
A burning and a shining light
    To a' this place. –

What was I, or my generation,
That I should get such exaltation?
I, wha deserv'd most just damnation,
    For broken laws
Sax thousand years ere my creation,
    Thro' Adam's cause!

When from my mother's womb I fell,
Thou might hae plunged me deep in hell,
To gnash my gooms, and weep, and wail,
    In burning lakes,
Where damned devils roar and yell
    Chain'd to their stakes. –

Yet I am here, a chosen sample,
To shew thy grace is great and ample:
I'm here, a pillar o' thy temple
    Strong as a rock,
A guide, a ruler and example
    To a' thy flock. –

O Lord thou kens what zeal I bear,
When drinkers drink, and swearers swear,
And singin' there, and dancin' here,
    Wi' great an' sma';
For I am keepet by thy fear,
    Free frae them a'. –

But yet – O Lord – confess I must –
At times I'm fash'd³ wi' fleshly lust;
And sometimes too, in warldly trust.
   Vile Self gets in;
But thou remembers we are dust,
   Defil'd wi' sin. –

O Lord – yestreen – thou kens – wi' Meg –
Thy pardon I sincerely beg!
O may't ne'er be a living plague,
   To my dishonor!
And I'll ne'er lift a lawless leg
   Again upon her. –

Besides, I farther maun avow,
Wi' Leezie's lass, three times – I trow –
But Lord, that Friday I was fou⁴
   When I cam near her;
Or else, thou kens, thy servant true
   Wad never steer⁵ her. –

Maybe thou lets this fleshly thorn
Buffet thy servant e'en and morn,
Lest he o'er proud and high should turn,
   That he's sae gifted;
If sae, thy hand maun e'en be borne
   Untill thou lift it. –

Lord bless thy Chosen in this place,
For here thou has a chosen race:
But God, confound their stubborn face,
   And blast their name,
Wha bring thy rulers to disgrace
   And open shame. –

---

³ bothered   ⁴ drunk   ⁵ molest

Lord mind Gaun Hamilton's deserts!
He drinks, and swears, and plays at cartes,
Yet has sae mony taking arts
   Wi' Great and Sma',
Frae God's ain priest the people's hearts
   He steals awa. –

And when we chasten'd him therefore,
Thou kens how he bred sic a splore,[6]
And set the warld in a roar
   O' laughin at us:
Curse thou his basket and his store,
   – Kail[7] and potatoes. –

Lord hear my earnest cry and prayer
Against that Presbytry of Ayr!
Thy strong right hand, Lord, make it bare
   Upon their heads!
Lord visit them, and dinna spare,
   For their misdeeds!

O Lord my God, that glib tongu'd Aiken!
My very heart and flesh are quaking
To think how I sat, sweating, shaking,
   And piss'd wi' dread,
While Auld wi' hingin lip gaed sneaking
   And hid his head!

Lord, in thy day o' vengeance try him!
Lord visit him that did employ him!
And pass not in thy mercy by them,
   Nor hear their prayer;
But for thy people's sake destroy them,
   And dinna spare!

[6] uproar   [7] cabbage

But Lord, remember me and mine
Wi' mercies temporal and divine!
That I for grace and gear[8] may shine,
   Excell'd by nane!
And a' the glory shall be thine!
   AMEN! AMEN!

[8] goods

CAROLINA OLIPHANT, LADY NAIRNE

Women with the social standing of Carolina Oliphant (1766–1845) did not publish poetry. She kept her hobby secret, even from her husband, and published her works anonymously or as Mrs Bogan of Bogan. She contributed to Robert Purdie's *The Scottish Minstrel*, which was published in six volumes between 1821 and 1824, and when she visited him it's said she disguised herself in an old, veiled cloak.

She was born in Gask, Perthshire; her father and grandfather fought with Bonnie Prince Charlie and she was named after the Young Pretender. Songs like 'Charlie is My Darling' and 'Will Ye No' Come Back Again' show her strong Jacobite sympathies; others, like 'The Laird o' Cockpen' and 'The Rowan Tree' are still widely known and popular.

At the age of forty-one she married her second cousin, Major William Murray Nairne, and they stayed in Edinburgh, where she made contact with Niel Gow's son Nathaniel, who is referred to in the fourth verse of 'Caller Herrin''. In 1824, a campaign by Sir Walter Scott, following the visit of King George IV, resulted in the restoration of peerages and titles which had been forfeited as a result of the 1745 Jacobite uprising; so Carolina Oliphant became Lady Nairne.

Nathaniel Gow's tune is said to echo the calls of the Newhaven fishwives and the bells of St Andrew's Kirk in Edinburgh. He was one of the king's herald trumpeters for Scotland and, like his father and brothers, was a prolific composer and performer. He died in 1831 and is buried in Greyfriar's Churchyard in an unmarked grave.

The song was later parodied by Robert Tannahill:

Ah, feechanie! They're no for me!
Gudewife, your herrin's stinkin';
O sic a smell! Jist fin' yersel',
I weel could ken them winkin'.

:CALLER HERRIN'

Wha'll buy my caller[1] herrin'?
   They're bonnie fish and halesome fairin';[2]
Wha'll buy my caller herrin',
   New drawn frae the Forth?

When ye were sleepin' on your pillows,
   Dream'd ye aught o' our puir fellows,
Darkling as they fac'd the billows,
   A' to fill the woven willows?
      Buy my caller herrin',
      New drawn frae the Forth.

Wha'll buy my caller herrin'?
   They're no brought here without brave darin';
Buy my caller herrin',
   Haul'd through wind and rain.
      Wha'll buy my caller herrin'? etc.

Wha'll buy my caller herrin'?
   Oh, ye may ca' them vulgar farin' –
Wives and mithers, maist despairin',
   Ca' them lives o' men.
      Wha'll buy my caller herrin'? etc.

When the creel o' herrin' passes,
   Ladies, clad in silks and laces,
Gather in their braw pelisses,[3]
   Cast their heads and screw their faces.
      Wha'll buy my caller herrin'? etc.

[1] fresh   [2] wholesome, fare   [3] cloaks

Caller herrin's no got lightlie: –
    Ye can trip the spring fu' tightlie;
Spite o' tauntin', flauntin', flingin',
    Gow has set you a' a-singing
        Wha'll buy my caller herrin'? etc.

Neebour wives, now tent[4] my tellin';
    When the bonnie fish ye're sellin',
At ae word be in yere dealin' –
    Truth will stand when a' thing's failin',
        Wha'll buy my caller herrin'?
           They're bonnie fish and halesome fairin';
        Wha'll buy my caller herrin',
           New drawn frae the Forth?

[4] heed

: *Wha'll buy my caller herrin'?*
They're no brought here without brave
darin';

JAMES HOGG   ⋮

James Hogg (1770–1835) was in his thirties when he made his name as a poet. Following the publication of his first novel *The Brownie of Bodsbeck* in 1818, he became increasingly interested in prose and, between 1819 and 1828, he contributed a series of stories and short prose pieces to *Blackwood's Magazine* under the general title of 'The Shepherd's Calendar'.

In these pieces Hogg recreates the oral tales he heard as a boy, where the main body of the text is in English but the rhythm and dialogue is Scots. 'The Brownie of Black Haggs' is not part of 'The Shepherd's Calendar' series but was published in *Blackwood's Magazine* in October 1828.

Following Sir Walter Scott's death in 1832, literature's crown passed to Professor John Wilson, one of the group who started *Blackwood's Magazine* in 1817. Wilson's novels mark the beginning of the nineteenth century's obsession with parish affairs and rural sentiment; and as Christopher North, with his co-editor, Walter Scott's son-in-law and biographer John Gibson Lockhart, Wilson contributed most of the 'Noctes Ambrosianae', a long-running series of conversational essays and monologues which often featured a version of their fellow contributor, James Hogg. Thinly disguised as The Shepherd, Hogg was portrayed as an ignorant simpleton, given to meaningless rants and discourse.

'I know that I have always been looked on by the learned part of the community as an intruder in the paths of literature,' Hogg wrote, 'and every opprobrium has been thrown on me from that quarter. The truth is that I am so. The walks of learning are occupied by a powerful aristocracy, who deem that province their own peculiar right; else, what would avail all their dear-bought collegiate honours and degrees? No wonder that they should view an intruder, from the humble and despised ranks of the community, with a jealous and indignant eye, and impede his progress with every means in their power.'

This attitude continued long after Hogg's death. George Sainsbury, Professor of English at Edinburgh University who retired in 1916, declared that Hogg could only have written *The Private Memoirs and Confessions of a Justified Sinner* with Lockhart's help.

....

:THE BROWNIE OF THE BLACK HAGGS

When the Sprots were lairds of Wheelhope, which is now a long time ago, there was one of the ladies who was very badly spoken of in the country. People did not just openly assert that Lady Wheelhope was a witch, but every one had an aversion even at hearing her named; and when by chance she happened to be mentioned, old men would shake their heads and say, 'Ah! let us alane o' her! The less ye meddle wi' her the better.' Auld wives would give over spinning, and, as a pretence for hearing what might be said about her, poke in the fire with the tongs, cocking up their ears all the while; and then, after some meaning coughs, hems, and haws, would haply say, 'Hech-wow, sirs! An a' be true that's said!' or something equally wise and decisive as that.

In short, Lady Wheelhope was accounted a very bad woman. She was an inexorable tyrant in her family, quarrelled with her servants, often cursing them, striking them, and turning them away; especially if they were religious, for these she could not endure, but suspected them of every thing bad. Whenever she found out any of the servant men of the laird's establishment for religious characters, she soon gave them up to the military, and got them shot; and several girls that were regular in their devotions, she was supposed to have popped off with poison. She was certainly a wicked woman, else many good people were mistaken in her character, and the poor persecuted Covenanters were obliged to unite in their prayers against her.

As for the laird, he was a big, dun-faced, pluffy body, that cared neither for good nor evil, and did not well know the one from the other.

He laughed at his lady's tantrums and barley-hoods; and the greater the rage that she got into, the laird thought it the better sport. One day, when two servant maids came running to him, in great agitation, and told him that his lady had felled one of their companions, the laird laughed heartily at them, and said he did not doubt it.

'Why, sir, how can you laugh?' said they. 'The poor girl is killed.'

'Very likely, very likely,' said the laird. 'Well, it will teach her to take care who she angers again.'

'And, sir, your lady will be hanged.'

'Very likely; well, it will learn her how to strike so rashly again – Ha, ha, ha! Will it not, Jessy?'

But when this same Jessy died suddenly one morning, the laird was greatly confounded, and seemed dimly to comprehend that there had been unfair play going. There was little doubt that she was taken off by poison; but whether the lady did it through jealousy or not, was never divulged; but it greatly bamboozled and astonished the poor laird, for his nerves failed him, and his whole frame became paralytic. He seems to have been exactly in the same state of mind with a colley that I once had. He was extremely fond of the gun as long as I did not kill any thing with her, (there being no game laws in Ettrick Forest in those days,) and he got a grand chase after the hares when I missed them. But there was one day that I chanced for a marvel to shoot one dead, a few paces before his nose. I'll never forget the astonishment that the poor beast manifested. He stared one while at the gun, and another while at the dead hare, and seemed to be drawing the conclusion, that if the case stood thus, there was no creature sure of its life. Finally, he took his tail between his legs, and ran away home, and never would face a gun all his life again.

So was it precisely with Laird Sprot of Wheelhope. As long as his lady's wrath produced only noise and splutter among the servants, he thought it fine sport; but when he saw what he believed the dreadful effects of it, he became like a barrel organ out of tune, and could only discourse one note, which he did to every one he met. 'I wish she mayna hae gotten something she has been the waur of.' This note he repeated early and late, night and day, sleeping and waking, alone and in company, from the moment that Jessy died till she was buried; and on going to the churchyard as chief mourner, he whispered it to her relations by the way. When they came to the grave, he took his stand at the head, nor would he give place to the girl's father; but there he stood, like a huge post, as though he neither saw nor heard; and when he had lowered her late comely head into the grave, and dropped the cord, he slowly lifted his hat with one hand, wiped his dim eyes with the back of the other, and said, in a deep tremulous tone, 'Poor lassie! I wish she didna get something she had been the waur of.'

This death made a great noise among the common people; but there was no protection for the life of the subject in those days; and provided a man or woman was a true loyal subject, and a real Anti-Covenanter, any of them might kill as many as they liked. So there was no one to take cognizance of the circumstances relating to the death of poor Jessy.

After this, the lady walked softly for the space of two or three years. She saw that she had rendered herself odious, and had entirely lost her husband's countenance, which she liked worst of all. But the evil propensity could not be overcome; and a poor boy, whom the laird, out of sheer compassion, had taken into his service, being found dead one morning, the country people could no longer be restrained; so they went in a body to the Sheriff, and insisted on an investigation. It was proved that she detested the boy, had often threatened him, and had given him brose and butter the afternoon before he died; but the cause was ultimately dismissed, and the pursuers fined.

No one can tell to what height of wickedness she might now have proceeded, had not a check of a very singular kind been laid upon her. Among the servants that came home at the next term, was one who called himself Merodach; and a strange person he was. He had the form of a boy, but the features of one a hundred years old, save that his eyes had a brilliancy and restlessness, which was very extraordinary, bearing a strong resemblance to the eyes of a well-known species of monkey. He was forward and perverse in all his actions, and disregarded the pleasure or displeasure of any person; but he performed his work well, and with apparent ease. From the moment that he entered the house, the lady conceived a mortal antipathy against him, and besought the laird to turn him away. But the laird, of himself, never turned away any body, and moreover he had hired him for a trivial wage, and the fellow neither wanted activity nor perseverance. The natural consequence of this arrangement was, that the lady instantly set herself to make Merodach's life as bitter as it was possible, in order to get early quit of a domestic every way so disgusting. Her hatred of him was not like a common antipathy entertained by one human being against another, – she hated him as one might hate a toad or an adder; and his occupation of jotteryman (as the laird termed his servant of all work) keeping him always about her hand, it must have proved highly disagreeable.

She scolded him, she raged at him, but he only mocked her wrath, and giggled and laughed at her, with the most provoking derision. She tried to fell him again and again, but never, with all her address, could she hit him; and never did she make a blow at him, that she did not repent it. She was heavy and unwieldy, and he as quick in his motions as a monkey; besides, he generally had her in such an ungovernable rage, that when she flew at him, she hardly knew what she was doing. At one time she guided her blow towards him, and he at the same instant avoided it with such dexterity, that she knocked down the chief hind, or foresman; and then Merodach giggled so heartily, that, lifting the kitchen poker, she threw it at him with a full design of knocking out his brains; but the missle only broke every plate and ashet on the kitchen dresser.

She then hasted to the laird, crying bitterly, and telling him she would not suffer that wretch Merodach, as she called him, to stay another night in the family. 'Why, then, put him away, and trouble me no more about him,' said the laird.

'Put him away!' exclaimed she; 'I have already ordered him away a hundred times, and charged him never to let me see his horrible face again; but he only flouts me, and tells me he'll see me at the devil first.'

The pertinacity of the fellow amused the laird exceedingly; his dim eyes turned upwards into his head with delight; he then looked two ways at once, turned round his back, and laughed till the tears ran down his dun cheeks, but he could only articulate 'You're fitted now.'

The lady's agony of rage still increasing from this derision, she flew on the laird, and said he was not worthy the name of a man, if he did not turn away that pestilence, after the way he had abused her.

'Why, Shusy, my dear, what has he done to you?'

'What done to me! has he not caused me to knock down John Thomson, and I do not know if ever he will come to life again?'

'Have you felled your favourite John Thomson?' said the laird, laughing more heartily than before; 'you might have done a worse deed than that. But what evil has John done?'

'And has he not broke every plate and dish on the whole dresser?' continued the lady, disregarding the laird's question; 'and for all this devastation, he only mocks at my displeasure, – absolutely mocks me, – and if you do not have him turned away, and hanged or shot for his deeds, you are not worthy the name of man.'

'O alack! What a devastation among the china metal!' said the laird; and calling on Merodach, he said, 'Tell me, thou evil Merodach of Babylon, how thou dared'st knock down thy lady's favourite servant, John Thomson?'

'Not I, your honour. It was my lady herself, who got into such a furious rage at me, that she mistook her man, and felled Mr Thomson; and the good man's skull is fractured.'

'That was very odd,' said the laird, chuckling; 'I do not comprehend it. But then, what the devil set you on smashing all my lady's delft and china ware? – That was a most infamous and provoking action.'

'It was she herself, your honour. Sorry would I have been to have broken one dish belonging to the house. I take all the house-servants to witness, that my lady smashed all the dishes with a poker, and now lays the blame on me.'

The laird turned his dim and delighted eyes on his lady, who was crying with vexation and rage, and seemed meditating another personal attack on the culprit, which he did not at all appear to shun, but rather encourage. She, however, vented her wrath in threatenings of the most deep and desperate revenge, the creature all the while assuring her that she would be foiled, and that in all her encounters and contests with him, she would uniformly come to the worst. He was resolved to do his duty, and there before his master he defied her.

The laird thought more than he considered it prudent to reveal; but he had little doubt that his wife would wreak that vengeance on his jotteryman which she avowed, and as little of her capability. He almost shuddered when he recollected one who had taken *something that she had been the waur of.*

In a word, the Lady of Wheelhope's inveterate malignity against this one object, was like the rod of Moses, that swallowed up the rest of the serpents. All her wicked and evil propensities seemed to be superseded by it, if not utterly absorbed in its virtues. The rest of the family now lived in comparative peace and quietness; for early and late her malevolence was venting itself against the jotteryman, and him alone. It was a delirium of hatred and vengeance, on which the whole bent and bias of her inclination was set. She could not stay from the creature's presence, for in the intervals when absent from him, she spent her breath in curses and execrations, and then not able to rest, she ran again to seek him, her eyes gleaming with the anticipated delights of vengeance, while, ever and anon, all the scaith, the ridicule, and the harm, redounded on herself.

Was it not strange that she could not get quit of this sole annoyance of her life? One would have thought she easily might. But by this time there was nothing farther from her intention; she wanted vengeance, full, adequate, and delicious vengeance, on her audacious opponent. But he was a strange and terrible creature, and the means of retaliation came always, as it were, to his hand.

Bread and sweet milk was the only fare that Merodach cared for, and he having bargained for that, would not want it, though he often got it with a curse and with ill will. The lady having intentionally kept back his wonted allowance for some days, on the Sabbath morning follow-ing, she set him down a bowl of rich sweet milk, well drugged with a deadly poison, and then she lingered in a little anteroom to watch the success of her grand plot, and prevent any other creature from tasting of the potion. Merodach came in, and the house-maid says to him. 'There is your breakfast, creature.'

'Oho! my lady has been liberal this morning,' said he; 'but I am beforehand with her. – Here, little Missie, you seem very hungry to-day – take you my breakfast.' And with that he set the beverage down to the lady's little favourite spaniel. It so happened that the lady's only son came at that instant into the anteroom, seeking her, and teazing his mamma about something which took her attention from the hall-table for a space. When she looked again, and saw Missie lapping up the sweet milk, she burst from her lobby like a dragon, screaming as if her head had been on fire, kicked the bowl and the remainder of its contents against the wall, and lifting Missie in her bosom, she retreated hastily, crying all the way.

'Ha, ha, ha – I have you now!' cried Merodach, as she vanished from the hall.

Poor Missie died immediately, and very privately; indeed, she would have died and been buried, and never one have seen her, save her mis-tress, had not Merodach, by a luck that never failed him, popped his nose over the flower garden wall, just as his lady was laying her favourite in a grave of her own digging. She, not perceiving her tormentor, plied on at her task, apostrophizing the insensate little carcass, – 'Ah! poor dear little creature, thou hast had a hard fortune, and hast drank of the bitter potion that was not intended for thee; but he shall drink it three times double, for thy sake!'

'Is that little Missie?' said the eldrich voice of the jotteryman, close at the lady's ear. She uttered a loud scream, and sunk down on the bank. 'Alack for poor little Missie!' continued the creature in a tone of mockery, 'My heart is sorry for Missie. What has befallen her – whose breakfast cup did she drink?'

'Hence with thee, thou fiend!' cried the lady; 'what right hast thou to intrude on thy mistress's privacy? Thy turn is coming yet, or may the nature of woman change within me.'

'It is changed already,' said the creature, grinning with delight; 'I have thee now, I have thee now! And were it not to shew my superiority over thee, which I do every hour, I should soon see thee strapped like a mad cat, or a worrying bratch.[1] What wilt thou try next?'

'I will cut thy throat, and if I die for it, will rejoice in the deed; a deed of charity to all that dwell on the face of the earth. Go about thy business.'

'I have warned thee before, dame, and I now warn thee again, that all thy mischief meditated against me will fall double on thine own head.'

'I want none of your warning, and none of your instructions, fiendish cur. Hence with your elvish face, and take care of yourself.'

It would be too disgusting and horrible to relate or read all the incidents that fell out between this unaccountable couple. Their enmity against each other had no end, and no mitigation; and scarcely a single day passed over on which her acts of malevolent ingenuity did not terminate fatally for some favourite thing of the lady's, while all these doings never failed to appear as her own act. Scarcely was there a thing, animate or inanimate, on which she set a value, left to her, that was not destroyed; and yet scarcely one hour or minute could she remain absent from her tormentor, and all the while, it seems, solely for the purpose of tormenting him.

But while all the rest of the establishment enjoyed peace and quietness from the fury of their termagant dame, matters still grew worse and worse between the fascinated pair. The lady haunted the menial, in

[1] a bitch hound

the same manner as the raven haunts the eagle, for a perpetual quarrel, though the former knows that in every encounter she is to come off the loser. But now noises were heard on the stairs by night, and it was whispered among the menials, that the lady had been seeking Merodach's bed by night, on some horrible intent. Several of them would have sworn that they had seen her passing and repassing on the stair after midnight, when all was quiet; but then it was likewise well known, that Merodach slept with well fastened doors, and a companion in another bed in the same room, whose bed, too, was nearest the door. Nobody cared much what became of the jotteryman, for he was an unsocial and disagreeable person; but some one told him what they had seen, and hinted a suspicion of the lady's intent. But the creature only bit his upper lip, winked with his eyes, and said, 'She had better let alone; she will be the first to rue that.'

Not long after this, to the horror of the family and the whole country side, the laird's only son was found murdered in his bed one morning, under circumstances that manifested the most fiendish cruelty and inveteracy on the part of his destroyer. As soon as the atrocious act was divulged, the lady fell into convulsions, and lost her reason; and happy had it been for her had she never recovered either the use of reason, or her corporeal functions any more, for there was blood upon her hand, which she took no care to conceal, and there was too little doubt that it was the blood of her own innocent and beloved boy, the sole heir and hope of the family.

This blow deprived the laird of all power of action; but the lady had a brother, a man of the law, who came and instantly proceeded to an investigation of this unaccountable murder; but before the Sheriff arrived, the housekeeper took the lady's brother aside, and told him he had better not go on with the scrutiny, for she was sure the crime would be brought home to her unfortunate mistress; and after examining into several corroborative circumstances, and viewing the state of the raving maniac, with the blood on her hand and arm, he made the investigation a very short one, declaring the domestics all exculpated.

The laird attended his boy's funeral, and laid his head in the grave, but appeared exactly like a man walking in a trance, an automaton, without feelings or sensations, oftentimes gazing at the funeral procession, as on something he could not comprehend. And when the death-bell of the parish church fell a-tolling, as the corpse approached the kirk-stile, he cast a dim eye up towards the belfry, and said hastily, 'What, what's that? Och ay, we're just in time, just in time.' And often was he hammering over the name of 'Evil Merodach, King of Babylon,' to himself. He seemed to have some far-fetched conception that his unaccountable jotteryman[2] had a hand in the death of his only son, and other lesser calamities, although the evidence in favour of Merodach's innocence was as usual quite decisive.

This grievous mistake of Lady Wheelhope (for every land-ward laird's wife was then styled Lady) can only be accounted for, by suppos-ing her in a state of derangement, or rather under some evil influence, over which she had no control; and to a person in such a state, the mis-take was not so very unnatural. The mansion-house of Wheelhope was old and irregular. The stair had four acute turns, all the same, and four landing-places, all the same. In the uppermost chamber slept the two domestics, – Merodach in the bed farthest in, and in the chamber imme-diately below that, which was exactly similar, slept the young laird and his tutor, the former in the bed farthest in; and thus, in the turmoil of raging passions, her own hand made herself childless.

Merodach was expelled the family forthwith, but refused to accept of his wages, which the man of law pressed upon him, for fear of farther mischief; but he went away in apparent sullenness and discontent, no one knowing whither.

When his dismissal was announced to the lady, who was watched day and night in her chamber, the news had such an effect on her, that her whole frame seemed electrified; the horrors of remorse vanished, and another passion, which I neither can comprehend nor define, took the sole possession of her distempered spirit. 'He *must* not go! – He *shall* not go!' she exclaimed. 'No, no, no – he shall not – he shall not – he shall not!' and then she instantly set herself about making ready to follow him, uttering all the while the most diabolical expression, indicative of anticipated vengeance. – 'Oh, could I but snap his nerves one by one, and birl among his vitals! Could I but slice his heart off piecemeal in small messes, and see his blood lopper[3] and bubble, and spin away in purple slays; and then to see him grin, and grin, and grin, and grin! Oh – oh – oh – How beautiful and grand a sight it would be to see him grin, and grin, and grin!' And in such a style would she run on for hours together.

[2] an orra man, an odd-job-man　　　[3] ripple

She thought of nothing, she spake of nothing, but the discarded jot-teryman, whom most people now began to regard as a creature that was not canny. They had seen him eat, and drink, and work like other people; still he had that about him that was not like other men. He was a boy in form, and an antediluvian in feature. Some thought he was a mule, between a Jew and an ape; some a wizard, some a kelpie, or a fairy, but most of all, that he was really and truly a Brownie. What he was I do not know, and therefore will not pretend to say; but be that as it may, in spite of locks and keys, watching and waking, the Lady of Wheelhope soon made her escape and eloped after him. The attendants, indeed, would have made oath that she was carried away by some invisible hand, for that it was impossible she could have escaped on foot like other people; and this edition of the story took in the country; but sensible people viewed the matter in another light.

As for instance, when Wattie Blythe, the laird's old shepherd, came in from the hill one morning, his wife Bessie thus accosted him. – 'His presence be about us, Wattie Blythe! have ye heard what has happened at the ha'? Things are aye turning waur and waur there, and it looks like as if Providence had gi'en up our laird's house to destruction. This grand estate maun now gang frae the Sprots, for it has finished them.'

'Na, na, Bessie, it isna the estate tha has finished the Sprots, but the Sprots that hae finished it, an' themsells into the boot. They hae been a wicked and degenerate race, an' aye the langer the waur, till they hae reached the utmost bounds o' earthly wickedness; an' it's time the deil were looking after his ain.'

'Ah, Wattie Blythe, ye never said a truer say. An' that's just the very point where your story ends, and mine commences; for hasna the deil, or the fairies, or the brownies, ta'en away our lady bodily, an' the haill country is running and riding in search o' her; and there is twenty hunder merks offered to the first that can find her, an' bring her safe back. They hae ta'en her away, skin an' bane, body an' soul, an' a', Wattie!'

'Hech-wow! but that is awsome! And where is it thought they have ta'en her to, Bessie?'

'O, they hae some guess at that frae her ain hints afore. It is thought they hae carried her after that Satan of a creature, wha wrought sae muckle wae about the house. It is for him they are a' looking, for they ken weel, that where they get the tane they will get the tither.'

'Whew! Is that the gate o't, Bessie? Why, then, the awfu' story is nouther mair nor less than this, that the leddy has made a lopment, as they ca't, and run away after a blackgaird jotteryman. Hech-wow! wae's me for human frailty! Bu that's just the gate! When aince the deil gets in the point o' his finger, he will soon have in his haill hand. Ay, he wants but a hair to make a tether of, ony day. I hae seen her a braw sonsy lass, but even then I feared she was devoted to destruction, for she aye mockit at religion, Bessie, an' that's no a good mark of a young body. An' she made a' its servants her enemies; an' think you these good men's prayers were a' to blaw away i' the wind, and be nae mair regarded? Na, na, Bessie, my woman, take ye this mark baith o' our ain bairns and ither folk's – If ever ye see a young body that disregards the Sabbath, and makes a mock at the ordinances o' religion, ye will never see that body come to muckle good. A braw hand she has made o' her gibes an' jeers at religion, an' her mockeries o' the poor persecuted hill-folk! – sunk down by degrees into the very dregs o' sin and misery! run away after a scullion!'[4]

'Fy, fy, Wattie, how can ye say sae? It was weel kenn'd that she hatit him wi' a perfect an' mortal hatred, an' tried to make away wi' him mae ways nor ane.'

'Aha, Bessie; but nipping an' scarting[5] are Scots folk's wooing; an' though it is but right that we suspend our judgments, there will naebody persuade me, if she be found alang wi' the creature, but that she has run away after him in the natural way, on her twa shanks, without help either frae fairy or brownie.'

'I'll never believe sic a thing of any woman born, let be a lady weel up in years.'

'Od help ye, Bessie! ye dinna ken the stretch o' corrupt nature. The best o' us, when left to oursells, are nae better than strayed sheep, that will never find the way back to their ain pastures; an' of a' things made o' mortal flesh, a wicked woman is the warst.'

'Alack-a-day! we get the blame o' muckle that we little deserve. But, Wattie, keep ye a gayan sharp look-out about the cleuchs[6] and the caves o' our glen, or hope, as ye ca't; for the lady kens them a' gayan weel; and gin the twenty hunder merks wad come our way, it might gang a waur gate. It wad tocher a' our bonny lasses.'

'Ay, weel I wat, Bessie, that's nae lee. And now, when ye bring me amind o't, the L-forgie me gin I didna hear a creature up in Brock-holes

---

[4] rascal   [5] scratching   [6] gorges

this morning, skirling as if something war cutting its throat. It gars a'
the hairs stand on my head when I think it may hae been our leddy, an'
the droich[7] of a creature murdering her. I took it for a battle of wulcats,
and wished they might pu' out ane anither's thrapples; but when I think
on it again, they war unco like some o' our leddy's unearthly screams.'

'His presence be about us, Wattie! Haste ye. Pit on your bonnet –
take your staff in your hand, and gang an' see what it is.'

'Shame fa' me, if I daur gang, Bessie.'

'Hout, Wattie, trust in the Lord.'

'Aweel, sae I do. But ane's no to throw himself ower a linn, an' trust
that the Lord's to kep him in a blanket; nor hing himself up in a raip, an'
expect the Lord to come and cut him down. An' it's nae muckle safer for
an auld stiff man to gang away out to a wild remote place, where there
is ae body murdering another. – What is that I hear, Bessie? Haud the
lang tongue o' you, and rin to the door, an' see what noise that is.'

Bessie ran to the door, but soon returned an altered creature, with
her mouth wide open, and her eyes set in her head.

'It is them, Wattie! it is them! His presence be about us! What will
we do?'

'Them? whaten them?'

'Why, that blackguard creature, coming here, leading our leddy be
the hair o' the head, an' yerking her wi' a stick. I am terrified out o' my
wits. What will we do?'

'We'll *see* what they *say*,' said Wattie, manifestly in as great terror
as his wife; and by a natural impulse, or as a last resource, he opened
the Bible, not knowing what he did, and then hurried on his spectacles;
but before he got two leaves turned over, the two entered, a frightful-
looking couple indeed. Merodach, with his old withered face, and ferret
eyes, leading the Lady of Wheelhope by the long hair, which was mixed
with grey, and whose face was all bloated with wounds and bruises, and
having stripes of blood on her garments.

'How's this! – How's this, sirs?' said Wattie Blythe.

'Close that book, and I will tell you, goodman,' said Merodach.

'I can hear what you hae to say wi' the beuk open, sir,' said Wattie,
turning over the leaves, as if looking for some particular passage, but
apparently not knowing what he was doing. 'It is a shamefu' business

[7] dwarf

this, but some will hae to answer for't. My leddy, I am unco grieved to see you in sic a plight. Ye hae surely been dooms[8] sair left to yoursell.'

The lady shook her head, uttered a feeble hollow laugh, and fixed her eyes on Merodach. But such a look! It almost frightened the simple aged couple out of their senses. It was not a look of love nor of hatred exclusively; neither was it of desire or disgust, but it was a combination of them all. It was such a look as one fiend would cast on another, in whose everlasting destruction he rejoiced. Wattie was glad to take his eyes from such countenances, and look into the Bible, that firm foundation of all his hopes and all his joy.

'I request that you will shut that book, sir,' said the horrible creature; 'or if you do not, I will shut it for you with a vengeance;' and with that he seized it, and flung it against the wall. Bessie uttered a scream, and Wattie was quite paralysed; and although he seemed disposed to run after his best friend, as he called it, the hellish looks of the Brownie interposed, and glued him to his seat.

'Hear what I have to say first,' said the creature, 'and then pore your fill on that precious book of yours. One concern at a time is enough. I came to do you a service. Here, take this cursed, wretched woman, whom you style your lady, and deliver her up to the lawful authorities, to be restored to her husband and her place in society. She is come upon one that hates her, and never said one kind word to her in his life, and though I have beat her like a dog, still she clings to me, and will not depart, so enchanted is she with the laudable purpose of cutting my throat. Tell your master and her brother, that I am not to be burdened with their maniac. I have scourged, I have spurned and kicked her, afflicting her night and day, and yet from my side she will not depart. Take her. Claim the reward in full, and your fortune is made, and so farewell.'

The creature bowed and went away, but the moment his back was turned the lady fell a-screaming and struggling like one in an agony, and, in spite of all the old couple's exertions, she forced herself out of their hands, and ran after the retreating Merodach. When he saw better would not be, he turned upon her, and, by one blow with his stick, struck her down; and, not content with that, he continued to kick and baste her in such a manner as to all appearance would have killed

[8] very

twenty ordinary persons. The poor devoted dame could do nothing, but now and then utter a squeak like a half-worried cat, and writhe and grovel on the sward, till Wattie and his wife came up and withheld her tormentor from further violence. He then bound her hands behind her back with a strong cord, and delivered her once more to the charge of the old couple, who contrived to hold her by that means and take her home.

Wattie had not the face to take her into the hall, but into one of the outhouses, where he brought her brother to receive her. The man of the law was manifestly vexed at her reappearance, and scrupled not to testify his dissatisfaction; for when Wattie told him how the wretch had abused his sister, and that, had it not been for Bessie's inteference and his own, the lady would have been killed outright,

'Why, Walter, it is a great pity that he did not kill her outright,' said he. 'What good can her life now do to her, or of what value is her life to any creature living? After one has lived to disgrace all connected with them, the sooner they are taken off the better.'

The man, however, paid old Walter down his two thousand merks, a great fortune for one like him in those days; and not to dwell longer on this unnatural story, I shall only add, very shortly, that the Lady of Wheelhope soon made her escape once more, and flew, as by an irresistible charm, to her tormentor. Her friends looked no more after her; and the last time she was seen alive, it was following the uncouth creature up the water of Daur, weary, wounded, and lame, while he was all the way beating her, as a piece of excellent amusement. A few days after that, her body was found among some wild haggs, in a place called Crook-burn, by a party of the persecuted Covenanters that were in hiding there, some of the very men whom she had exerted herself to destroy, and who had been driven, like David of old, to pray for a curse and earthly punishment upon her. They buried her like a dog at the Yetts of Keppel, and rolled three huge stones upon her grave, which are lying there to this day. When they found her corpse, it was mangled and wounded in a most shocking manner, the fiendish creature having manifestly tormented her to death. He was never more seen or heard of in this kingdom, though all that country-side was kept in terror for him many years afterwards; and to this day, they will tell you of THE BROWNIE OF THE BLACK HAGGS, which title he seems to have acquired after his disappearance.

This story was told to me by an old man, named Adam Halliday, whose great grandfather, Thomas Halliday, was one of those that found the body and buried it. It is many years since I heard it; but, however ridiculous it may appear, I remember it made a dreadful impression on my young mind. I never heard any story like it, save one of an old foxhound that pursued a fox through the Grampians for a fortnight, and when at last discovered by the Duke of Athole's people, neither of them could run, but the hound was still continuing to walk after the fox, and when the latter lay down the other lay down beside him, and looked at him steadily all the while, though unable to do him the least harm. The passion of inveterate malice seems to have influenced these two exactly alike. But, upon the whole, I scarcely believe the tale can be true.

MOUNT BENGER, *Sept.* 10, 1828.

ANON.

When Francis James Child was compiling his monumental work, *The English and Scottish Popular Ballads*, he urged collectors to record even the barest fragment. 'Something must still be left in the memory of men, or better, of *women*, who have been the chief preservers of ballad-poetry,' he said.

Balladry is principally a female genre; the finest examples have been transmitted by women. Anna Brown, a minister's wife from Falkland who died in 1810, was an important source to early collectors. Scott's main informant for *The Minstrelsy of the Scottish Border* was James Hogg's mother, Margaret Laidlaw; she, needless to say, influenced her son. A Mrs Gillespie was the Rev. James Duncan's main informant, Gavin Greig collected most of his material from Belle Robertson and Hamish Henderson's principal source was Jeannie Robertson (no relation). Nor were women simple carriers. In folk song, women rarely adopt a subservient or secondary role. They are usually the protagonists and many songs are written from a woman's perspective.

This version of 'The Twa Corbies' comes from Scott's *Minstrelsy of the Scottish Borders*, having been collected by Charles Kirkpatrick Sharp 'from tradition by a lady'. The ballad was given a new lease of life when Morris Blythman fitted a Breton dance tune to words that previously existed on the page – a suitable marriage, given that *corbeau* is French for crow.

: THE TWA CORBIES

As I was walking all alane,
I heard twa corbies[1] making a mane;[2]
The tane unto the t'other say,
'Where sall we gang and dine to-day?'

'In behint yon auld fail dyke,[3]
I wot there lies a new slain knight;
And naebody kens that he lies there,
But his hawk, his hound, and lady fair.

'His hound is to the hunting gane,
His hawk to fetch the wild-fowl hame,
His lady's ta'en another mate,
So we may mak our dinner sweet.

'Ye'll sit on his white hause-bane,[4]
And I'll pike[5] out his bonny blue een;
Wi ae lock o his gowden hair
We'll theek[6] our nest when it grows bare.

'Mony a one for him makes mane,[7]
But nane sall ken where he is gane;
Oer his white banes, when they are bare,
The wind sall blaw for evermair.'

---

[1] crows [2] talking together [3] turf wall [4] collar bone
[5] peck [6] thatch [7] laments

ANON.   :

According to the American ballad scholar Bernard Bronson, eighteenth-century Scotland was 'a nation of ballad singers and ballad lovers. How much earlier it had been so, no one knows; but it is a fact that what we today know as British balladry at its best is a mass of texts taken down by interested persons from living Scottish tradition in the latter half of the eighteenth century, or learned then transmitted to print or manuscript early in the following century.'

It is scarcely surprising that while the more genteel segments of our society were manufacturing ersatz tales of heroism and grandeur, the feeling that much of our identity and language was being lost or subsumed in a counterfeit culture forced others to search and record the real stuff. From the beginning writers, notably Burns and Scott, were involved in ballad preservation and found them a constant inspiration. When we take into account how elusive the oral tradition can be and that broadsides and chapbooks had a chancy survival rate, we clearly do not have the whole picture. Collectors obviously gathered a small sample of what existed.

Edwin Muir said ballads contain the greatest poetry Scotland has produced. 'They bring us back again to the Scottish people and its part in the making of Scotland; for it was the people who created these magnificent poems,' he wrote. 'The greatest poetry of most countries has been written by the educated middle and upper classes; the greatest poetry of Scotland has come from the people.'

Muir's continual reference to the poetry of the ballads presupposes he never heard them sung or that he considered the tunes unimportant. Until relatively recently, ballad study had a literary bias, which resulted in bawdry and humour being overlooked, even though these aspects appealed to singers and audiences.

'We should never forget that the ballad is a sung genre with a whole musical dimension that is not caught by the printed text,' says Emily Lyle. Hamish Henderson obviously loved singing 'Lang Johnnie More'. He relished the story and sang with a smile, emphasising his favourite lines with swinging arms, exaggerating phrases like 'wi a trumpet in his hands'.

The popularity of Scott's *Minstrelsy of the Scottish Border* gave rise to the mistaken belief that most Scottish ballads were from the Borders. Aberdeenshire has always been the place where ballads are found, including many in Scott's collection, and its geography often features in the texts. This version is from Gavin Greig and Alexander Keith's *Last Leaves of Traditional Ballads and Ballad Airs* and was taken from Belle Robertson. The editors concede that a fuller version, some fifty verses long, exists in Peter Buchan's *Ancient Ballads and Songs of the North of Scotland*.

....

:LANG JOHNNIE MORE

There lives a lad in Rhynie's lands,
    An' anither on Auchindore,
But the bonniest lad among them a'
    Was lang Johnnie More.
        A riddle a in aldinadie,
        A riddle a in aldinee.

Young Johnnie was a clever youth,
    Sturdy, stoot an' strang,
An' the sword that hung by Johnnie's side
    Was fuily ten feet lang.

Young Johnnie was a clever youth,
    A sturdy, stoot an' wight,[1]
He was full three yards aboot the waist,
    An' fourteen fit o height.

[1] courageous

An' if a' be true that they do say,
    An' if a' be true we hear
Young Johnnie's on to fair England
    The king's standard to bear.

He hadna been in fair England
    A year but barely three,
Till the fairest lady in a' London
    Fell in love wi young Johnnie.

Word's gane up an' word's gane doon
    An' word's gane to the king,
That the muckle Scot had fa'en in love
    Wi his daughter, Lady Jean.

'An a' be true that they do say
    An' that you tell to me,
That wighty Scot shall strait the rope
    An' hangit he shall be.'

But oot it spoke young Johnnie then,
    This words pronouncèd he:
'While I hae strength to wield my blade
    Ye daurna a' hang me.'

But the English dogs is cunnin rogues,
    An' room him they did creep,
They've gien him drams o laudamy,
    Till he fell fast asleep.

Fan Johnnie wauken'd fae his sleep
    A sorry man was he,
Wi his jaws an' hands in iron bands
    An' his feet in fetters three.

'Faur will I get a bonnie boy,
    That will win baith meat an' fee,
An' will rin on to my uncle
    At the fit o Bennachie?'

'O here am I, a bonnie boy,
    That will win baith meat an' fee,
An' will rin on to your uncle
    At the fit o Bennachie.'

'For faur ye fin' the brigs broken,
    Ye'll bend your bow an' swim,
An' faur ye fin' the grass growin
    Ye'll slack your shoes an' rin.

'Fan ye come on to Bennachie
    Ye'll bide neither to chap nor ca',
Weel will ye ken auld Johnnie there,
    Three fit abeen them a'.

'Ye'll gie him this broad letter
    Sealed wi my faith an' troth,
An' ye'll bid him bring alang wi him
    The body Jock o Noth.'

Faur he fan' the brigs broken,
    He bent his bow an' swam,
An' faur he fan' the grass growin
    He slackit his shoes an' ran.

Fan he cam on to Bennachie
    He bade neither to chap nor ca',
Weel did he ken auld Johnnie there,
    Three fit abeen them a'.

'Fat news, fat news, my bonnie boy,
    Ye never was here before?'–
'Nae news, nae news, but a broad letter
    Fae your nephew Johnnie More.

'Ye tak here this broad letter,
    Sealed wi his oath an' troth,
An' ye're bidden bring alang wi ye
    The body Jock o Noth.'

Bennachie lies very low,
    An' the Tap o Noth stands high,
But for a' the distance that lies atween
    They heard auld Johnnie cry.

Upon the plains the chieftains met,
    Twa grizzly guests to see,
They were three fit atween each brow,
    An' their shoulders broad yards three.

This men they ran ower hills an' dales,
    An' over mountains high,
An' they arrived at fair England
    At the dyin o the day.

When they arrived at fair London
    The gates were lockèd in,
An' wha saw they but the trumpeter.
    Wi his trumpet in his han'.

'Fat's the maitter,' auld Johnnie says,
    'O fat's the maitter within,
That the drums do beat an' the bells do ring
    An' mak sic a doleful din?'

'Naething's the maitter,' the keeper said,
    'Naething's the maitter to thee,
But a wighty Scot's to strait the rope,
    An' tomorrow he maun dee.'

'Open the gates,' auld Johnnie said,
    'Open the gates, I say.'–
The tremblin keeper smiled an' said,
    'But we have not the key.'

'Open the gates,' auld Johnnie said,
    'Open the gates, I say,
Or there is a body at my back
    Fae Scotland's brought the key.'

'Open the gates,' said Jock o Noth,
    'Open them at my call,'
An' wi his fit he has dung² in
    Three yard-breadths o the wall.

'Ye may chance to wear us oot,
    Or we may chance to fail,
For ye see that we are weighèd doon
    Wi weighty coats o mail.'

They are doon thro fair London,
    An' doon by the town hall,
An' there they saw young Johnnie More
    Stand on the English wall.

'Ye're welcome here, my uncle dear,
    Ye're welcome here to me,
Ye loose the knot an' slack the rope,
    An' tak me fae the tree.'

² struck

'Faur is the lady?' auld Johnnie cried.
    'Sae fain I wad her see,
For I hae sworn a solemn oath,
    She's go to Bennachie.'

'O tak the lady,' the king he says,
    'Ye're welcome to her for me,
For I never thocht to see sic men
    Fae the fit o Bennachie.'

'If I had known,' said Jock o Noth,
    'That ye'd wonder sae much at me,
I sud hae brocht Sir John o Echt an' Park,
    He's thirty fit an' three.'

'But wae betide that little wee boy,
    That tidings brocht to thee;
Let all England say what they will,
    Sae hangit he shall be.'

'O if ye hang that little wee boy
    That tidings brought to me,
We shall attend the burial,
    An' rewarded ye shall be.'

'O tak the lady,' the king he said,
    'Ye're welcome to her for me,
O tak the lady,' the king he said,
    'An' the boy he shall go free.'

'A priest, a priest,' young Johnnie cried,
    'To join my love an' me.'
'A clerk, a clerk,' the king he cried,
    'To seal her tocher wi.'

But oot it spak auld Johnnie then,
    This words pronouncèd he:
'O he has lands an' rents enow,
    An' he'll seek nae gowd fae thee.

'He has lands an' rents enow,
    He has thirty ploughs an' three,
Likewise fa's heir to my estate
    At the fit o Bennachie.'

'Hae ye ony masons,' says Jock o Noth,
    'Ony at your call,
Hae ye ony masons in this place
    To build up your broken wall?'

'I've plenty masons in this place,
    An' plenty at my call,
But ye may from whence ye came,
    Never mind my broken wall.'

They've ta'en the lady by the han',
    An' set her prison free;
Wi drums beatin an' fifes playin,
    They're on to Bennachie.

SIR WALTER SCOTT   :

Sir Walter Scott (1771–1832) is not a single-issue writer. His work is voluminous, in places complex; and much the same can be said for his life and political opinions. Like any human being of substance, he is contradictory and diverse.

Few of his novels are strong on psychological analysis. The song and story tradition he loved injected the best of them with a social and historical dimension that is especially evident in his characters. They are rarely introspective yet their speech provides them with an energy and dynamism; it gives them presence and provides a roundness they would otherwise lack.

And, if we have shaped Burns in our own image, to what extent have we fitted Scott into a similar mould? It is often forgotten that the ordinary Scot had no access to Scottish history until Scott popularised some aspects through his fiction. And it could be argued that the stemming of the tide which threatened to engulf Scotland as North Britain was jointly achieved by Burns and Scott, spreading knowledge both of the Scots language and the old Scots ways of rural life as well as the actions and decisions which shaped her destiny in the dubious years.

Burns felt the Scots way of life was under threat. He especially loathed and continually battled with the remnants of an older Scotland where intellectual curiosity and passion had been replaced by ignorance and tolerance. And Scott feared that the things which in his opinion had made Scotland Scotland were being swept away in a tide of modernity. He may have dressed us up for His Majesty's visit but what does that say for us, the ones who have willingly embraced his symbols while denigrating their creator?

: WANDERING WILLIE'S TALE

Ye maun have heard of Sir Robert Redgauntlet of that Ilk, who lived in these parts before the dear years. The country will lang mind him; and our fathers used to draw breath thick if ever they heard him named. He was out wi' the Hielandmen in Montrose's time; and again he was in the hills wi' Glencairn in the saxteen hundred and fifty-twa; and sae when King Charles the Second came in, wha was in sic favour as the Laird of Redgauntlet? He was knighted at Lonon court, wi' the king's ain sword; and being a red-hot prelatist, he came down here, rampauging like a lion, with commissions of lieutenancy (and of lunacy, for what I ken) to put down a' the Whigs and Covenanters in the country. Wild wark they made of it; for the Whigs were as dour as the Cavaliers were fierce, and it was which should first tire the other. Redgauntlet was ay for the strong hand; and his name is kend as wide in the country as Claverhouse's or Tam Dalyell's. Glen, nor dargle, nor mountain, nor cave, could hide the puir hill-folk when Redgauntlet was out with bugle and bloodhound after them, as if they had been sae mony deer. And troth when they fand them, they didna mak muckle mair ceremony than a Hielandman wi' a roebuck–it was just, 'Will ye tak the test?'–if not, 'Make ready–present–fire!'–and there lay the recusant.

Far and wide was Sir Robert hated and feared. Men thought he had a direct compact with Satan–that he was proof against steel–and that bullets happed aff his buff-coat like hailstanes from a hearth–that he had a mear that would turn a hare on the side of Carrifra-gawns[1]–and muckle to the same purpose, of whilk mair anon. The best blessing they wared on him was, 'Deil scowp wi' Redgauntlet!' He wasna a bad master to his ain folk, though, and was weel aneugh liked by his tenants; and as for the lackies and troopers that raid out wi' him to the persecutions, as the Whigs caa'd those killing times, they wad hae drunken themsells blind to his health at ony time.

Now you are to ken that my gudesire lived on Redgauntlet's grund–they ca' the place Primrose Knowe. We had lived on the grund,

---

[1] A precipitous side of a mountain in Moffatdale.

and under the Redgauntlets, since the riding days, and lang before. It was a pleasant bit; and I think the air is callerer and fresher there than onywhere else in the country. It's a' deserted now; and I sat on the broken door-cheek three days since, and was glad I couldna see the plight the place was in; but that's a' wide o' the mark. There dwelt my gudesire, Steenie Steenson, a rambling, rattling chiel' he had been in his young days, and could play weel on the pipes; he was famous at 'Hoopers and Girders'–a' Cumberland couldna touch him at 'Jockie Lattin'–and he had the finest finger for the back-lilt between Berwick and Carlisle. The like o' Steenie wasna the sort that they made Whigs o'. And so he became a Tory, as they ca' it, which we now ca' Jacobites, just out of a kind of needcessity, that he might belang to some side or other. He had nae ill will to the Whig bodies, and liked little to see the blude rin, though, being obliged to follow Sir Robert in hunting and hoisting, watching and warding, he saw muckle mischief, and maybe did some, that he couldna avoid.

Now Steenie was a kind of favourite with his master, and kend a' the folks about the castle, and was often sent for to play the pipes when they were at their merriment. Auld Dougal MacCallum, the butler, that had followed Sir Robert through gude and ill, thick and thin, pool and stream, was specially fond of the pipes, an ay gae my gudesire his gude word wi' the laird; for Dougal could turn his master round his finger.

Weel, round came the Revolution, and it had like to have broken the hearts baith of Dougal and his master. But the change was not a'thegether sae great as they feared, and other folk thought for. The Whigs made an unco crawing what they wad do with their auld enemies, and in special wi' Sir Robert Redgauntlet. But there were ower mony great folks dipped in the same doings, to make a spick and span new warld. So Parliament passed it a' ower easy; and Sir Robert, bating that he was held to hunting foxes instead of Covenanters, remained just the man he was.[2] His revel was as loud, and his hall as weel lighted,

---

[2] The caution and moderation of King William III, and his principles of unlimited toleration, deprived the Cameronians of the opportunity they ardently desired, to retaliate the injuries which they had received during the reign of prelacy, and purify the land, as they called it, from the pollution of blood. They esteemed the Revolution, therefore, only a half measure, which neither comprehended the rebuilding the Kirk in its full splendour, nor the revenge of the death of the Saints on their persecutors.

as ever it had been, though maybe he lacked the fines of the non-conformists, that used to come to stock his larder and cellar; for it is certain he began to be keener about the rents than his tenants used to find him before, and they behoved to be prompt to the rent-day, or else the laird wasna pleased. And he was sic an awsome body, that naebody cared to anger him; for the oaths he swore, and the rage that he used to get into, and the looks that he put on, made men sometimes think him a devil incarnate.

Weel, my gudesire was nae manager–no that he was a very great misguider–but he hadna the saving gift, and he got twa terms' rent in arrear. He got the first brash at Whitsunday put ower wi' fair word and piping; but when Martinmas came, there was a summons from the grund-officer to come wi' the rent on a day preceese, or else Steenie behoved to flit. Sair wark he had to get the siller; but he was weel-freended, and at last he got the haill scraped thegether–a thousand merks–the maist of it was from a neighbour they ca'd Laurie Lapraik–a sly tod. Laurie had walth o' gear–could hunt wi' the hound and rin wi' the hare–and be Whig or Tory, saunt or sinner, as the wind stood. He was a professor in this Revolution warld, but he liked an orra sough of this warld, and a tune on the pipes weel aneugh at a bytime; and abune a', he thought he had gude security for the siller he lent my gudesire ower the stocking at Primrose Knowe.

Away trots my gudesire to Redgauntlet Castle wi' a heavy purse and a light heart, glad to be out of the laird's danger. Weel, the first thing he learned at the castle was, that Sir Robert had fretted himsell into a fit of the gout, because he did not appear before twelve o'clock. It wasna a'thegether for sake of the money, Dougal thought; but because he didna like to part wi' my gudesire aff the grund. Dougal was glad to see Steenie, and brought him into the great oak parlour, and there sat the laird his leesome lane, excepting that he had beside him a great, ill-favoured jackanape, that was a special pet of his; a cankered beast it was, and mony an ill-natured trick it played–ill to please it was, and easily angered–ran about the haill castle, chattering and yowling, and pinching, and biting folk, specially before ill weather, or disturbances in the state. Sir Robert caa'd it Major Weir, after the warlock that was burnt;[3] and few folk liked either the name or the conditions of the creature–they thought there was something in it by ordinar–and my

[3] A celebrated wizard, executed at Edinburgh for sorcery and other crimes.

gudesire was not just easy in mind when the door shut on him, and he saw himself in the room wi' naebody but the laird, Dougal Mac Callum, and the major, a thing that hadna chanced to him before.

Sir Robert sat, or, I should say, lay, in a great armed chair, wi' his grand velvet gown, and his feet on a cradle; for he had baith gout and gravel, and his face looked as gash and ghastly as Satan's. Major Weir sat opposite him, in a red laced coat, and the laird's wig on his head; and ay as Sir Robert girned wi' pain, the jackanape girned too, like a sheep's-head between a pair of tangs—an ill-faur'd, fearsome couple they were. The laird's buff-coat was hung on a pin behind him, and his broadsword and his pistols within reach; for he keepit up the auld fashion of having the weapons ready, and a horse saddled day and night, just as he used to do when he was able to loup on horseback, and away after ony of the hill-folk he could get speerings of. Some said it was for fear of the Whigs taking vengeance, but I judge it was just his auld custom—he wasna gien to fear onything. The rental-book, wi' its black cover and brass clasps, was lying beside him; and a book of sculduddry sangs was put betwixt the leaves, to keep it open at the place where it evidence against the Goodman of Primrose Knowe as behind the hand with his mails and duties. Sir Robert gave my gudesire a look, as would have withered his heart in his bosom. Ye maun ken he had a way of bending his brows, that men saw the visible mark of a horseshoe in his forehead, deep dinted, as if it had been stamped there.

Are ye come light-handed, ye son of a toom whistle?' said Sir Robert. 'Zounds! if you are—'

My gudesire, with as gude a countenance as he could put on, made a leg, and placed the bag of money on the table wi' a dash, like a man that does something clever. The laird drew it to him hastily—'Is it all here, Steenie, man?'

'Your honour will find it right,' said my gudesire.

'Here, Dougal,' said the laird, 'gie Steenie a tass of brandy down-stairs, till I count the siller and write the receipt.'

But they werena weel out of the room, when Sir Robert gied a yelloch that garr'd the castle rock. Back ran Dougal—in flew the livery-men—yell on yell gied the laird, ilk ane mair awfu' than the ither. My gudesire knew not whether to stand or flee, but he ventured back into the parlour, where a' was gaun hirdy-girdie—naebody to say come in', or 'gae out.' Terribly the laird roared for cauld water to his feet, and wine to cool his throat; and Hell, hell, hell, and its flames, was ay the word in his mouth. They brought him water, and when they plunged his swollen feet into the tub, he cried out it was burning; and folk say that it *did* bubble and sparkle like a seething cauldron. He flung the cup at Dougal's head, and said he had given him blood instead of burgundy; and, sure aneugh, the lass washed clotted blood aff the carpet the neist day. The jackanape they caa'd Major Weir, it jibbered and cried as if it was mocking its master; my gudesire's head was like to turn–he forgot baith siller and receipt, and downstairs he banged; but as he ran, the shrieks came faint and fainter; there was a deep-drawn shivering groan, and word gaed through the castle that the laird was dead.

Weel, away came my gudesire, wi' his finger in his mouth, and his best hope was that Dougal had seen the money-bag, and heard the laird speak of writing the receipt. The young laird, now Sir John, came from Edinburgh, to see things put to rights. Sir John and his father never gree'd weel. Sir John had been bred an advocate, and afterwards sat in the last Scots Parliament and voted for the Union, having gotten, it was thought, a rug of the compensations–if his father could have come out of his grave, he would have brained him for it on his awn hearthstane. Some thought it was easier counting with the auld rough knight than the fair-spoken young ane–but mair of that anon.

Dougal MacCallum, poor body, neither grat nor grained, but gaed about the house looking like a corpse, but directing, as was his duty, a' the order of the grand funeral. Now, Dougal looked ay waur and waur when night was coming, and was ay the last to gang to his bed, whilk was in a little round just opposite the chamber of dais, whilk his master occupied while he was living, and where he now lay in state, as they caa'd it, weel-a-day! The night before the funeral, Dougal could keep his awn counsel nae langer; he came doun with his proud spirit, and fairly asked auld Hutcheon to sit in his room with him for an hour. When they were in the round, Dougal took ae tass of brandy to himsell, and gave another to Hutcheon, and wished him all health and lang life, and said that, for himsell, he wasna lang for this world; for that, every night since Sir Robert's death, his silver call had sounded from the state chamber, just as it used to do at nights in his lifetime, to call Dougal to help to turn him in his bed. Dougal said that being alone with the dead on that floor of the tower (for naebody cared to wake Sir Robert Redgauntlet like another corpse) he had never daured to answer the call, but that now his conscience checked him for neglecting his duty; for, 'though death breaks service,' said MacCallum, 'it shall never break my service to Sir Robert; and I will answer his next whistle, so be you will stand by me, Hutcheon.'

Hutcheon had nae will to the wark, but he had stood by Dougal in battle and broil, and he wad not fail him at this pinch; so down the carles sat ower a stoup of brandy, and Hutcheon, who was something of a clerk, would have read a chapter of the Bible; but Dougal would hear naething but a blaud of Davie Lindsay, whilk was the waur preparation.

When midnight came, and the house was quiet as the grave, sure enough the silver whistle sounded as sharp and shrill as if Sir Robert was blowing it, and up got the twa auld serving-men, and tottered into the room where the dead man lay. Hutcheon saw aneugh at the first glance; for there were torches in the room, which showed him the foul fiend, in his ain shape, sitting on the laird's coffin! Ower he cowped as if he had been dead. He could not tell how lang he lay in a trance at the door, but when he gathered himself, he cried on his neighbour, and getting nae answer, raised the house, where Dougal was found lying dead within twa steps of the bed where his master's coffin was placed. As for the whistle, it was gaen anes and ay; but mony a time was it heard at the top of the house on the bartizan, and amang the auld chimneys and turrets where the howlets have their nests. Sir John hushed the matter up, and the funeral passed over without mair bogle-wark.

But when a' was ower, and the laird was beginning to settle his affairs, every tenant was called up for his arrears, and my gudesire for the full sum that stood against him in the rental-book. Weel, away he trots to the castle, to tell his story, and there he is introduced to Sir John, sitting in his father's chair, in deep mourning, with weepers and hanging cravat, and a small walking rapier by his side, instead of the auld broadsword that had a hundredweight of steel about it, what with blade, chape, and basket-hilt. I have heard their communing so often tauld over, that I almost think I was there myself, though I couldna be born at the time. (In fact, Alan, my companion mimicked, with a good deal of humour, the flattering, conciliating tone of the tenant's address, and the hypocritical melancholy of the laird's reply. His grandfather, he said, had, while he spoke, his eye fixed on the rental-book, as if it were a mastiff-dog that he was afraid would spring up and bite him.)

'I wuss ye joy, sir, of the head seat, and the white loaf, and the braid lairdship. Your father was a kind man to friends and followers; muckle grace to you, Sir John, to fill his shoon–his boots, I suld say, for he seldom wore shoon, unless it were muils when he had the gout.'

'Aye, Steenie,' quoth the laird, sighing deeply, and putting his napkin to his een, 'his was a sudden call, and he will be missed in the country; no time to set his house in order–weel prepared Godward, no doubt, which is the root of the matter–but left us behind a tangled hesp to wind, Steenie. Hem! hem! We maun go to business, Steenie; much to do, and little time to do it in.'

Here he opened the fatal volume. I have heard of a thing they call Doomsday Book–I am clear it has been a rental of back-ganging tenants.

'Stephen,' said Sir John, still in the same soft, sleekit tone of voice–'Stephen Stevenson, or Steenson, ye are down here for a year's rent behind the hand–due at last term.'

Stephen. 'Please your honour, Sir John, I paid it to your father.'

Sir John. 'Ye took a receipt, then, doubtless, Stephen; and can produce it?'

Stephen. 'Indeed I hadna time, an it like your honour; for nae sooner had I set doun the siller, and just as his honour, Sir Robert, that's gaen, drew it till him to count it, and write out the receipt, he was ta'en wi' the pains that removed him.'

'That was unlucky,' said Sir John, after a pause. 'But ye maybe paid it in the presence of somebody. I want but a *talis qualis* evidence, Stephen. I would go ower strictly to work with no poor man.'

Stephen. 'Troth, Sir John, there was naebody in the room but Dougal MacCallum the butler. But, as your honour kens, he has e'en followed his auld master.'

'Very unlucky again, Stephen,' said Sir John, without altering his voice a single note. 'The man to whom ye paid the money is dead–and the man who witnessed the payment is dead too–and the siller, which would have been to the fore, is neither seen nor heard tell of in the repositories. How am I to believe a' this?'

Stephen. 'I dinna ken, your honour; but there is a bit memorandum note of the very coins; for, God help me! I had to borrow out of twenty purses; and I am sure that ilka man there set down will take his grit oath for what purpose I borrowed the money.'

Sir John. 'I have little doubt ye *borrowed* the money, Steenie. It is the payment to my father that I want to have some proof of.'

Stephen. 'The siller maun be about the house, Sir John. And since your honour never got it, and his honour that was canna have taen it wi' him, maybe some of the family may have seen it.'

Sir John. 'We will examine the servants, Stephen; that is but reasonable.'

But lackey and lass, and page and groom, all denied stoutly that they had ever seen such a bag of money as my gudesire described. What was waur, he had unluckily not mentioned to any living soul of them his purpose of paying his rent. Ae quean had noticed something under his arm, but she took it for the pipes.

Sir John Redgauntlet ordered the servants out of the room, and then said to my gudesire, 'Now, Steenie, ye see ye have fair play; and, as I have little doubt ye ken better where to find the siller than ony other body, I beg, in fair terms, and for your own sake, that you will end this fasherie; for, Stephen, ye maun pay or flit.'

'The Lord forgie your opinion,' said Stephen, driven almost to his wit's end—'I am an honest man.'

'So am I, Stephen,' said his honour; 'and so are all the folks in the house, I hope. But if there be a knave amongst us, it must be he that tells the story he cannot prove.' He paused, and then added, mair sternly, 'If I understand your trick, sir, you want to take advantage of some malicious reports concerning things in this family, and particularly respecting my father's sudden death, thereby to cheat me out of the money, and perhaps take away my character, by insinuating that I have received the rent I am demanding. Where do you suppose this money to be? I insist upon knowing.'

My gudesire saw everything look so muckle against him, that he grew nearly desperate—however, he shifted from one foot to another, looked to every corner of the room, and made no answer.

'Speak out, sirrah,' said the laird, assuming a look of his father's, a very particular ane, which he had when he was angry—it seemed as if the wrinkles of his frown made that selfsame fearful shape of a horse's shoe in the middle of his brow—'Speak out, sir! I *will* know your thoughts;—do you suppose that I have this money?'

'Far be it frae me to say so,' said Stephen.

'Do you charge any of my people with having taken it?'

'I wad be laith to charge them that may be innocent,' said my gudesire; 'and if there be any one that is guilty, I have nae proof.'

'Somewhere the money must be, if there is a word of truth in your story,' said Sir John; 'I ask where you think it is—and demand a correct answer?'

'In hell, if you *will* have my thoughts of it,' said my gudesire, driven to extremity, 'in hell! with your father, his jackanape, and his silver whistle.'

Down the stairs he ran (for the parlour was nae place for him after such a word) and he heard the laird swearing blood and wounds behind him, as fast as ever did Sir Robert, and roaring for the bailie and the baron-officer.

Away rode my gudesire to his chief creditor (him they ca'd Laurie Lapraik) to try if he could make onything out of him; but when he tauld his story, he got but the worst word in his wame–thief, beggar and dyvour, were the saftest terms; and to the boot of these hard terms, Laurie brought up the auld story of his dipping his hand in the blood of God's saunts, just as if a tenant could have helped riding with the laird, and that a laird like Sir Robert Redgauntlet. My gudesire was, by this time, far beyond the bounds of patience, and, while he and Laurie were at deil speed the liars, he was wanchancie aneugh to abuse Lapraik's doctrine as weel as the man, and said things that garr'd folks' flesh grue that heard them;–he wasna just himsell, and he had lived wi' a wild set in his day.

At last they parted, and my gudesire was to ride hame through the wood of Pitmurkie, that is a' fou of black firs, as they say. I ken the wood, but the firs may be black or white for what I can tell. At the entry of the wood there is a wild common, and on the edge of the common, a little lonely change-house, that was keepit then by an ostler-wife, they suld hae caa'd her Tibbie Faw, and there puir Steenie cried for a mutchkin of brandy, for he had had no refreshment the haill day. Tibbie was earnest wi' him to take a bite of meat, but he couldna think o't, nor would he take his foot out of the stirrup, and took off the brandy wholely at twa draughts, and named a toast at each:–the first was the memory of Sir Robert Redgauntlet, and might he never lie quiet in his grave till he had righted his poor bond-tenant; and the second was a health to Man's Enemy, if he would but get him back the pock of siller or tell him what came o't, for he saw the haill world was like to regard him as a thief and a cheat, and he took that waur than even the ruin of his house and hauld.

On he rode, little caring where. It was a dark night turned, and the trees made it yet darker, and he let the beast take its ain road through the wood; when all of a sudden, from tired and wearied that it was before, the nag began to spring and flee, and stend, that my gudesire could hardly keep the saddle. Upon the whilk, a horseman, suddenly riding up beside him, said, 'That's a mettle beast of yours, freend; will you sell him?' So saying, he touched the horse's neck with his riding-wand, and it fell into its auld neigh-ho of a stumbling trot. 'But his spunk's soon out of him, I think,' continued the stranger, 'and that is like mony a man's courage, that thinks he wad do great things till he come to the proof.'

My gudesire scarce listened to this, but spurred his horse, with 'Gude e'en to you, freend.'

But it's like the stranger was ane that doesna lightly yield his point; for, ride as Steenie liked, he was ay beside him at the selfsame pace. At last my gudesire, Steenie Steenson, grew half angry, and, to say the truth, half feared.

'What is it that ye want with me, freend?' he said. 'If ye be a robber, I have nae money; if ye be a leal man, wanting company, I have nae heart to mirth or speaking; and if ye want to ken the road, I scarce ken it mysell.'

'If you will tell me your grief,' said the stranger, 'I am one that, though I have been sair miscaa'd in the world, am the only hand for helping my freends.'

So my gudesire, to ease his ain heart, mair than from any hope of help, told him the story from beginning to end.

'It's a hard pinch,' said the stranger; 'but I think I can help you.'

'If you could lend the money, sir, and take a lang day–I ken nae other help on earth,' said my gudesire.

'But there may be some under the earth,' said the stranger. 'Come, I'll be frank wi' you; I could lend you the money on bond, but you would maybe scruple my terms. Now, I can tell you, that your auld laird is dis-turbed in his grave by your curses, and the wailing of your family, and if ye daur venture to go to see him, he will give you the receipt.'

My gudesire's hair stood on end at this proposal, but he thought his companion might be some humoursome chield that was trying to frighten him, and might end with lending him the money. Besides, he was bauld wi' brandy, and desperate wi' distress; and he said he had courage to go to the gate of hell, and a step farther, for that receipt. The stranger laughed.

Weel, they rode on through the thickest of the wood, when, all of a sudden, the horse stopped at the door of a great house; and, but that he knew the place was ten miles off, my father would have thought he was at Redgauntlet Castle. They rode into the outer courtyard, through the muckle faulding yetts and aneath the auld portcullis; and the whole front of the house was lighted, and there were pipes and fiddles, and as much dancing and deray within as used to be at Sir Robert's house at Pace and Yule, and such high seasons. They lap off, and my gudesire, as seemed to him, fastening his horse to the very ring he had tied him to that morning, when he gaed to wait on the young Sir John.

'God!' said my gudesire, 'if Sir Robert's death be but a dream!'

He knocked at the ha' door just as he was wont and his auld acquaintance, Dougal MacCallum—just after his wont, too—came to open the door, and said, 'Piper Steenie, are ye there, lad? Sir Robert has been crying for you.'

My gudesire was like a man in a dream—he looked for the stranger, but he was gane for the time. At last he just tried to say, 'Ha! Dougal Driveower, are ye living? I thought ye had been dead.'

'Never fash yoursell wi' me,' said Dougal, 'but look to yoursell; and see ye tak naething frae ony body here, neither meat, drink, or siller, except just the receipt that is your ain.'

So saying, he led the way out through halls and trances that were weel kend to my gudesire, and into the auld oak parlour; and there was as much singing of profane sangs, and birling of red wine, and speaking blasphemy and sculduddry, as had ever been in Redgauntlet Castle when it was at the blithest.

But, Lord take us in keeping, what a set of ghastly revellers they were that sat around that table! My gudesire kend mony that had long before gane to their place, for often had he piped to the most part in the hall of Redgauntlet. There was the fierce Middleton, and the dissolute Rothes, and the crafty Lauderdale; and Dalyell, with his bald head and a beard to his girdle; and Earlshall, with Cameron's blude on his hand; and wild Bonshaw, that tied blessed Mr Cargill's limbs till the blude sprung; and Dunbarton Douglas, the twice-turned traitor baith to country and king.

There was the Bluidy Advocate MacKenyie, who, for his worldly wit and wisdom had been to the rest as a god. And there was Claverhouse, as beautiful as when he lived, with his long, dark, curled locks streaming down over his laced buff-coat, and his left hand always on his right spule-blade, to hide the wound that the silver bullet had made. He sat apart from them all, and looked at them with a melancholy, haughty countenance; while the rest hallooed, and sang, and laughed, that the room rang. But their smiles were fearfully contorted from time to time; and their laugh passed into such wild sounds as made my gudesire's very nails grow blue, and chilled the marrow in his banes.

They that waited at the table were just the wicked serving-men and troopers, that had done their work and cruel bidding on earth. There was the Lang Lad of the Nethertown, that helped to take Argyle; and the bishop's summoner, that they called the Deil's Rattle-bag; and the wicked guardsmen in their laced coats; and the savage Highland Amorites, that shed blood like water; and many a proud serving-man, haughty of heart and bloody of hand, cringing to the rich, and making them wickeder than they would be; grinding the poor to powder, when the rich had broken them to fragments. And mony, mony mair were coming and ganging, a' as busy in their vocation as if they had been alive.

Sir Robert Redgauntlet, in the midst of a' this fearful riot, cried, wi' a voice like thunder, on Steenie Piper to come to the board-head where he was sitting; his legs stretched out before him, and swathed up with flannel, with his holster pistols aside him, while the great broadsword rested against his chair, just as my gudesire had seen him the last time upon earth–the very cushion for the jackanape was close to him, but the creature itself was not there–it wasna its hour, it's likely; for he heard them say as he came forward, 'Is not the major come yet?' And another answered, 'The jackanapes will be here betimes the morn.' And when my gudesire came forward, Sir Robert, or his ghaist, or the deevil in his likeness, said, 'Weel, piper, hae ye settled wi' my son for the year's rent?'

With much ado my father gat breath to say that Sir John would not settle without his honour's receipt.

'Ye shall hae that for a tune of the pipes, Steenie,' said the appearance of Sir Robert–'Play us up "Weel hoddled, Luckie".'

Now this was a tune my gudesire learned frae a warlock, that heard it when they were worshipping Satan at their meetings, and my gudesire had sometimes played it at the ranting suppers in Redgauntlet

Castle, but never very willingly; and now he grew cauld at the very name of it, and said, for excuse, he hadna his pipes wi' him.

'MacCallum, ye limb of Beelzebub,' said the fearfu' Sir Robert, 'bring Steenie the pipes that I am keeping for him!'

MacCallum brought a pair of pipes which might have served the piper of Donald of the Isles. But he gave my gudesire a nudge as he offered them; and looking secretly and closely, Steenie saw that the chanter was of steel, and heated to a white heat; so he had fair warning not to trust his fingers with it. So he excused himself again, and said he was faint and frightened, and had not wind aneugh to fill the bag.

'Then ye maun eat and drink, Steenie,' said the figure; 'for we do little else here; and it's ill speaking between a fou man and a fasting.'

Now these were the very words that the bloody Earl of Douglas said to keep the king's messenger in hand while he cut the head off MacLellan of Bombie, at the Threave Castle, and that put Steenie mair and mair on his guard. So he spoke up like a man, and said he came neither to eat, or drink, or make minstrelsy; but simply for his ain–to ken what was come o' the money he had paid, and to get a discharge for it; and he was so stout-hearted by this time that he charged Sir Robert for conscience-sake (he had no power to say the holy name) and as he hoped for peace and rest, to spread no snares for him, but just to give him his ain.

The appearance gnashed its teeth and laughed, but it took from a large pocket-book the receipt, and handed it to Steenie. 'There is your receipt, ye pitiful cur; and for the money, my dog-whelp of a son may go look for it in the Cat's Cradle.'

My gudesire uttered many thanks, and was about to retire when Sir Robert roared aloud, 'Stop, though, thou sack-doudling son of a whore! I am not done with thee. HERE we do nothing for nothing; and you must return on this very day twelvemonth, to pay your master the homage that you owe me for my protection.'

My father's tongue was loosed of a suddenty, and he said aloud, 'I refer mysell to God's pleasure, and not to yours.'

He had no sooner uttered the word than all was dark around him; and he sank on the earth with such a sudden shock, that he lost both breath and sense.

How lang Steenie lay there, he could not tell; but when he came to himsell, he was lying in the auld kirkyard of Redgauntlet parochine just at the door of the family aisle, and the scutcheon of the auld knight, Sir Robert, hanging over his head. There was a deep morning fog on grass and gravestane around him, and his horse was feeding quietly beside the minister's twa cows. Steenie would have thought the whole was a dream, but he had the receipt in his hand, fairly written and signed by the auld laird; only the last letters of his name were a little disorderly, written like one seized with sudden pain.

Sorely troubled in his mind, he left that dreary place, rode through the mist to Redgauntlet Castle, and with much ado he got speech of the laird.

'Well, you dyvour bankrupt,' was the first word, 'have you brought me my rent?'

'No,' answered my gudesire, 'I have not; but I have brought your honour Sir Robert's receipt for it.'

'How, sirrah? Sir Robert's receipt! You told me he had not given you one.'

'Will your honour please to see if that bit line is right?'

Sir John looked at every line, and at every letter, with much attention; and at last, at the date, which my gudesire had not observed–'*From my appointed place,*' he read, '*this twenty-fifth of November.*'–'What!–That is yesterday!–Villain, thou must have gone to hell for this!'

'I got it from your honour's father–whether he be in heaven or hell, I know not,' said Steenie.

'I will delate you for a warlock to the Privy Council!' said Sir John, 'I will send you to your master, the devil, with the help of a tar-barrel and a torch!'

'I intend to delate mysell to the Presbytery,' said Steenie, 'and tell them all I have seen last night, whilk are things fitter for them to judge of than a borrel man like me.'

Sir John paused, composed himself, and desired to hear the full history; and my gudesire told it him from point to point, as I have told it you–word for word, neither more nor less.

Sir John was silent again for a long time, and at last he said, very composedly, 'Steenie, this story of yours concerns the honour of many a noble family besides mine; and if it be a leasing-making, to keep yourself out of my danger, the least you can expect is to have a redhot iron driven through your tongue, and that will be as bad as scaulding your fingers wi' a redhot chanter. But yet it may be true, Steenie; and if the money cast up, I shall not know what to think of it. But where shall we find the Cat's Cradle? There are cats enough about the old house, but I think they kitten without the ceremony of bed or cradle.'

'We were best ask Hutcheon,' said my gudesire; 'he kens a' the odd corners about as weel as–another serving-man that is now gane, and that I wad not like to name.'

Aweel, Hutcheon, when he was asked, told them, that a ruinous turret, lang disused, next to the clock-house, only accessible by a ladder, for the opening was on the outside, and far above the battlements, was called of old the Cat's Cradle.

'There will I go immediately,' said Sir John; and he took (with what purpose, Heaven kens) one of his father's pistols from the hall-table, where they had lain since the night he died, and hastened to the battlements.

It was a dangerous place to climb, for the ladder was auld and frail, and wanted ane or twa rounds. However, up got Sir John, and entered at the turret-door, where his body stopped the only little light that was in the bit turret. Something flees at him wi' a vengeance, maist dang him back ower–bang gaed the knight's pistol, and Hutcheon, that held the ladder, and my gudesire that stood beside him, hears a loud skelloch. A minute after, Sir John flings the body of the jackanape down to them, and cries that the siller is fund, and that they should come up and help him. And there was the bag of siller sure eneugh, and mony orra things besides, that had been missing for mony a day. And Sir John, when he had riped the turret weel, led my gudesire into the dining-parlour, and took him by the hand and spoke kindly to him, and said he was sorry he should have doubted his word and that he would hereafter be a good master to him to make amends.

'And now, Steenie,' said Sir John, 'although this vision of yours tend, on the whole, to my father's credit, as an honest man, that he should, even after his death, desire to see justice done to a poor man like you, yet you are sensible that ill-dispositioned men might make bad con-structions upon it, concerning his soul's health. So, I think, we had better lay the haill dirdum on that ill-deedie creature, Major Weir, and say naething about your dream in the wood of Pitmurkie. You had taken ower muckle brandy to be very certain about onything; and, Steenie, this receipt' (his hand shook while he held it out)–'it's but a queer kind of document, and we will do best, I think, to put it quietly in the fire.'

'Od, but for as queer as it is, it's a' the voucher I have for my rent,' said my gudesire, who was afraid, it may be, of losing the benefit of Sir Robert's discharge.

'I will bear the contents to your credit in the rental-book, and give you a discharge under my own hand,' said Sir John, 'and that on the spot. And, Steenie, if you can hold your tongue about this matter, you shall sit, from this term downward, at an easier rent.'

'Mony thanks to your honour,' said Steenie, who saw easily in what corner the wind was; 'doubtless I will be conformable to all your honour's commands; only I would willingly speak wi' some powerful minister on the subject, for I do not like the sort of soumons of appointment whilk your honour's father–'

'Do not call the phantom my father!' said Sir John, interrupting him. 'Weel, then, the thing that was so like him,' said my gudesire; 'he spoke of my coming back to see him this time twelvemonth, and it's a weight on my conscience.'

'Aweel, then,' said Sir John, 'if you be so much distressed in mind, you may speak to our minister of the parish; he is a douce man, regards the honour of our family, and the mair that he may look for some patronage from me.'

Wi' that, my father readily agreed that the receipt should be burnt, and the laird threw it into the chimney with his ain hand. Burn it would not for them, though; but away it flew up the lum, wi' a lang train of sparks at its tail, and a hissing noise like a squib.

My gudesire gaed down to the Manse, and the minister, when he had heard the story, said it was his real opinion that though my gudesire had gaen very far in tampering with dangerous matters, yet, as he had refused the devil's arles (for such was the offer of meat and drink) and had refused to do homage by piping at his bidding, he hoped, that if he held a circumspect walk hereafter, Satan could take little advantage by what was come and gane. And, indeed, my gudesire, of his ain accord, lang foreswore baith the pipes and the brandy–it was not even till the year was out, and the fatal day past, that he would so much as take the fiddle, or drink usquebaugh or tippeny.

Sir John made up his story about the jackanape as he liked himsell; and some believe till this day there was no more in the matter than the filching nature of the brute. Indeed, ye'll no hinder some to threap that it was nane o' the auld Enemy that Dougal and my gudesire saw in the laird's room, but only that wanchancy creature, the major, capering on the coffin; and that, as to the blawing on the laird's whistle that was heard after he was dead, the filthy brute could do that as weel as the laird himsell, if no better. But Heaven kens the truth, whilk first came out by the minister's wife, after Sir John and her ain gudeman were baith in the moulds. And then my gudesire, wha was failed in his limbs, but not in his judgement or memory–at least nothing to speak of–was obliged to tell the real narrative to his friends, for the credit of his good name. He might else have been charged for a warlock.

The shades of evening were growing thicker around us as my conductor finished his long narrative with this moral–'Ye see, birkie, it is nae chancy thing to tak a stranger traveller for a guide, when you are in an uncouth land.'

'I should not have made that inference,' said I. 'Your grandfather's adventure was fortunate for himself, whom it saved from ruin and distress; and fortunate for his landlord also, whom it prevented from committing a gross act of injustice.'

'Aye, but they had baith to sup the sauce o't sooner or later,' said Wandering Willie–'what was fristed wasna forgiven. Sir John died before he was much over threescore; and it was just like of a moment's illness. And for my gudesire, though he departed in fullness of life, yet there was my father, a yauld man of forty-five, fell down betwixt the stilts of his pleugh, and rase never again, and left nae bairn but me, a puir sightless, fatherless, motherless creature, could neither work nor want. Things gaed weel aneugh at first; for Sir Redwald Redgauntlet, the only son of Sir John, and the oye of auld Sir Robert, and, waes me! the last of the honourable house, took the farm aff our hands, and brought me into his household to have care of me. He liked music, and I had the best teachers baith England and Scotland could gie me. Mony a merry year was I wi' him; but waes me! he gaed out with other pretty men in the Forty-five–I'll say nae mair about it–My head never settled weel since I lost him; and if I say another word about it, deil a bar will I have the heart to play the night. 'Look out, my gentle chap,' he resumed in a different tone, 'ye should see the lights at Brokenburn Glen by this time.'

ROBERT TANNAHILL   :

The American folklorist Alan Lomax lived in London from 1950 to 1958. Apart from his fieldwork, he produced numerous broadcasts of traditional music for BBC radio and, in 1953 with David Attenborough, he produced the first television broadcast of traditional music of the British Isles.

He persuaded the BBC to hire Peter Kennedy and Seamus Ennis as staff field recorders and, for some fifteen years, they produced a weekly half-hour Sunday morning radio programme called *As I Roved Out*. In 1957 they featured a song, 'Wild Mountain Thyme', sung by Francis McPeake of Belfast. The song is a variant of Robert Tannahill's 'The Braes of Balquither'.

Tannahill (1774–1810) was the fifth of eight children. At the age of twelve, he was apprenticed to his father and worked as a weaver all his life. In 1800 he and his brother travelled to Bolton, where he worked for two years, returning when he heard of his father's terminal illness.

He composed new lyrics to existing airs and had a love of Irish song. At the request of a local theatre manager, he wrote a prologue for Ramsay's *The Gentle Shepherd* and in 1807 found enough subscribers to published *The Soldiers Return, a Scottish Interlude in Two Acts, With Other Poems and Songs*. His play was based on the Ramsay original and the published edition contained thirty-three poems. The edition sold out in weeks and in 1810 James Hogg visited Tannahill in Paisley. They spent much of the day in the Bourock, a back room of the Sun Tavern, with three other acquaintances – one of whom, James Barr, noted the contrast of 'the one healthy, lively and off-hand; the other delicate, quiet and unassuming'.

Tannahill walked Hogg and Barr back to Glasgow, as far as Crookston Road. William Motherwell describes the parting he did not witness with Tannahill grasping Hogg's hand, tears in his eyes, declaring, 'Farewell; we shall never meet again. Farewell; I shall never see you more.'

Motherwell is known to exaggerate; but for some time Tannahill had been prone to bouts of melancholy. When a new poetry collection was rejected by two publishers, Tannahill destroyed his manuscripts and on 17 May 1810 his body was found in a culvert of the Candren Burn, his coat and silver watch on the ground nearby.

:THE SIMMER GLOAMIN'

TUNE: *Alex Donn's Strathspey*

The midges dance aboon the burn,
    The dew begins to fa',
The pairtricks down the rushy howm,[1]
    Set up their e'ening ca':
Now loud and clear the blackbird's sang
    Rings through the briery shaw,
While fleeting gay, the swallows play
    Around the castle wa'.

Beneath the gowden gloamin' sky
    The mavis[2] mends his lay,
The redbreast pours its sweetest strains,
    To charm the lingering day:
While weary yeldrins[3] seem to wail
    Their little nestlings torn,
The merry wren, frae den to den,
    Gaes jinkin' through the thorn.

The roses fauld their silken leaves,
    The foxglove shuts its bell,
The honey-suckle and the birk[4]
    Spread fragrance through the dell:
Let others crowd the giddy court
    Of mirth and revelry,
The simple joys that nature yields
    Are dearer far to me.

[1] a stretch of low-lying land beside a river   [2] thrush   [3] yellowhammers
[4] birch

ANON.

In 1818, at the age of sixteen, Robert Chambers (1802–71) opened a bookstall in Leith Walk. His stock consisted of remnants from his father's library and his own collection. In 1819 his elder brother William (1800–83) also started a bookselling business and, while William experimented with his hand-press, Robert explored the Old Town closes. In 1824 he produced *Traditions of Edinburgh*, printed, bound and published by his brother and the reason Sir Walter Scott called at the shop to meet the author, telling his friends he was surprised at 'where the boy got all the information'.

As Robert Chalmers reported, Scott 'then called upon me one day with Mr Lockhart. I was overwhelmed with the honour, for Sir Walter Scott was almost an object of worship to me. I could not utter a word.' Scott followed his visit by sending 'sixteen folio pages, in his usual close handwriting, and containing all the reminiscences he could at that time summon up of old persons and things in Edinburgh . . . When I was preparing a subsequent work *The Popular Rhymes of Scotland*, he sent me whole sheets of his recollections, with appropriate explanations.'

The Popular Rhymes of Scotland was published in 1826 and a two-volume edition of *Scottish Songs* appeared in 1829. In 1832 they launched the weekly, sixteen-page *Chambers's Edinburgh Journal*. It was an immediate success and within a few years had a circulation of 84,000. By the end of the nineteenth century, W. & R. Chambers was one of the largest English-language publishers in the world.

Robert Chambers is the main source for many Scots folktales, especially the familiar wonder tales such as 'The Red Etin' and 'Whuppity Stoorie'. Without *Popular Rhymes of Scotland* and the chapter on 'Fireside Nursery Tales' which he added to later editions, it's likely many tales would be lost or exist in a less sympathetic form. He combines an understanding of the oral tradition with an obvious love of the stories and, although his texts are not verbatim transcriptions, they convey the energy and eccentricities of the spoken tale – something notably missing from later anglicised versions.

: THE BLACK BULL OF NORROWAY

In Norroway, langsyne, there lived a certain lady, and she had three dochters. The auldest o' them said to her mither: 'Mither, bake me a bannock, and roast me a collop,[1] for I'm gaun awa' to spotch[2] my fortune.' Her mither did sae; and the dochter gaed awa' to an auld witch washerwife and telled her purpose. The auld wife bade her stay that day, and gang and look out o' her back door, and see what she could see. She saw nocht the first day. The second day she did the same, and saw nocht. On the third day she looked again, and saw a coach-and-six coming alang the road. She ran in and telled the auld wife what she saw. 'Aweel,' quo' the auld wife, 'yon's for you.' Sae they took her into the coach, and galloped aff.

The second dochter next says to her mither: 'Mither, bake me a bannock, and roast me a collop, for I'm gaun awa' to spotch my fortune.' Her mither did sae; and awa' she gaed to the auld wife, as her sister had dune. On the third day she looked out o' the back door, and saw a coach-and-four coming alang the road. 'Aweel,' quo' the auld wife, 'yon's for you.' Sae they took her in, and aff they set.

The third dochter says to her mither: 'Mither, bake me a bannock, and roast me a collop, for I'm gaun awa' to spotch my fortune.' Her mither did sae; and awa' she gaed to the auld witch wife. She bade her look out o' her back door, and see what she could see. She did sae; and when she came back, said she saw nocht. The second day she did the same, and saw nocht. The third day she looked again, and on coming back, said to the auld wife she saw nocht but a muckle Black Bull coming crooning[3] alang the road. 'Aweel,' quo' the auld wife, 'yon's for you.' On hearing this she was next to distracted wi' grief and terror; but she was lifted up and set on his back, and awa' they went.

Aye they travelled, and on they travelled, till the lady grew faint wi' hunger. 'Eat out o' my right lug,' says the Black Bull, 'and drink out o' my

---

[1] slice of meat   [2] poach or seek trifles   [3] roaring

left lug, and set by your leavings.' Sae she did as he said, and was wonderfully refreshed. And lang they gaed, and sair they rade, till they came in sight o' a very big and bonny castle. 'Yonder we maun be this night,' quo' the bull, 'for my auld brither lives yonder;' and presently they were at the place. They lifted her aff his back, and took her in, and sent him away to a park for the night. In the morning, when they brought the bull hame, they took the lady into a fine shining parlour, and gave her a beautiful apple, telling her no to break it till she was in the greatest strait ever mortal was in in the world, and that wad bring her out o't. Again she was lifted on the bull's back, and after she had ridden far, and far'er than I can tell, they came in sight o' a far bonnier castle, and far farther awa' than the last. Says the bull till her: 'Yonder we maun be the night, for my second brither lives yonder;' and they were at the place directly. They lifted her down and took her in, and sent the bull to the field for the night. In the morning they took the lady into a fine and rich room, and gave her the finest pear she had ever seen, bidding her no to break it till she was in the greatest strait ever mortal could be in, and that wad get her out o't. Again she was lifted and set on his back, and awa' they went. And lang they rade, and sair they rade, till they came in sight o' the far biggest castle, and far farthest aff, they had yet seen. 'We maun be yonder the night,' says the bull, 'for my young brither lives yonder;' and they were there directly. They lifted her down, took her in, and sent the bull to the field for the night. In the morning they took her into a room, the finest of a', and gied her a plum, telling her no to break it till she was in the greatest strait mortal could be in, and that wad get her out o't. Presently they brought hame the bull, set the lady on his back, and awa' they went.

And aye they rade, and on they rade, till they came to a dark and ugsome[4] glen, where they stopped, and the lady lighted down. Says the bull to her: 'Here ye maun stay till I gang and fight the deil. Ye maun seat yoursel' on that stane, and move neither hand nor fit till I come back, else I'll never find ye again. And if everything round about ye turns blue, I hae beaten the deil; but should a' things turn red, he'll hae conquered me.' She set hersel' down on the stane, and by and by a' round her turned blue. O'ercome wi' joy, she lifted the ae fit and crossed it owre the ither, sae glad was she that her companion was victorious. The bull returned and sought for, but never could find her.

[4] repellent

Lang she sat, and aye she grat, till she wearied. At last she rase and gaed awa', she kendna whaur till. On she wandered, till she came to a great hill o' glass, that she tried a' she could to climb, but wasna able. Round the bottom o' the hill she gaed, sabbing and seeking a passage owre, till at last she came to a smith's house; and the smith promised, if she wad serve him seven years, he wad make her airn[5] shoon, wherewi' she could climb owre the glassy hill. At seven years' end she got her aim shoon, clamb the glassy hill, and chanced to come to the auld washerwife's habitation. There she was telled of a gallant young knight that had given in some bluidy sarks to wash, and whaever washed thae sarks was to be his wife. The auld wife had washed till she was tired, and then she set to her dochter, and baith washed, and they washed, and they better washed, in hopes of getting the young knight; but a' they could do, they couldna bring out a stain. At length they set the stranger damosel to wark; and whenever she began, the stains came out pure and clean, and the auld wife made the knight believe it was her dochter had washed the sarks. So the knight and the eldest dochter were to be married, and the stranger damosel was distracted at the thought of it, for she was deeply in love wi' him. So she bethought her of her apple, and breaking it, found it filled with gold and precious jewellery, the richest she had ever seen. 'All these,' she said to the eldest dochter, 'I will give you, on condition that you put off your marriage for ae day, and allow me to go into his room alone at night.' So the lady consented; but meanwhile the auld wife had prepared a sleeping drink, and given it to the knight, wha drank it, and never wakened till next morning. The lee-lang night the damosel sabbed and sang:

'Seven lang years I served for thee,
The glassy hill I clamb for thee,
The bluidy shirt I wrang for thee;
And wilt thou no wauken and turn to me?'

Next day she kentna what to do for grief. She then brak the pear, and fan't filled wi' jewellery far richer than the contents o' the apple. Wi' thae jewels she bargained for permission to be a second night in the young knight's chamber; but the auld wife gied him anither sleeping drink, and he again sleepit till morning. A' night she kept sighing and singing as before:

[5] iron

'Seven lang years I served for thee,' &c.

Still he sleepit, and she nearly lost hope a'thegither. But that day, when he was out at the hunting, somebody asked him what noise and moaning was yon they heard all last night in his bedchamber. He said he heardna ony noise. But they assured him there was sae; and he resolved to keep waking that night to try what he could hear. That being the third night, and the damosel being between hope and despair, she brak her plum, and it held far the richest jewellery of the three. She bargained as before; and the auld wife, as before, took in the sleeping drink to the young knight's chamber; but he telled her he couldna drink it that night without sweetening. And when she gaed awa' for some honey to sweeten it wi', he poured out the drink, and sae made the auld wife think he had drunk it. They a' went to bed again, and the damosel began, as before, singing:

'Seven lang years I served for thee,
The glassy hill I clamb for thee,
The bluidy shirt I wrang for thee;
And wilt thou no wauken and turn to me?'

He heard, and turned to her. And she telled him a' that had befa'en her, and he telled her a' that had happened to him. And he caused the auld washerwife and her dochter to be burnt. And they were married, and he and she are living happy till this day, for aught I ken.

: *'Mither, bake me a bannock, and roast
me a collop, for I'm gaun awa'
to spotch my fortune.'*

JOHN GALT

Following his marriage to Elizabeth Tilloch in 1813, John Galt (1779–1839) took to full-time writing and contributed regularly to the *Monthly Magazine*. Around this time, he offered Archibald Constable a novel 'but he gave me no encouragement to proceed: Scottish novels, he said, would not do'.

Blackwood's Magazine serialised Galt's first novel, *The Ayrshire Legatees*, in 1820. The anonymous series proved so popular that they published the book in 1821 and asked for more. Galt sent the piece Constable had rejected and William Blackwood published *Annals of the Parish* immediately. Sir Walter Scott's *Waverley* had appeared in 1814 and Scottish novels were now popular.

In many ways, this typifies Galt's life and reputation. He has always been overshadowed by Scott yet, when regarded in his own right, a fresh and original voice emerges.

Galt's novels are inventive, intelligent and varied. The group he called *Tales of the West* are set in the Ayrshire of his youth. He saw them as theoretical histories, observations and sketches rather than novels, presenting a view of Scottish rural life that could otherwise be missed. The stories adopt a similar approach. The action is often viewed through a single narrator, which allows for shrewd and comic observations and crafty satire.

: THE HOWDIE:
AN AUTOBIOGRAPHY

PART I—ANENT BIRTHS

When my gudeman departed this life, he left me with a heavy handful of seven childer, the youngest but a baby at the breast, and the elder a lassie scant of eight years old. With such a small family what could a lanely widow woman do? Greatly was I grieved, not only for the loss of our bread-winner, but the quenching of that cheerful light which was my solace and comfort in straitened circumstances, and in the many cold and dark hours which the needs of our necessitous condition obliged us to endure.

James Blithe was my first and only Jo; and but for that armed man, Poverty, who sat ever demanding at our hearth, there never was a brittle minute in the course of our wedded life. It was my pleasure to gladden him at home, when out-of-door vexations ruffled his temper; which seldom came to pass, for he was an honest young man, and pleasant among those with whom his lot was cast. I have often, since his death, thought, in calling him to mind, that it was by his natural sweet nature that the Lord was pleased, when He took him to Himself, to awaken the sympathy of others for me and the bairns, in our utmost distress.

He was the head gairdner to the Laird of Rigs, as his father had been before him; and the family had him in great respect. Besides many a present of useful things which they gave to us, when we were married, they came to our wedding; a compliment that James often said was like the smell of the sweet briar in a lown[1] and dewy evening, a cherishment that seasoned happiness. It was not however till he was taken away that I experienced the extent of their kindness. The ladies of the family were most particular to me; the Laird himself, on the Sabbath after the burial, paid me a very edifying visit; and to the old Leddy Dowager, his mother, I owe the meal that has ever since been in the basin, by which I have been enabled to bring up my childer in the fear of the Lord.

The Leddy was really a managing motherly character; no grass grew beneath her feet when she had a turn to do, as was testified by my case:

---

[1] peaceful

for when the minister's wife put it into her head that I might do well in the midwife-line, Mrs Forceps being then in her declining years, she lost no time in getting me made, in the language of the church and gospel, her helper and successor. A blessing it was at the time, and the whole parish has, with a constancy of purpose, continued to treat me far above my deserts; for I have ever been sure of a shortcoming in my best endeavours to give satisfaction. But it's not to speak of the difficulties that the hand of a considerate Providence has laid upon me with a sore weight for an earthly nature to bear, that I have sat down to indite this history book. I only intend hereby to show, how many strange things have come to pass in my douce way of life; and sure am I that in every calling, no matter however humble, peradventures will take place that ought to be recorded for the instruction, even of the wisest. Having said this, I will now proceed with my story.

All the har'st before the year of dearth, Mrs Forceps, my predecessor, had been in an ailing condition; insomuch that, on the Halloween, she was laid up, and never after was taken out of her bed a living woman. Thus it came to pass that, before the turn of the year, the midwifery business of our countryside came into my hands in the natural way.

I cannot tell how it happened that there was little to do in the way of trade all that winter; but it began to grow into a fashion that the genteeler order of ladies went into the towns to have there han'lings among the doctors. It was soon seen, however, that they had nothing to boast of by that manœuvre, for their gudemen thought the cost overcame the profit; and thus, although that was to a certainty a niggardly year, and great part of the next no better, it pleased the Lord, by the scanty upshot of the har'st before spoken of, that, whatever the ladies thought of the doctors, their husbands kept the warm side of frugality towards me and other poor women that had nothing to depend upon but the skill of their ten fingers.

Mrs Forceps being out of the way, I was called in; and my first case was with an elderly woman that was long thought by all her friends to be past bearing; but when she herself came to me and rehearsed the state she was in, with a great sough for fear, instead of a bairn, it might turn out a tympathy,[2] I called to her mind how Sarah the Patriarchess, the wife of Abraham, was more than fourscore before Isaac was born: which was to her great consolation; for she was a pious woman in the main, and could discern in that miracle of Scripture an admonition to her to be of good cheer.

[2] tumor

From that night, poor Mrs Houselycat grew an altered woman; and her gudeman, Thomas Houselycat, was as caidgy a man as could be, at the prospect of having an Isaac in his old age; for neither he nor his wife had the least doubt that they were to be blest with a man-child. At last the fulness of time came; and Thomas having provided a jar of cinnamon brandy for the occasion, I was duly called in.

Well do I remember the night that worthy Thomas himself came for me, with a lantern or a bowit[3] in his hand. It was pitch-dark; the winds rampaged among the trees, the sleet was just vicious, and every drop was as salt as pickle. He had his wife's shawl tied over his hat, by a great knot under the chin, and a pair of huggars[4] drawn over his shoes, and above his knees; he was just a curiosity to see coming for me.

I went with him; and to be sure when I got to the house, there was a gathering; young and old were there, all speaking together; widows and grannies giving advice, and new-married wives sitting in the expectation of getting insight. Really it was a ploy; and no wonder that there was such a collection; for Mrs Houselycat was a woman well-stricken in years, and it could not be looked upon as any thing less than an inadvertency that she was ordained to be again a mother. I very well remember that her youngest daughter of the first clecking[5] was there, a married woman, with a wean at her knee, I'se warrant a year-and-a-half old; it could both walk alone, and say many words almost as intelligible as the minister in the poopit, when it was a frosty morning; for the cold made him there shavelin-gabbit,[6] and every word he said was just an oppression to his feckless tongue.

By and by the birth came to pass: but, och on! the long faces that were about me when it took place; for instead of a lad-bairn it proved a lassie; and to increase the universal dismay at this come-to-pass, it turned out that the bairn's cleading[7] had, in a way out of the common, been prepared for a man child; which was the occasion of the innocent being, all the time of its nursing in appearance a very doubtful creature.

The foregoing case is the first that I could properly say was my own; for Mrs Forceps had a regular finger in the pie in all my heretofores. It was, however, good erls; for no sooner had I got Mrs Houselycat on her feet again, than I received a call from the head inns in the town, from a Captain's lady, that was overtaken there as the regiment was going through.

---

[3] hand lantern   [4] footless stockings   [5] brood, litter
[6] with a mouth like a spokeshave   [7] clothing

In this affair there was something that did not just please me in the conduct of Mrs Facings, as the gentlewoman was called; and I jaloused,[8] by what I saw with the tail of my eye, that she was no better than a light woman. However, in the way of trade, it does not do to stand on trifles of that sort; for ours is a religious trade, as witness what is said in the Bible of the midwives of the Hebrews; and if it pleased Providence to ordain children to be, it is no less an ordained duty of the midwife to help them into the world. But I had not long been satisfied in my own mind that the mother was no better than she should be, when my kinder feelings were sorely tried, for she had a most extraordinar severe time o't; and I had but a weak hope that she would get through. However, with my help and the grace of God, she did get through: and I never saw, before nor since, so brave a baby as was that night born.

Scarcely was the birth over, when Mrs Facings fell into a weakly dwam[9] that was very terrifying; and if the Captain was not her gude man, he was as concerned about her, as any true gudeman could be, and much more so than some I could name, who have the best of characters.

It so happened that this Mrs Facings had been, as I have said, overtaken on the road, and had nothing prepared for a sore foot, although she well knew that she had no time to spare. This was very calamitous, and what was to be done required a consideration. I was for wrapping the baby in a blanket till the morning, when I had no misdoubt of gathering among the ladies of the town a sufficient change of needfu' baby clouts;[10] but among other regimental clanjamphry[11] that were around this left-to-hersel' damsel, was a Mrs Gooseskin, the drum-major's wife, a most devising character. When I told her of our straits and jeopardy, she said to give myself no uneasiness, for she had seen a very good substitute for child-linen, and would set about making it without delay.

What she proposed to do was beyond my comprehension; but she soon returned into the room with a box in her hand, filled with soft-teazed wool, which she set down on a chair at the bed-stock, and covering it with an apron, she pressed the wool under the apron into a hollow shape, like a goldfinch's nest, wherein she laid the infant, and covering it up with the apron, she put more wool over it, and made it as snug as a silk-worm in a cocoon, as it has been described to me. The sight of this novelty was, however, an affliction, for if she had intended to smother the bairn, she could not have taken a more effectual

[8] guessed   [9] fit of illness   [10] nappies   [11] group, gathering

manner; and yet the baby lived and thrived, as I shall have occasion to rehearse.

Mrs Facings had a tedious recovery, and was not able to join him that in a sense was her gudeman, and the regiment, which was to me a great cause of affliction; for I thought that it might be said that her case was owing to my being a new hand, and not skilful enough. It thus came to pass that she, when able to stand the shake, was moved to private lodgings, where, for a season, she dwined and dwindled, and at last her life went clean out; but her orphan bairn was spared among us, and was a great means of causing a tenderness of heart to arise among the lasses, chiefly on account of its most thoughtless and ne'er-do-weel father, who never inquired after he left the town, concerning the puir thing; so that if there had not been a seed of charity bred by its orphan condition, nobody can tell what would have come of it. The saving hand of Providence was, however, manifested. Old Miss Peggy Needle, who had all her life been out of the body about cats and dogs, grew just extraordinar to make a pet, in the place of them all, of the laddie Willie Facings; but, as I have said, I will by and by have to tell more about him; so on that account I will make an end of the second head of my discourse, and proceed to the next, which was one of a most piteous kind.

In our parish there lived a young lad, a sticket[12] minister, not very alluring in his looks; indeed, to say the truth, he was by many, on account of them, thought to be no far short of a haverel;[13] for he was lank and most uncomely, being in-kneed; but, for all that, the minister said he was a young man of great parts, and had not only a streak of geni, but a vast deal of inordinate erudition. He went commonly by the name of Dominie Quarto; and it came to pass, that he set his affections on a weel-faured[14] lassie, the daughter of Mrs Stoups, who keepit the Thistle Inn. In this there was nothing wonderful, for she was a sweet maiden, and nobody ever saw her without wishing her well. But she could not abide the Dominie: and, indeed, it was no wonder, for he certainly was not a man to pleasure a woman's eye. Her affections were settled on a young lad called Jock Sym, a horse-couper,[15] a blithe heartsome young man, of a genteel manner, and in great repute, therefore, among the gentlemen.

He won Mally Stoups' heart; they were married, and, in the fulness of time thereafter, her pains came on, and I was sent to ease her. She lay in a back room, that looked into their pleasant garden. Half up the

---

[12] incapable, incapacitated   [13] fool   [14] good-looking   [15] horse trader

lower casement of the window, there was a white muslin curtain, made out of one of her mother's old-fashioned tamboured[16] aprons, drawn across from side to side, for the window had no shutters. It would be only to distress the reader to tell what she suffered. Long she struggled, and weak she grew; and a sough of her desperate case went up and down the town like the plague that walketh in darkness. Many came to enquire for her, both gentle and semple;[17] and it was thought that the Dominie would have been in the crowd of callers: but he came not.

In the midst of her suffering, when I was going about my business in the room, with the afflicted lying-in woman, I happened to give a glint to the window, and startled I was, to see, like a ghost, looking over the white curtain, the melancholious visage of Dominie Quarto, with watery eyes glistening like two stars in the candle light.

I told one of the women who happened to be in the way, to go out to the sorrowful young man, and tell him not to look in at the window; whereupon she went out, and remonstrated with him for some time. While she was gone, sweet Mally Stoups and her unborn baby were carried away to Abraham's bosom. This was a most unfortunate thing; and I went out before the straighting-board could be gotten, with a heavy heart, on account of my poor family, that might suffer, if I was found guilty of being to blame.

I had not gone beyond the threshold of the back-door that led into the garden, when I discerned a dark figure between me and the westling scad[18] of the setting moon. On going towards it, I was greatly surprised to find the weeping Dominie, who was keeping watch for the event there, and had just heard what had happened, by one of the women telling another.

This symptom of true love and tenderness made me forget my motherly anxieties, and I did all I could to console the poor lad; but he was not to be comforted, saying, 'It was a great trial when it was ordained that she should lie in the arms of Jock Sym, but it's far waur to think that the kirkyard hole is to be her bed, and her bridegroom the worm.'

Poor forlorn creature! I had not a word to say. Indeed, he made my heart swell in my bosom; and I could never forget the way in which he grat over my hand, that he took between both of his, as a dear thing, that he was prone to fondle and mourn over.

But this cutting grief did not end that night; on Sabbath evening following, as the custom is in our parish, Mrs Sym was ordained to be

[16] embroidered   [17] commonality   [18] a faint appearance of colour or light

interred; and there was a great gathering of freends and neighbours; for
both she and her gudeman were well thought of. Everybody expected the
Dominie would be there, for his faithfulness was spoken of by all pitiful
tongues; but he stayed away for pure grief; he hid himself from the day-
light and the light of every human eye. In the gloaming, however, after, as
the betherel[19] went to ring the eight o'clock bell, he saw the Dominie
standing with a downcast look, near the new grave, all which made baith
a long and a sad story, for many a day among us: I doubt if it's forgotten
yet. As for me, I never thought of it without a pang, but all trades have
their troubles and the death of a young wife and her unborn baby, in her
nineteenth year, is not one of the least that I have had to endure in mine.

But, although I met like many others in my outset both mortifica-
tions and difficulties, and what was worse than all, I could not say that I
was triumphant in my endeavours; yet, like the Doctors, either good
luck or experience made me gradually gather a repute for skill and dis-
cernment, insomuch that I became just wonderful for the request I was
in. It is therefore needless for me to make a strive for the entertainment
of the reader, by rehearsing all the han'lings that I had; but, as some of
them were of a notable kind, I will pass over the generality and only
make a Nota Bena here of those that were particular, as well as the
births of the babies that afterwards came to be something in the world.
Between the death of Mally Stoups and the Whitsunday of that year,
there was not much business in my line, not above two cases; but, on
the day after, I had a doing, no less than of twins in a farmer's family,
that was already overstocked with weans to a degree that was just a
hardship; but, in that case, there was a testimony that Providence never
sends mouths into the world without at the same time giving the
wherewithal to fill them.

James Mashlam was a decent, douce, hard-working, careful man,
and his wife was to all wives the very patron of frugality; but, with all
their ettling, they could scarcely make the two ends of the year to meet.
Owing to this, when it was heard in the parish that she had brought
forth a Jacob and Esau, there was a great condolence; and the birth that
ought to have caused both mirth and jocundity was not thought to be
a gentle dispensation. But short-sighted is the wisdom of man and even
of woman like-wise; for, from that day, James Mashlam began to
bud and prosper, and is now the toppingest man far or near; and his

[19] beadle

prosperity sprang out of what we all thought would be a narrowing of his straitened circumstances.

All the gentry of the country-side, when they heard the tydings, sent Mrs Mashlam many presents, and stocked her press with cleeding[20] for her and the family. It happened, also, that, at this time, there was a great concourse of Englishers at the castle with my Lord; and one of them, a rattling young gentleman, proposed that they should raise a subscription for a race-purse; promising, that, if his horse won, he would give the purse for the behoof of the twins. Thus it came to pass, that a shower of gold one morning fell on James Mashlam, as he was holding the plough; for that English ramplor's[21] horse, lo and behold! won the race, and he came over with all the company, with the purse in his hand full of golden guineas galloping upon James; and James and his wife sat cloking on this nest-egg, till they have hatched a fortune; for the harvest following, his eldest son was able to join the shearers, and from that day plenty, like a fat carlin, visited him daily. Year after year his childer that were of the male gender grew better and better helps: so that he enlarged his farm, and has since built the sclate house by the water side; that many a one, for its decent appearance, cannot but think it is surely the minister's manse.

From that time I too got a lift in the world; for it happened, that a grand lady, in the family way, came on a visit to the castle, and by some unaccountable accident she was prematurely brought to bed there. No doctor being at hand nearer than the burgh town, I was sent for and, before one could be brought, I had helped into the world the son and heir of an ancient family; for the which, I got ten golden guineas, a new gown that is still my best honesty, and a mutch that many a one came to see for it is made of a French lace. The lady insisted on me to wear it at the christening; which the Doctor was not overly pleased to hear tell of, thinking that I might in time clip the skirts of his practice.

For a long time after the deliverance of that lady I had a good deal to do in the cottars' houses; and lucky it was for me that I had got the guineas aforesaid, for the commonalty have not much to spare on an occasion; and I could not help thinking how wonderful are the ways of Providence, for the lady's gift enabled me to do my duty among the cottars with a lighter heart than I could have afforded to do had the benison been more stinted.

[20] clothes   [21] roving fellow

All the remainder of that year, the winter and the next spring, was without a remarkable: but just on the eve of summer, a very comical accident happened.

There was an old woman that come into the parish, nobody could tell how, and was called Lucky Nanse, who made her bread by distilling peppermint. Some said that now and then her house had the smell of whiskey; but how it came, whether from her still or the breath of her nostrils, was never made out to a moral certainty. This carlin had been in her day a by-ordinair woman, and was a soldier's widow forby.

At times she would tell stories of marvels she had seen in America, where she said there was a moose so big that a man could not lift its head. Once, when old Mr Izet, the precentor, to whom she was telling anent this beast, said it was not possible, she waxed very wroth, and knocking her neives[22] together in his face, she told him that he was no gentleman to misdoubt her honour: Mr Izet, who had not much of the sweet milk of human kindness in his nature, was so provoked at this freedom, that he snapped his fingers as he turned to go away, and said she was not better than a ne'er-do-weel camp-randy. If she was oil before she was flame now, and dancing with her arms extended, she looted down, and, grasping a gowpin of earth in each hand, she scattered it with an air to the wind, and cried with a desperate voice, that she did not value his opinion at the worth of that dirt.

By this time the uproar had disturbed the clachan, and at every door the women were looking out to see what was the hobble-show;[23] some with bairns in their arms and others with weans at their feet. Among the rest that happened to look out was Mrs Izet, who, on seeing the jeopardy that her gudeman was in, from that rabiator[24] woman, ran to take him under her protection. But it was a rash action for Lucky Nanse stood with her hands on her henches and daured her to approach, threatening, with some soldier-like words, that if she came near she would close her day-lights.

Mrs Izet was terrified, and stood still.

Home with you, said Nanse, ye mud[25] that ye are, to think yourself on a par with pipeclay, with other hetradox brags,[26] that were just a sport to hear. In the meantime, the precentor was walking homeward, and called to his wife to come away, and leave that tempest and whirlwind with her own wrack and carry.

---

[22] fists   [23] uproar   [24] scoundrel, a violent, useless person
[25] a small insignificant object   [26] defiant individuals

Lucky Nanse had, by this time, spent her ammunition, and, unable to find another word sufficiently vicious, she ran up to him and spat in his face.

Human nature could stand no more, and the precentor forgetting himself and his dignity in the parish, lifted his foot and gave her a kick, which caused her to fall on her back. There she lay sprawling and speechless, and made herself at last lie as like a corpse, as it was possible. Every body thought that she was surely grievously hurt, though Mr Izet said his foot never touched her; and a hand-barrow was got to carry her home. All present were in great dismay, for they thought Mr Izet had committed a murder and would be hanged in course of law; but I may be spared from describing the dolorosity[27] that was in our town that night.

Lucky Nanse being carried home on the barrow like a carcase, was put to bed; where, when she had lain some time, she opened a comical eye for a short space, and then to all intents and purposes seemed in the dead throes. It was just then that I, drawn into the house by the din of the straemash,[28] looked over a neighbour's shoulder; but no sooner did the artful woman see my face than she gave a skirle of agony, and cried that her time was come, and the pains of a mother were upon her; at which to hear, all the other women gave a shout, as if a miracle was before them, for Nanse was, to all appearance, threescore; but she for a while so enacted her stratagem that we were in a terrification lest it should be true. At last she seemed quite exhausted, and I thought she was in the natural way, when in a jiffy she bounced up with a derisive gaffaw, and drove us all pell-mell out of the house. The like of such a ploy had never been heard of in our countryside. I was, however, very angry to be made such a fool of in my profession before all the people, especially as it turned out that the old woman was only capering in her cups.

Sometime after this exploit another come-to-pass happened that had a different effect on the nerves of us all. This fell out by a sailor's wife, a young woman that came to lie in from Sandy-port with her mother, a most creditable widow, that kept a huckstry[29] shop for the sale of parliament cakes, candles, bone-combs, and prins, and earned a bawbee by the eydency[30] of her spinning wheel.

Mrs Spritsail, as the young woman was called, had a boding in her breast that she could not overcome, and was a pitiable object of despondency, from no cause; but women in her state are often troubled by

[27] low spirits, ill-temper   [28] uproar   [29] haggling   [30] diligence, busy

similar vapours. Hers, however, troubled everybody that came near her, and made her poor mother almost persuaded that she would not recover.

One night when she expected to be confined, I was called in: but such a night as that was! At the usual hour, the post woman, Martha Dauner, brought a letter to the old woman from Sandy-port, sealed with a black wafer; which, when Mrs Spritsail saw, she grew as pale as a clout,[31] and gave a deep sigh. Alas! it was a sigh of prophecy; for the letter was to tell that her husband, John Spritsail, had tumbled overboard the night before, and was drowned.

For some time the young widow sat like an image, making no moan: it was very frightful to see her. By and by, her time came on, and although it could not be said that her suffering was by common, she fell back again into that effigy state, which made her more dreadful to see than if she had been a ghost in its winding sheet; and she never moved from the posture she put herself in till all was over, and the living creature was turned into a clod of church-yard clay.

This for a quiet calamity is the most distressing in my chronicle, for it came about with little ceremony. Nobody was present with us but only her sorrowful mother, on whose lap I laid the naked new-born babe. Soon after, the young widow departed to join her gudeman in paradise; but as it is a mournful tale, it would only be to hurt the reader's tender feelings to make a more particular account.

All my peradventures were not, however, of the same doleful kind; and there is one that I should mention, for it was the cause of meikle jocosity at the time and for no short season after.

There lived in the parish a very old woman, upwards of fourscore: she was as bent in her body as a cow's horn, and she supported herself with a staff in one hand, and for balance held up her gown behind with the other; in short, she was a very antideluvian, something older than seemed the folk at that time of the earth.

This ancient crone was the grandmother to Lizzy Dadily, a light-headed winsome lassie, that went to service in Glasgow; but many months she had not been there when she came back again, all mouth and een; and on the same night her granny, old Maudelin, called on me. It was at the gloaming: I had not trimmed my crusie,[32] but I had just mended the fire, which had not broken out so that we conversed in an obscurity.

[31] cloth, a baby's nappy   [32] a boat-shaped oil lamp with a rush wick

Of the history of old Maudelin I had never before heard ony particulars; but her father, as she told me, was out in the rebellion of Mar's year, and if the true king had gotten his rights, she would not have been a needful woman. This I, however, jealouse was vanity; for although it could not be said that she was positively an ill-doer, it was well known in the town that old as she was, the conduct of her house in many points was not the best. Her daughter, the mother of Lizzy, was but a canary-headed creature. What became of her we never heard, for she went off with the soldiers one day, leaving Lizzy, a bastard bairn. How the old woman thereafter fenn't,[33] in her warsle with age and poverty, was to many a mystery, especially as it was now and then seen that she had a bank guinea note to change, and whom it cam frae was a marvel.

Lizzy coming home, her granny came to me, as I was saying, and after awhile conversing in the twilight about this and that, she told me that she was afraid her oe[34] had brought home her wark, and that she didna doubt they would need the sleight of my hand in a short time, for that Lizzy had only got a month's leave to try the benefit of her native air; that of Glasgow, as with most young women, not agreeing with her.

I was greatly taken aback to hear her talk in such a calm and methodical manner concerning Lizzy, whom I soon found was in that condition that would, I'm sure, have drawn tears of the heart's blood from every other grandmother in the clachan. Really I was not well pleased to hear the sinful carlin talk in such a good-e'en and good-morn way about a guilt of that nature; and I said to her, both hooly and fairly, that I was not sure if I could engage myself in the business, for it went against my righteous opinion to make myself a mean of filling the world with natural children.

The old woman was not just pleased to hear me say this, and without any honey on her lips, she replied,

'Widow Blithe, this is an unco strain! and what for will ye no do your duty to Lizzy Dadily; for I must have a reason, because the minister or the magistrates of the borough shall ken of this.'

I was to be sure a little confounded to hear the frail though bardy[35] old woman thus speak to her peremptors, but in my mild and methodical manner I answered and said,

'That no person in a trade with full hands ought to take a new turn; and although conscience, I would allow, had its weight with me, yet there was a stronger reason in my engagements to others.'

---

[33] subsisted   [34] grandchild   [35] fierce

'Very well,' said Maudelin, and hastily rising, she gave a rap with her staff, and said, 'that there soon would be news in the land that I would hear of;' and away she went, stotting out at the door, notwithstanding her age, like a birsled pea.

After she was gone, I began to reflect; and I cannot say that I had just an ease of mind, when I thought of what she had been telling anent her oe: but nothing more came to pass that night.

The following evening, however, about the same hour, who should darken my door but the minister himself, a most discreet man, who had always paid me a very sympathysing attention from the death of my gudeman; so I received him with the greatest respect, wondering what could bring him to see me at that doubtful hour. But no sooner had he taken a seat in the elbow chair than he made my hair stand on end at the wickedness and perfidy of the woman sec.

'Mrs Blithe,' said he, 'I have come to have a serious word with you, and to talk with you on a subject that is impossible for me to believe. Last night that old Maudelin, of whom the world speaks no good, came to me with her grand-daughter from Glasgow, both weeping very bitterly; the poor young lass had her apron tail at her face, and was in great distress.'

'What is the matter with you,' said I, quoth the minister; 'and thereupon the piteous grandmother told me that her oe had been beguiled by a false manufacturing gentleman, and was thereby constrained to come back in a state of ignominy that was heartbreaking.'

'Good Maudelin, in what can I help you in your calamity?'

'In nothing, nothing,' said she; 'but we are come to make a confession in time.'

'What confession? quo' I'—that said the minister.

'Oh, sir,' said she, 'it's dreadful, but your counselling may rescue us from a great guilt. I have just been with Widow Blithe, the midwife, to bespeak her helping hand; oh, sir, speir no questions.'

'But,' said the minister, 'this is not a business to be trifled with; what did Mrs Blithe say to you?'

'That Mrs Blithe,' replied Maudelin, 'is a hidden woman; she made sport of my poor Lizzy's misfortune, and said that the best I could do was to let her nip the craig[36] of the bairn in the hour of its birth.'

'Now, Mrs Blithe,' continued the Minister, 'is it possible that you could suggest such a crime?'

---

[36] neck, throat

I was speechless; blue sterns danced before my sight, my knees trembled, and the steadfast earth grew as it were coggly aneath my chair; at last I replied,

'That old woman, sir, is of a nature, as she is of age enough, to be a witch–she's no canny! to even me to murder! Sir, I commit myself into your hands and judgment.'

'Indeed, I thought,' said the minister, 'that you would never speak as Maudelin said you had done; but she told me to examine you myself, for that she was sure, if I was put to the straights of a question, I would tell the truth.'

'And you have heard the truth, sir,' cried I.

'I believe it,' said he; 'but, in addition to all she rehearsed, she told me that, unless you, Mrs Blithe, would do your duty to her injured oe, and free gratis for no fee at all, she would go before a magistrate, and swear you had egged her on to bathe her hands in innocent infant blood.'

'Mr Stipend,' cried I; 'the wickedness of the human heart is beyond the computations of man: this dreadful old woman is, I'll not say what; but oh, sir, what am I to do; for if she makes a perjury to a magistrate my trade is gone, and my dear bairns driven to iniquity and beggary?'

Then the minister shook his head, and said, 'It was, to be sure, a great trial, for a worthy woman like me, to be so squeezed in the vice of malice and malignity; but a calm sough in all troubles was true wisdom, and that I ought to comply with the deceitful carlin's terms.'

Thus it came to pass, that, after the bastard brat was born, the old wife made a brag of how she had spirited the worthy minister to terrify me. Everybody laughed at her souple trick: but to me it was, for many a day, a heartburning; though, to the laive of the parish, it was a great mean, as I have said, of daffin and merriment.

No doubt, it will be seen, by the foregoing, that, although in a sense I had reason to be thankful that Providence, with the help of the laird's leddy-mother, had enabled me to make a bit of bread for my family, yet, it was not always without a trouble and an anxiety. Indeed, when I think on what I have come through in my profession, though it be one of the learned, and the world not able to do without it, I have often thought that I could not wish waur to my deadliest enemy than a kittle case of midwifery; for surely it is a very obstetrical business, and far above a woman with common talons to practise. But it would be to make a wearisome tale were I to lengthen my story; and so I mean just to tell of another accident that happened to me last year, and then to make an end, with a word or two of improvement on what shall have been said; afterwards I will give some account of what happened to those that, through my instrumentality, were brought to be a credit to themselves and an ornament to the world. Some, it is very true, were not just of that stamp; for, as the impartial sun shines alike on the wicked and the worthy, I have had to deal with those whose use I never could see, more than that of an apple that falleth from the tree, and perisheth with rottenness.

The case that I have to conclude with was in some sort mystical; and long it was before I got an interpretation thereof. It happened thus:–

One morning in the fall of the year and before break of day, when I was lying wakerife in my bed, I heard a knuckling on the pane of the window and got up to inquire the cause. This was by the porter of the Thistle Inns, seeking my help for a leddy at the crying, that had come to their house since midnight and could go no further.

I made no more ado, but dressed myself off-hand, and went to the Inns; where, to be sure, there was a leddy, for any thing that I then knew to the contrary, in great difficulty. Who she was, and where she had come from, I heard not; nor did I speir; nor did I see her face; for over her whole head she had a muslin apron so thrown and tied, that her face was concealed; and no persuasion could get her to remove that veil. It was therefore plain to me that she wished herself, even in my hands, not to be known; but she did not seem to jalouse that the very obstinacy about the veil would be a cause to make me think that she was afraid I would know her. I was not, however, overly-curious; for, among the other good advices that I got when I was about to take up the trade, from the leddy of Rigs, my patron, I was enjoined never to be inquisitive anent family secrets; which I have, with a very scrupulous care, always adhered to; and thus it happened, that, although the leddy made herself so strange as to make me suspicious that all was not right, I said nothing but I opened both my eyes and my ears.

She had with her an elderly woman; and, before she came to the worst, I could gather from their discourse, that the lady's husband was expected every day from some foreign land. By and by, what with putting one thing together with another, and eiking out with the help of my own imagination, I was fain to guess that she would not be ill pleased to be quit of her burden before the Major came home.

Nothing beyond this patch-work of hints then occurred. She had an easy time of it; and, before the sun was up, she was the mother of a bonny bairn. But what surprised me was, that, in less than an hour after the birth, she was so wonderful hale and hearty, that she spoke of travelling another stage in the course of the day, and of leaving Mrs Smith, that was with her, behind to take care of the babby; indeed, this was settled; and, before noon, at twelve o'clock, she was ready to step into the post-chaise that she had ordered to take herself forward–but mark the upshot.

When she was dressed and ready for the road–really she was a stout woman–another chaise drew up at the Inn's door, and, on looking from the window to see who was in it, she gave a shriek and staggered back to a sofa, upon which she fell like one that had been dumbfoundered.

In the chaise I saw only an elderly weather-beaten gentleman, who, as soon as the horses were changed, pursued his journey. The moment he was off, this mysterious mother called the lady-nurse with the babby, and they spoke for a time in whispers. Then her chaise was brought out and in she stepped, causing me to go with her for a stage. I did so and she very liberally gave me a five pound note of the Royal Bank and made me, without allowing me to alight, return back with the retour-chaise; for the which, on my account, she settled with the driver. But there the story did not rest, as I shall have occasion to rehearse by and by.

Part II–Anent Bairns

Although I have not in the foregoing head of my subject mentioned every extraordinary han'ling that came to me, yet I have noted the most remarkable; and made it plain to my readers by that swatch of my professional work, that it is not an easy thing to be a midwife with repute, without the inheritance from nature of good common sense and discretion, over and above skill and experience. I shall now dedicate this second head, to a make-mention of such things as I have heard and known anent the bairns, that in their entrance into this world, came by the grace of God through my hands.

And here, in the first place, and at the very outset, it behoves me to make an observe, that neither omen nor symptom occurs at a birth, by which any reasonable person or gossip present can foretell what the native, as the unchristened baby is then called, may be ordained to come through in the course of the future. No doubt this generality, like every rule, has an exception; but I am no disposed to think the exceptions often kent-speckle; for although I have heard many a well-doing sagacious carlin notice the remarkables she had seen at some births, I am yet bound to say that my experience has never taught me to discern in what way a-come-to-pass in the life of the man was begotten of the uncos at the birth of the child.

But while I say this, let me no be misunderstood as throwing any doubt on the fact, that births sometimes are, and have been, in all ages, attended with signs and wonders manifest. I am only stating the truth it has fallen out in the course of my own experience; for I never misdoubt that it's in the power of Providence to work miracles and cause marvels, when a child is ordained with a superfluity of head-rope. I only maintain, that it is not a constancy in nature to be regular in that way, and that many prodigies happen at the times of births, of which it would not be a facile thing for a very wise prophet to expound the use. Indeed, my observes would go to the clean contrary; for I have noted that, for the most part, the births which have happened in dread and strange circumstances, were not a hair's-breadth better, than those of the commonest clamjamphry. Indeed, I had a very notable instance of this kind in the very first year of my setting up for myself, and that was when James Cuiffy's wife lay in of her eldest born.

James, as all the parish well knew, was not a man to lead the children of Israel through the Red Sea, nor she a Deborah to sing of butter in a lordly dish; but they were decent folk; and when the fulness of her time was come, it behoved her to be put to bed, and my helping hand to be called for. Accordingly I went.

It was the gloaming when James came for me; and as we walked o'er the craft together, the summer lightning ayont the hills began to skimmer in a woolly cloud: but we thought little o't, for the day had been very warm, and that flabbing of the fire was but a natural outcoming of the same cause.

We had not, however, been under the shelter of the roof many minutes, when we heard a-far off, like the ruff of a drum or the hurl of a cart of stones tumbled on the causey, a clap of thunder, and then we heard another and another, just like a sea-fight of Royal Georges in the skies, till the din grew so desperate, that the crying woman could no more be heard than if she had been a stone image of agony.

I'll no say that I was not in a terrification. James Cuiffy took to his Bible, but the poor wife needed all my help. At last the bairn was born; and just as it came into the world, the thunder rampaged, as if the Prince of the Powers of the air had gaen by himself; and in the same minute, a thunder-bolt fell doun the lum, scattered the fire about the house, whiskit out of the window, clove like a wedge the apple-tree at the house-end, and slew nine sucking pigs and the mother grumphy, as if they had been no better than the host of Sennacherib; which every body must allow was most awful: but for all that, nothing afterwards came to pass; and the bairn that was born, instead of turning out a necromancer or a geni, as we had so much reason to expect, was, from the breast, as silly as a windlestraw. Was not this a plain proof that they are but of a weak credulity who have faith in freats of that kind?

I met, likewise, not in the next year, but in the year after, nearer to this time, another delusion of the same uncertainty. Mrs Gallon, the excise-man's wife, was overtaken with her pains, of all places in the world, in the kirk, on a Sabbath afternoon. They came on her suddenly, and she gave a skirle that took the breath with terror from the minister, as he was enlarging with great bir on the ninth clause of the seventh head of his discourse. Every body stood up. The whole congregation rose upon the seats, and in every face was pale consternation. At last the minister said, that on account of the visible working of Providence in the midst of us, yea in the very kirk itself, the congregation should skail: whereupon skail they did; so that in a short time I had completed my work, in which I was assisted by some decent ladies staying to lend me their Christian assistance; which they did, by standing in a circle round the table seat where the ploy was going on, with their backs to the crying mother, holding out their gowns in a minaway fashion, as the maids of honour are said to do, when the queen is bringing forth a prince in public.

The bairn being born, it was not taken out of the kirk till the minister himself was brought back, and baptized it with a scriptural name; for it was every body's opinion that surely in time it would be a brave minister, and become a great and shining light in the Lord's vineyard to us all. But it is often the will and pleasure of Providence to hamper in the fulfilment the carnal wishes of corrupt human nature. Matthew Gallon had not in after life the seed of a godly element in his whole carcase; quite the contrary, for he turned out the most rank ringing enemy that was ever in our country-side; and when he came to years of discretion, which in a sense he never did, he fled the country as a soldier, and for some splore with the Session, though he was born in the kirk;–another plain fact that shows how little reason there is in some cases to believe that births and prognostifications have no natural connexion. Not that I would condumaciously maintain that there is no meaning in signs sometimes, and may be I have had a demonstration; but it was a sober advice that the auld leddy of Rigs gave me, when she put me in a way of business, to be guarded in the use of my worldy wisdom, and never to allow my tongue to describe what my eyes saw or my ears heard at an occasion, except I was well convinced it would pleasure the family.

'No conscientious midwife', said she, 'will ever make causey-talk of what happens at a birth, if it's of a nature to work dule by repetition on the fortunes of the bairn;' and this certainly was most orthodox, for I have never forgotten her counsel.

I have, however, an affair in my mind at this time; and as I shall mention no names, there can be no harm done in speaking of it here; for it is a thing that would perplex a philosopher or a mathematical man, and stagger the self-conceit of an unbeliever.

There was a young Miss that had occasion to come over the moor by herself one day, and in doing so she met with a hurt; what that hurt was, no body ever heard; but it could not be doubted that it was something most extraordinar; for, when she got home, she took to her bed and was very unwell for several days, and her een were blear't with greeting. At last, on the Sabbath-day following, her mother foregathert with me in coming from the kirk; and the day being showery, she proposed to rest in my house as she passed the door, till a shower that she saw coming would blow over. In doing this, and we being by ourselves, I speired in a civil manner for her daughter; and from less to more she told me something that I shall not rehearse, and, with the tear in her eye, she entreated advice; but I could give her none, for I thought her daughter had been donsie;[37] so no more was said anent it; but the poor lassie from that day fell as it were into a dwining, and never went out; insomuch that before six months were come and gone, she was laid up in her bed, and there was a wally-wallying on her account throughout the parish, none doubting that she was in a sore way, if not past hope.

In this state was her sad condition, when they had an occasion for a gradawa[38] at my Lord's; and as he changed horses at the Cross Keys

---

[37] silly, dreamy   [38] a doctor

when he passed through our town, I said to several of the neighbours, to advise the mother that this was a fine opportunity she ought not to neglect, but should consult him anent her dochter. Accordingly, on the doctor returning from the castle, she called him in; and when he had consulted the ailing lassie as to her complaint, every body rejoiced to hear that he made light of it, and said that she would be as well as ever in a month or two; for that all she had to complain of was but a weakness common to womankind, and that a change of air was the best thing that could be done for her.

Maybe I had given an advice to the same effect quietly before, and therefore was none displeased to hear, when it came to pass, that shortly after, the mother and Miss were off one morning, for the benefit of the air of Glasgow, in a retour chaise, by break of day, before anybody was up. To be sure some of the neighbours thought it an odd thing that they should have thought of going to that town for a beneficial air; but as the report soon after came out to the town that the sick lassie was growing brawly, the wonder soon blew over, for it was known that the air of a close town is very good in some cases of the asthma.

By and by, it might be six weeks or two months after, aiblins more, when the mother and the daughter came back, the latter as slimb as a popular tree, and blooming like a rose. Such a recovery after such an illness was little short of a miracle, for the day of their return was just ten months from the day and date of her hurt.

It is needless for me to say what were my secret thoughts on this occasion, especially when I heard the skill of the gradawa extolled, and far less how content I was when, in the year following, the old lady went herself on a jaunt into the East Country to see a sick cousin, a widow woman with only a bairn, and brought the bairn away with her on the death of the parent. It was most charitable of her so to do, and nothing could exceed the love and ecstasy with which Miss received it from the arms of her mother. Had it been her ain bairn she could not have dandalized it more!

Soon after this the young lady fell in with a soldier officer, that was sent to recruit in the borough, and married him on a short acquaintance, and went away with him a regimenting to Ireland; but 'my cousin's wee fatherless and motherless orphan,' as the old pawkie carlin used to call the bairn, stayed with her, and grew in time to be a ranting birkie; and in the end, my lord hearing of his spirit, sent for him one day to the castle, and in the end bought for him a commission, in the most generous manner, such as well befitted a rich young lord to do; and afterwards, in the army, his promotion was as rapid as if he had more than merit to help him.

Now, is not this a thing to cause a marvelling; for I, that maybe had it in my power to have given an explanation, was never called on so to do; for everything came to pass about it in such an ordained-like way, that really I was sometimes at a loss what to think, and said to myself surely I have dreamt a dream; for, although it could not be said to have been a case of prognostications, it was undoubtedly one of a most kittle sort in many particulars. Remembering, however, the prudent admonition I had received from the auld leddy of Rigs, I shall say no more at present, but keep a calm sough.

It is no doubt the even-down fact that I had no hand in bringing 'my cousin's wee fatherless and motherless orphan' into the world, but maybe I might have had, if all the outs and ins of the story were told. As that, however, is not fitting, I have just said enough to let the courteous reader see, though it be as in a glass darkly, that my profession is no without the need of common sense in its handlings, and that I have not earned a long character for prudence in the line without ettle, nor been without jobs that cannot be spoken of, but, like this, in a far-off manner. But it behoves me, before I go farther, to request the reader to turn back to where I have made mention of the poor deserted bairn, Willy Facings; how he was born in an unprepared hurry, and how his mother departed this life, while his ne'er-do-weel father went away like a knotless thread. I do not know how it happened, but come to pass it did, that I took a kindness for the forsaken creature, insomuch that, if his luck had been no better with Miss Peggy Needle, it was my intent to have brought him up with my own weans; for he was a winsome thing from the hour of his birth, and made every day a warmer nest for his image in my heart. His cordial temper was a mean devised by Providence as a compensation to him for the need that was in its own courses, that he would never enjoy a parent's love.

When Miss Peggy had skailed the byke of her cats, and taken Billy, as he came to be called, home to her house, there was a wonderment both in the borough-town and our clachan how it was possible for her, an inexperienced old maid, to manage the bairn; for by this time he was weaned, and was as rampler a creature as could well be, and she was a most prejinct and mim[39] lady. But, notwithstanding her natural

[39] prim

mimness and prejinkity, she was just out of the body with love and tenderness towards him, and kept him all day at her foot, playing in the inside of a stool whamled up-side down.

It was the sagacious opinion of every one, and particularly both of the doctor and Mr Stipend, the minister, that the bairn would soon tire out the patience of Miss Peggy; but we are all short-sighted mortals, for instead of tiring her, she every day grew fonder and fonder of him, and hired a lassie to look after him, as soon as he could tottle. Nay, she bought a green parrot for him from a sailor, when he was able to run about; and no mother could be so taken up with her own get as kind-hearted Miss Peggy was with him, her darling Dagon; for although the parrot was a most outstrapolous beast, and skrighed at times with louder desperation than a pea-hen in a passion, she yet so loved it on his account, that one day when it bit her lip to the bleeding, she only put it in its cage, and said, as she wiped her mouth, that it was 'a sorrow.'

By and by Miss Peggy put Billy to the school; but, by that time, the condumacious laddie had got the upper hand of her, and would not learn his lesson, unless she would give him an apple or sweeties; and yet, for all that, she was out of the body about him, in so much that the minister was obligated to remonstrate with her on such indulgence; telling her she would be the ruin of the boy, fine creature as he was, if she did not bridle him, and intended to leave him a legacy.

In short, Miss Peggy and her pet were just a world's wonder, when, at last, Captain Facings, seven years after Billy's birth, being sent by the king to Glasgow, came out, one Sunday to our town, and sent for me to learn what had become of his bairn. Though I recollected him at the first sight, yet, for a matter of policy, I thought it convenient to pretend doubtful of my memory, till, I trow, I had made him sensible of his sin in deserting his poor baby. At long and length I made him to know the blessing that had been conferred by the fancy of Miss Peggy, on the deserted child, and took him myself to her house. But, judge of my consternation, and his likewise, when, on introducing him to her as the father of Billy, whom I well recollected, she grew very huffy at me, and utterly denied that Billy was any such boy as I had described, and foundled over him, and was really in a comical distress, till, from less to more, she grew, at last, as obstinate as a graven image, and was not sparing in the words she made use of to get us out of her habitation.

But, not to summer and winter on this very unforeseen come-to-pass, the Captain and I went to the minister, and there made a confession of the whole tot of the story. Upon which he advised the Captain to leave Billy with Miss Peggy, who was a single lady, not ill-off in the world; and he would, from time to time, see that justice was done to the bairn. They then made a paction concerning Billy's education; and, after a sore struggle, Miss Peggy, by the minister's exhortation, was brought to consent that her pet should be sent to a boarding-school, on condition that she was to be allowed to pay for him.

This was not difficult to be agreed to; and, some weeks after, Bill was accordingly sent to the academy at Green Knowes, where he turned out a perfect delight; and Miss Peggy sent him every week, by the carrier, a cake, or some other dainty. At last, the year ran round, and the vacance being at hand, Bill sent word by the carrier, that he was coming home to spend the time with Mamma, as he called Miss Peggy. Great was her joy at the tidings; she set her house in order, and had, at least, twenty weans, the best sort in the neighbourhood, for a ploy to meet him. But, och hone! when Billy came, he was grown such a big creature, that he no longer seemed the same laddie; and, at the sight of him, Miss Peggy began to weep and wail, crying, that it was an imposition they were attempting to put upon her, by sending another callan. However, she became, in the course of the night, pretty well convinced that he was indeed her pet; and, from that time, though he was but eight years old, she turned over a new leaf in her treatment.

Nothing less would serve her, seeing him grown so tall, than that he should be transmogrified into a gentleman; and, accordingly, although he was not yet even a stripling–for that's a man-child in his teens–she sent for a taylor next day and had him put into long clothes, with top boots; and she bought him a watch, and just made him into a curiosity, that nowhere else could be seen.

When he was dressed in his new clothes and fine boots, he went out to show himself to all Miss Peggy's neighbours; and, it happened, that, in going along, he fell in with a number of other childer, who were sliding down a heap of mixed lime, and the thoughtless brat joined them; by which he rubbed two holes in the bottom of his breeks, spoiled his new boots, and, when the holes felt cold behind, he made his hat into a seat, and went careering up the heap and down the slope with it, as if he had been a charioteer.

Everybody who saw the result concluded that certainly now Miss Peggy's favour was gone from him for ever. But she, instead of being angry, just exclaimed and demonstrated with gladness over him; saying, that, till this disaster, she had still suspected that he might turn out an imposture. Was there ever such infatuation? But, as I shall have to speak more anent him hereafter, I need not here say how he was sent back to the academy, on the minister's advice, just dress'd like another laddie.

: *Home with you, said Nanse, ye mud*
that ye are, to think yourself on a par
with pipeclay, with other hetradox brags,
that were just a sport to hear.

ALICIA ANNE SPOTTISWOODE OF THAT ILK (LADY JOHN SCOTT)

Throughout the nineteenth century, a number of middle- and upper-class women produced songs in Scots, often reworking traditional verses picked up from broadsides or setting their own words to existing tunes.

These pieces present an individual view of the world; often bland and observational, they rarely challenge established conventions. The love songs celebrate rural charm, individual beauty and the subject's suitability for marriage, which may be deplored as an institution but only because it curtails individual freedom. As in 'Durrisdeer', love triumphs over death, where a happy reunion is anticipated, or happier times, free from worldly cares, are recalled. But the most popular genre was Jacobite songs, with their potent mixture of glamour, loss and nationalism.

These contrast sharply with the work of writers like Janet Little, Ellen Johnston and Marion Bernstein, which was generally dismissed because of the writers' lack of formal education or their political opinions, especially on subjects such as marriage, drink and women's rights.

Alicia Anne Spottiswoode (1810–1900) was born in Berwickshire and married Lord John Scott, whose brother was the fifth Duke of Buccleuch. She was a collector of traditional songs and often based her work on older pieces. The best known of her attributed compositions is 'Annie Laurie', which was originally a poem by William Douglas of Fingland, set to the tune 'Kempie Kaye'. Spottiswoode altered the words and melody and added a third verse.

:DURRISDEER

We'll meet nae mair at sunset, when the weary day is dune,
Nor wander hame thegither, by the lee licht o' the mune!
I'll hear your step nae longer amang the dewy corn,
For we'll meet nae mair, my bonniest, either at eve or morn.

The yellow broom is waving, abune the sunny brae,
And the rowan berries dancing, where the sparkling waters play.
Tho' a' is bright and bonnie, it's an eerie place to me,
For we'll meet nae mair, my dearest, either by burn or tree.

Far up into the wild hills, there's a kirkyard auld and still,
Where the frosts lie ilka morning, and the mists hang low and chill,
And there ye sleep in silence, while I wander here my lane,
Till we meet ance mair in Heaven, never to part again.

JANET HAMILTON

Janet Hamilton (1795–1873) started work when she was seven, and was thirteen when she married John Hamilton. She was, according to George Eyre-Todd, 'one of those remarkable women in humble life of whom Scotland has produced so strong a crop'.

'On a cold February morning in the year 1809 we started on foot early for Glasgow. We went to the house of an acquaintance of my husband, and told him we had come to be married. He sent his porter to the Rev. Dr Lockhart, of College Church . . . who asked if we had anyone to witness the marriage. Our answer was in the negative. The porter and Betty, the housemaid, were called in to witness – the knot was tied which has never yet been loosed. I never saw the Doctor's face, and I can pass my word he never saw mine. We then returned to the friend's house, got some refreshment, took the road home again on foot, arrived after dark, got in unperceived by any of my girlish companions, had a cup of tea with a few of the old neighbours, and at the breakfast table next morning we took stock of our worldly gear. Our humble household plenishing was all paid, and my husband had a Spanish dollar, and on that and our two pair of hands we started, and though many battles and bustles have had to be encountered, with the help of a good kind God, we have always been able to keep the wolf from the door.'

She started work when her family moved to Langloan, Coatbridge, where her father was a shoemaker. Janet's husband worked for her father and the couple had ten children. She taught them all to read, having taught herself at the age of five, and was fifty-four before she taught herself to write. For the last eighteen years of her life she was blind; a daughter read to her and a son transcribed her work.

Janet Hamilton wrote a number of essays and prose pieces, as well
as poetry in both Scots and English on a wide range of social, political
and religious subjects.

Na, na, I wunna pairt wi' that,
I downa gi'e it up;
O' Scotlan's hamely mither tongue
I canna quat the grup.
It's 'bedded in my very heart,
Ye needna rive an' rug;
It's in my e'e an' on my tongue,
An' singin' in my lug.

(*Auld Mither Scotlan': A Lay of the Doric*)

. . . .

: OOR LOCATION

A hunner funnels bleezin', reekin',
Cóal an' ironstane charrin', smeekin';
Navvies, miners, keepers, fillers,
Puddlers, rollers, iron millers;
Reestit, reekit, raggit laddies,
Firemen, enginemen, an' paddies;
Boatmen, banksmen, rough and rattlin',
'Bout the wecht wi' colliers battlin',
Sweatin', swearin', fechtin' drinkin',
Change-house bells an' gill-stoups clinkin';
Police—ready men and willin'–
Aye at han' whan stoups are fillin',
Clerks, an' counter-loupers plenty,
Wi' trim moustache and whiskers dainty–
Chaps that winna staun at trifles,
Min' ye they can han'le rifles.

'Bout the wives in oor location,
An' the lassies' botheration,
Some are decent, some are dandies,
An' a gey wheen drucken randies,
Aye tae neebors' hooses sailin',
Greetin' bairns ahint them trailin',
Gaun for nouther bread nor butter,
Just tae drink an' rin the cutter.
Oh, the dreadfu' curse o' drinkin'!
Men are ill, but tae my thinkin',
Lukin' through the drucken fock,
There's a Jenny for ilk Jock.
Oh the dool an' desolation,
An' the havoc in the nation,
Wrocht by dirty, drucken wives!
Oh hoo mony bairnies' lives
Lost ilk year through their neglec';
Like a millstane roun' the neck
O' the strugglin', toilin' masses
Hing drucken wives an' wanton lassies.
Tae see sae mony unwed mithers
Is sure a shame that taps a' ithers.

An' noo I'm fairly set a-gaun,
On baith the whisky-shop and pawn;
I'll speak my min'—and whatfor no?
Frae whence cums misery, want, an' wo,
The ruin, crime, disgrace, an' shame,
That quenches a' the lichts o' hame?
Ye needna speer, the feck ot's drawn
Out o' the change-hoose an' the pawn.

Sin and death, as poets tell,
On ilk side the doors o' hell
Wait tae haurl mortals in;
Death gets a' that's catcht by sin:
There are doors whaur death an' sin
Draw their tens o' thoosan's in;
Thick and thrang we see them gaun,
First the dram-shop, then the pawn;
Owre a' kin's o' ruination,
Drink's the king in oor location.

P. HATELY WADDELL

For more than 200 years the Authorised Version of the Bible was the most widely read book in Scotland. It was consulted privately, read at family worship and heard at every service in every Kirk. In a religious age, when the word of God was absolute, the word of God was English. The prestige and status of Scots was inevitably diminished, especially in the minds of those who spoke it.

It is impossible to imagine any other book having such an effect on linguistic development. The triple blow of the court and the parliament's removal to London and the Reformed Kirk's adoption of the King James Bible, clearly stifled the development of Scots prose at a time when the status of the language was already in decline.

In 1871 the Rev. Dr Peter Hately Waddell, LLD (1817–91) produced *Psalms frae Hebrew intil Scottis*. It was, as his title page proclaims, a new translation from the original source, rather than being based on an English version.

Waddell was a Free Church minister at the time of the Disruption in 1843. He disagreed on a point of ecclesiastical government and left the same year, founding a church for himself at Girvan, known as the Church of the Future, where he preached for nineteen years. In 1862 he came to Glasgow and, still independent of other denominations, founded Trades' Hall Congregation.

As chairman at the Burns's Centenary celebration in the Alloway cottage in 1859, he delivered an address comparing Burns with the Psalmist David – the main difference being that 'the Hebrew had no humour'. Burns, he concluded, was the foremost lyricist since David.

:THE 23RD PSALM

The LORD *is* my herd, nae want sal fa' me:

He louts me till lie amang green howes; he airts me atowre by the lown watirs:

He waukens my wa'-gaen saul; he weises me roun, for his ain name's sake, intil right roddins.

Na! tho' I gang thro' the dead-mirk-dail; *e'en thar*, sal I dread nae skaithin: for yersel *are* nar-by me; yer stok an' yer stay haud me baith fu' cheerie.

My buird ye hae hansell'd in face o' my faes; ye hae drookit my head wi' oyle; my bicker is *fu' an'* skailin.

E'en sae, sal gude-guidin an' gude-gree gang wi' me, ilk day o' my livin; an' evir mair syne, i' the LORD's ain howff, *at lang last*, sal I mak bydan.

WILLIAM ALEXANDER   :

William Alexander (1826–94) lost a leg at the age of twenty and in 1852 began a career in journalism on the *Aberdeen Free Press*, where his novel *Johnny Gibb of Gushetneuk* was serialised.

Johnny Gibb is set at the time of the 1843 Disruption, when English was the language of ecclesiastical debate but ministers addressed their congregations in Doric. Like other writers of his day, Alexander's narrative is in English and his dialogue reproduces the voices of Messrs Muggart, Pinkshule, Langchafts, Tawse and Sleekaboot.

Alexander serialised a number of novels, including *The Laird of Drammochdyle*, which, like much of his work, tilts towards John Galt's influence, especially in the way he records social and economic change through characters who struggle to make sense of the confusion of a Scottish community. *The Laird of Drammochdyle* anticipates other Scottish novels in the way that public respectability becomes a cloak for self-interest and the rising bourgeoisie destroy traditional community values.

'Baubie Huie's Bastard Geet' is clearly written for a local audience who would recognise the authenticity of the dialogue and the accuracy of the detail. The social and communal morality of the times are upheld and, though the young Jock Huie may not be accepted across the community, the very subject and its open treatment is a world away from the supposed country values espoused by the Kailyard writers where sentimentality and moral censure would surely have obscured the very human circumstances.

: BAUBIE HUIE'S BASTARD GEET

I

JACK HUIE'S HOUSEHOLD–BAUBIE ENTERS LIFE

I am not prepared to say how far Baubie Huie's own up-bringing had been a model of judicious parental nurture. There was ground to fear that it had not been at all times regulated by an enlightened regard to the principle laid down by King Solomon, concerning the training of children. Jock Huie had a muckle sma' faimily, crammed into limited space, in so far as the matter of house accommodation was concerned. It was a little, clay-built, 'rape-thackit' cot in which Jock, with Eppie, his wife, and their family dwelt; and the 'creatures' came so thickly, and in such multitude, that Jock, who was a 'darger,'[1] and did 'days' warks' here and there, as he could find them, experienced rather queer sensations when an unusually 'coorse' day happened to coop him up at home among the 'smatterie' of youngsters.

'Saul o' me, 'oman,' would Jock exclaim, when patience had reached its limit; 'the din o' that bairns o' yours wud rive a heid o' steen[2]–gar them be quaet, aw'm sayin', or I'll hae to tak' a horse fup to them.'

'Haud yer tongue, man; gin ye war amo' them fae screek o' day till gloamin' licht's I am, ye mith speak. Fat can be creatures dee fan they canna get leuket owre a door?' Eppie would reply.

Notwithstanding his formidable threat, Jock Huie rarely lifted his hand in the way of active correction of his offspring. His wife, who was not indisposed to govern a little more sharply if she could, knew of only one way of enforcing obedience, or some approach thereto, when matters had come to a decided pass of the character indicated, and which may be best described in plain English as indiscriminate chastisement, applied with sufficient heartiness though it might be quite as much in accordance with the dictates of temper as of calm reason. And so it came to pass that, as most of the youthful Huies were gifted with pretty definite wills of their own, the progress of physical development on their part might be taken, in a general way, as indicative, in inverse proportion, of the measure of moral and mental sway which the parental will was able to exercise over them.

[1] casual labourer   [2] stone

All that by the way, however. Jock Huie got his family brought up as he best could, and off his hands mainly; and he, personally, continued his dargin' with perhaps a little less vir[3] than aforetime. Jock was a man of large bones and strong bodily frame; when thirty he had physical strength that seemed equal to any task, and endurance against which no amount of rough usage appeared to tell with evil effect. But after all, men of Jock Huie's class do not wear long. Jock was now a man only a few years past fifty; yet digging in wet drains and ditches, and eating a bit of oat cake, washed down with 'treacle ale,' to his dinner, day by day, had procured for him a very appreciable touch of 'rheumatics,' and other indications that he had fairly passed his prime.

And Baubie, his eldest daughter, though not the eldest member of his family, for Jock had various sons older than she–Baubie had grown up–a buxom, ruddy-cheeked 'quine' of nineteen. She was servan' lass to the farmer of Brigfit–Briggies in short.

I remember very distinctly a bonnie summer gloamin at that time. It was gey late owre i' the evenin'. Baubie had milket the kye, seyt the milk, and wash'n up her dishes. Her day's work was at last fairly done, and why should not Baubie go out to the Toon Loan to enjoy the quiet scene as the cool dews of evening began to fall upon the landscape around the cosy, old-fashioned farm 'steading' of Brigfit.

It matters nothing in this narration where I had been that evening, further than to say that, as I pursued my journey homeward, the road took me past the corner of Briggies' stable, where, altogether unexpect-edly to me, I encountered Baubie Hule 'in maiden meditation fancy free.' Though Baubie's junior by a twelvemonth or so, I had developed since we two had last met from a mere herd loon into a sort of rawish second or third horseman. We had known each other more or less from infancy, Baubie and I, and our talk during the short parley that now ensued had a tinge of the byegone time in it; though, of course, we could not help giving fulfilment, in our own way, to the saying that out of the abundance of the heart, the mouth speaketh; and, naturally enough, at that season of life, that which most occupied our hearts was the present as it bore on our respective positions and prospects.

My own notion (it may be said in confidence) was that I was climb-ing up the pathway to maturity of life and definiteness of position with creditable alacrity; but in this direction I speedily found that Baubie

[3] energy

Huie had fairly out-distanced me. Why, here was the very same 'quine' who, almost the last time I saw her, was lugging along a big, sulky bairn, half her own size, wrapped in an old tartan plaid, and her weather-bleached hair hanging loosely about her shoulders–and that bairn her own younger brother–that very quine, giggling and tossing her head knowingly as she spoke, in what seemed a tone of half masculine licence, about the 'chiels' that were more or less familiarly known as sweethearts among young women in the neighbourhood of Brigfit. In matters of love and courtship, I was, it must be confessed, an entire novice; whereas in such affairs, it was obvious, Baubie had become an adept; and if I had been somewhat put out by the ready candour with which she criticised the physical appearance and general bearing of this and the other young man–hangers on after Baubie, I was given to understand–I was nothing short of completely 'flabbergasted' when, just as we were parting, she said–

'Dinna ye never gae fae hame at even, min? Ye mith come owre the gate some nicht an' see's.'

What my confused and stuttering reply amounted to I cannot really say–something grotesquely stupid, no doubt. What it called forth on Bauble's part, at any rate, was another round of giggling and the exclamation, as she turned off toward the dwelling-house of Brigfit–

'Weel, weel, Robbie, a' nicht wi' you; an' a file o' the morn's mornin'.'–This was simply the slang form of saying 'good night' among persons of Baubie's class. And she added–'I'll need awa' in; for there's Briggies, the aul' snot, at the ga'le o' the hoose–he'll be barrin' 's oot again, eenoo.'

Now, far be it from me to say that Baubie was a vicious or immodest young woman. I really am not prepared to say that she was anything of the sort. She had simply got the training that hundreds in her station of life in these northern shires do–home training that is. And after she left the parental roof, her experiences had been the common experiences of her class–that is to associate freely with promiscuous assemblages of farm-servants, male and female; mainly older than herself, without any supervision worth mentioning, as she moved from one situation to another. And how could Baubie, as an apt enough scholar, do other than imbibe the spirit and habits of those in whose companionship she lived day by day? Baubie was simply the natural product of the system under which she had been reared. Her moral tone, as indexed by her speech, might not be very high; and yet, after all, it is very possible to have the mere verbal proprieties fully attended to, where the innate morality is no whit better. Coarseness in the outer form, which is thrust on the view of all, is bad enough; depravity in the inner spirit, which is frequently concealed from many, may be a good deal worse.

Brigfit was a decent man; a very decent man, for he was an elder in the parish kirk, and a bachelor of good repute. He was a careful, industrious farmer, the extent of whose haudin enabled him to 'ca' twa pair.' Briggies was none of your stylish gentlemen farmers; he needed neither gig nor 'shalt'[4] to meet his personal convenience, but did his ordinary business journeys regularly on foot. And he stood on reasonably amicable terms with his servants; but he sought little of their confidence, and as little did he give to them of his own. Only Briggies had certain inflexible rules, and one was that his household should be in bed every night by nine o'clock in winter, and an hour later in summer; when he would himself solemnly put the bar on the door, and then walk as solemnly along to the 'horn en' '[5] to seek repose.

Briggies was a very early riser, and as it was his hand that usually put the bar on the door at night, so, honest man, was it his hand that ordinarily took it off in the morning in time to see that the household proper and the occupants of the outside 'chaum'er,' consisting of the male servants, were stirring to begin the labours of the day in due season. According to Baubie Huie's account, the bar was sometimes tampered with during the interval by the 'deems;'[6] only if matters were gone about quietly enough, Briggies, whether or not he might suspect aught in that way, usually said nothing.

'Augh, Robbie, man! Fear't for Briggies kennin? Peer bodie! fan onything comes in's noddle aboot's nowte[7] beasts he canna get rest, but'll be up an' paumerin[8] aboot the toon' o' the seelence o' the nicht, fan it's as mark's pick in winter, forbye o' the simmer evenin's. So ae nicht i' the spring time that me an' my neebour hedna been wuntin to gae to oor beds, we pits oot the lamp in gweed time, an' sits still, as quaet's pussy, till Briggies hed on the bar an' away till 's bed. I'm nae sayin' gin onybody was in ahin that or no, but lang aifter the wee oor hed struck'n, me an' Jinse was thereoot. I suppose the chiels hed made mair noise nor they sud 'a deen, caperin' owre the causeway wi' their muckle tacketie beets. At ony rate in a blink there was Briggies oot an' roon to

---

[4] pony   [5] best part of the house   [6] young serving women   [7] cattle
[8] ambling

the byres wi' the booet[9] in 's han'. Fan he hed glampit aboot amo' the beasts till he was satisfeet, he gaes awa' to the hoose again; an' we wusna lang o' bein' aifter 'im. But fudder or no he had leuket ben to the kitchie to see gin we wus there, he had pitten the bar siccar aneuch on upo' the door this time, I can tell ye; an' nae an in cud we win for near an oor, till we got an aul' ledder an' pat it up to the en' o' the hoose, an' syne I made oot to creep in at the ga'le winnochie—Fat did he say aifterhin? Feint a thing. Briggies never loot on, though he cudna but 'a hed 's ain think, 'cause gin he didna hear huz, he be 't till 'a kent "gyaun oot" that the bar sudna 'a been aff 'o the door at that time o' nicht.'

In this wise did Baubie Huie keep up the colloquy, my own side of which, candour compels me to say, was very badly sustained; for had I been ever so willing to take my part, the requisite fluency and *abandon* had not been attained, to say nothing of the utter absence of knowledge germane to the subject in hand, and personally acquired.

As a matter of course, I did not accept Baubie Huie's invitation to visit Brigfit. If the truth were to be told, I was too much of a greenhorn; one who would have been accurately described by Baubie and her associates as utterly destitute of 'spunk.' My Mentor of that date, a vigorous fellow of some eight and twenty years, whose habits might be not incorrectly described by the word 'haiveless,'[10] whose speech was at least as free, as refined, and who occupied the responsible position of first horseman, did not indeed hesitate to characterise my behaviour in relation to such matters, generally, in almost those very words. He knew Bauble Huie, moreover, and his estimate of Baubie was expressed in the words—'Sang, she's a richt quine yon, min; there's nae a deem i' the pairt'll haud 'er nain wi' ye better nor she'll dee; an' she's a fell ticht gweed-leukin hizzie tee,' which, no doubt, was a perfectly accurate description according to the notions entertained by the speaker of the qualities desirable in the female sex.

However these things may be, Baubie Huie continued to perform her convenanted duties to the farmer of Brigfit; and, so far as known, yielding the elder average satisfaction as a servant during the summer 'half-year.'

---

[9] lantern   [10] useless

II

BAUBIE RETURNS HOME

It was nearing the term of Martinmas, and Jock Huie, who had been laid off work for several days by a 'beel't thoom,'[11] was discussing his winter prospect with Eppie, his wife. Meal was 'fell chape,' and the potato crop untouched by disease; but Jock's opinion was that, as prices were low for the farmer, feein' would be slack. Cattle were down too, and though the price of beef and mutton was a purely abstract question for him personally–he being a strict vegetarian in practice, not by choice but of necessity–Jock was economist enough to know that the fact bore adversely on the farmer's ability to employ labour; so that, altogether, with a superfluity of regular servants unengaged, and a paucity of work for the common 'darger' in the shape of current farming improvements going on, he did not regard the aspect of things as cheering for his class.

'Aw howp neen o' that loons o' ours 'll throw themsel's oot o' a place,' said Jock. 'Wud ye think ony o' them wud be bidin'?'

'That wud be hard to say, man,' replied Eppie.

'That widdifus[12] o' young chiels 's aye sae saucy to speak till,' said Jock; whether he meant that the sauciness would be exhibited in the concrete from his own sons toward himself, or if the remark applied to the bearing of servant chiels generally on the point under consideration, was not clear. 'But better to them tak' a sma' waage nor lippen to orra wark; an' hae to lie aboot idle the half o' the winter.'

'Weel ken we that,' said Eppie, with a tolerably lively recollection of her experiences in having previously had one or two of her sons 'at hame' during the winter season. 'Mere ate-meats till Can'lesmas; I'm seer fowk hae's little need o' that; but creaturs'll tak' their nain gate for a' that.'

'Aw howp Baubie's bidin' wi' Briggies, ony wye,' added Jock.

'I ken naething aboot it,' said Eppie, in a tone that might be described as dry; 'Baubie's gey an' gweed at keepin' 'er coonsel till 'ersel.'

It was only a fortnight to the term, and Jock would not be kept long in suspense regarding those questions affecting the family arrangements on which he had thus incidentally touched. In point of fact, his mind was set at rest so far when only half the fortnight had run. For the feeing market came in during that period, and as Jock's thumb had not

[11] festered thumb   [12] rascals

yet allowed him to resume work, he 'took a step doon' to the market, where he had the satisfaction of finding that his sons had all formed engagements as regular farm servants. As for Baubie, though Jock learned on sufficient authority that she was present in the market, he failed to 'meet in' with her. Concerning Baubie's intended movements, he learnt, too, that she was *not* staying with Briggie's; Briggies himself had indeed told him so; but beyond that Jock's enquiries on the subject did not produce any enlightenment for him.

Subsequently to the feeing market, Jock Huie had once and again reverted to the subject of Baubie's strange behaviour in keeping the family in ignorance of her movements and intentions, but without drawing forth much in the way of response from his wife beyond what she had generally expressed in her previous remark.

The afternoon of the term day had come, and servants who were flittin' were moving here and there. I cannot state the nature of the ruminations that had passed, or were passing, through the mind of either Jock Huie or his wife Eppie concerning their daughter Baubie; but Jock, honest man, had just left his cottage in the grey gloamin to go to the smiddy and get his tramp-pick sharpened with the view of resuming work next day in full vigour, when Baubie dressed in her Sunday garments, and carrying a small bundle, entered. There was a brief pause; and then Baubie's mother, in a distinct and very deliberate tone, said–

'Weel, Baubie, 'oman; an' *ye're* here neist.'

At these words, Baubie, who had just laid aside her bundle, threw herself down beside it, on the top of the family 'deece,'[13] is with the remark,

'Aye; faur ither wud aw gae?'

And then she proceeded silently to untie the strings of her bonnet. Neither Baubie nor her mother was extremely agitated, but there was a certain measure of restrained feeling operating upon both the one and the other. The mother felt that a faithful discharge of the maternal duty demanded that she should give utterance to a reproof as severe as she could properly frame, accompanied by reproaches, bearing on the special wickedness and ingratitude of the daughter; and, on the part of the daughter along with a vague sense of the fitness of all this, in a general way, there were indications of a volcanic state of temper, which might burst out with considerable, if misplaced fierceness, on comparatively

[13] couch

slight provocation. And wherefore create a scene of verbal violence; for deep down, below those irascible feelings, did there not lurk in Eppie Huie's bosom a kind of latent sense that if such crises as that which had now emerged were not to be regarded as absolutely certain, they were assuredly to be looked upon as very much in the nature of events inevitable in the ordinary history of the family? And thus it was that Eppie Huie, virtually accepting the situation as part of the common lot, went no further than a general rasping away at details, and the consequences arising out of the main fact.

'Weel, weel, Baubie, 'oman, ye've begun to gae the aul' gate in braw time–ye'll fin't a hard road to yersel', as weel's to them 't 's near conneckit wi' you. Fat gar't ye keep oot o' yer fader's sicht at the market–haudin 'im gyaun like a wull stirk seekin' ye, an' makin' a feel o' 'im?'

'Aw'm seer ye needna speer that–'s gin ye hedna kent to tell 'im yersel'.'

'That's a bonnie story to set up noo, ye limmer[14]–that I sud say the like,' said Eppie with some heat. 'Didnin ye deny't i' my face the vera last time that ye was here?'

'H-mph! an' aw daursay ye believ't 's!'

'Weel, Baubie, 'oman, it's a sair say 't we sud be forc't to tak' for a muckle black lee fat's been threepit,[15] an' yea-threepit i' oor witters be' them that's sibbest til 's.'

To this observation Baubie made no reply: and after a short silence Eppie Huie continued in a dreary monotone–

'Ay, ay! An' this is fat folk get for toilin' themsel's to deith feshin up a faimily! There's little aneuch o' peace or rest for's till oor heid be aneth the green sod–jist oot o' ae tribble till anither. Little did I or yer peer fader think short syne that *ye* was to be hame to be a burden till 's.'

'Aw ha'ena been a burden yet ony wye,' said Baubie with some sharpness, 'ye needna be sae ready speakin' that gate.'

To this retort Eppie Huie made some reply to the effect that others similarly circumstanced had uttered such brave words, and that time would tell in Baubie's case as it had told in theirs. She then rose and put some water in a small pot, which she hung upon the 'crook' over the turf fire, in the light of which Baubie and she had hitherto sat.

'Fa 's the fader o' 't than?' said Eppie Huie, as she turned about from completing the operation just mentioned; but though the words were

---

[14] give, a playful term   [15] assented

uttered in a very distinct as well as abrupt tone, there was no answer till she repeated her question in the form of a sharp 'Aw'm sayin'?'

'Ye'll ken that a-time aneuch,' answered Baubie.

'Ken 't a-time aneuch!–an' you here'–

'Ay an' me here–an' fat aboot it? *It* winna be here the morn, nor yet the morn's morn,' said Baubie in a harder and more reckless tone than she had yet assumed.

Eppie Huie had, no doubt, a sense of being baffled, more or less. She resumed her seat, uttering as she did so, something between a sigh and a groan. There was nothing more said until the water in the little pot having now got to 'the boil,' Eppie rose, and lighting the rush wick in the little black lamp that hung on the shoulder of the 'swye' from which the crook depended, proceeded to 'mak' the sowens.'[16] When the lamp had been lighted, Baubie rose from her place on the deece, and lifting her bonnet, which now lay beside her, and her bundle, said,

'A'm gyaun awa' to my bed.'

'Ye better wyte an' get yer sipper–the sowens'll be ready eenoo.'

'Aw'm nae wuntin' nae sipper,' said Baubie, turning to go as she spoke. 'There's nae things lyin' i' the mid-hoose bed, is there?'

'Naething; oonless it be the muckle basket, wi' some o' yer breeders' half-dry't claes. Tak' that bit fir i' yer han'–ye'll need it, ony wye, to lat ye see to haud aff o' the tubs an' the basket.'

And Baubie went off to bed forthwith, notwithstanding a sort of second invitation, as she was lighting the fir, to wait for some supper. I rather think that after all she did not relish the comparative light so much as the comparative darkness. And then if she stayed to get even the first practicable mouthful of 'sowens,' was there not considerable risk that Jock Huie, her father, might drop in upon her on his return from the smiddy? Not that Baubie had an unreasonable sensitive dread of facing her father. But having now got over what she would have called 'the warst o' 't,' with her mother, she felt that her mother, being on the whole so well 'posted up,' might be left with advantage to break the ice, at least, to the old man.

When Jock Huie returned from the smiddy that evening, an event that happened in about half an hour after his daughter Baubie had gone to bed, he seemed to be moody, and in a measure out of temper.

[16] porridge

He put aside his bonnet, and sat down in his usual corner, while Eppie set the small table for his supper, only one or two remarks of a very commonplace sort having been made up to that point.

'Ye'll better saw awa', man; they've been made this file,' said Eppie, as she lifted the dish with the 'sowens' to the table from the heartstone, where it had been placed in order to retain warmth in the mess.

'Aw'm sayin', 'oman,' quoth Jock, apparently oblivious to his wife's invitation, 'div ye ken onything about that jaud[17] Baubie—there's something or anither nae richt, ere she wud haud oot o' fowk's road this gate?'

'Baubie's *here*, man,' said Eppie Huie; and the brevity of her speech was more than made up by the significance of the words and the tone in which they were uttered.

'Here?' exclaimed Jock in a tone of inquiry, and looking towards his wife as he spoke.

'She's till 'er bed i' the mid-hoose,' said Eppie in reply; and, perceiving that Jock's look was only half answered, she added, 'Aw daursay she wasna owre fain to see you.'

'Fat!' cried Jock, 'she'll be wi' a geet to some chiel, is she?'

'Ou ye needna speer,' said Eppie in a tone of 'dowie' resignation.

'Weel, that does cowe the gowan[18]—a quine[19] o' little mair nor nineteen! But aw mith 'a been seer o' 't. It wasna for naething that she was playin' hide-an'-seek wi' me yon gate. Brawlie kent I that she was i' the market wi' a set o' them. Deil speed them a', weel-a-wat!'

Jock Huie was not a model man exactly in point of moral sentiment; neither was he a man of keen sensibility. But he did nevertheless possess a certain capability of sincere, if it might be uncultured feeling; and he now placed his rough, weather-beaten face against the horny palms of his two hands, and, resting his two elbows on his knees, gave utterance to a prolonged 'Hoch-hey!' Jock maintained this attitude for sometime, and probably would have maintained it a good deal longer, but for the practical view of matters taken by his wife, and the practical advice urgently pressed upon him by her when her patience had got exhausted:–

'Aw'm sayin', man, ye needna connach[20] yer sipper; that'll dee nae gweed to naebody.–Tak' your sowens! Ye're lattin them grow stiff wi' caul', for a' the cribble 't aw was at keepin' them het to you.'

* * *

[17] jade   [18] beats everything   [19] girl   [20] waste

Thus admonished, Jock Huie took his supper in silence; and, thereafter, with little more talk beyond one or two questions from Jock of a like nature with those which had been so ineffectually addressed to Baubie by her mother, the husband and wife retired to bed.

III

THE GEET'S ADVENT–INITIAL DIFFICULTIES IN ACQUIRING AN ECCLESIASTICAL STATUS

That Jock Huie's daughter, Baubie, had returned home to her father and mother was a fact about which there could be no manner of doubt or equivocation; as to the cause of Baubie's return, there was a general concurrence of opinion in the neighbourhood; indeed, it had been a point settled long before, among elderly and sagacious females who knew her, that Baubie would speedily appear in her true colours. Yet there were a few of this same class of people in whose sides Baubie was still somewhat of a thorn. For when the first few days were over after her return, so far from shrinking out of their sight, Baubie flung herself across their path at the most unexpected times, and exhibited an unmistakeable readiness to meet their friendly criticisms with a prompt retort. Or was it a staring personal scrutiny–well, Baubie was almost ostentatiously ready to stand that ordeal, and stare with the best of her starers in return. Baubie was perfectly able to take care of herself, and if a young woman of her spirit chose to remain six months out of the 'hire house,' whose business was that but her own? Baubie would like to know that.

It is not to be supposed that this bravado went far in the way of deceiving any but very inexperienced people, if it deceived even them, which is more than doubtful. And in the nature of the case, it would at any rate deceive no one very long.

It was just at Candlemas when it was reported that Jock Huie had become a grandfather; a genealogical dignity the attainment of which did not seem to excite in Jock's breast any particular feeling of elation. Such an idea as that of apprehension lest the line of Huies in his branch should become extinct had certainly never troubled Jock to the extent that would have made him anxious to welcome a grandchild, legitimate or illegitimate; and the belief that this particular bairn was born to be a direct and positive burden upon him hardly tended to make its advent either auspicious or cheering. Jock knew full well the 'tyauve'[21] he had had in bringing up his own family proper; and now, ere the obstreperous squalling of the younger of them was well out of his ears, why here was another sample of the race, ready to renew and continue all that turmoil and uproar, by night and by day, from which his small hut had never been free for a good twenty years of his lifetime.

'An' it's a laddie, ye say, that the quine Huie's gotten?'

'A laddie; an' a-wat a richt protty[22] gate-farrin[23] bairnie 's ever ye saw wi' yer twa een.'

'Fan came' 't hame no?'

'It was jist the streen, nae langer gane. Aifter 't was weel gloam't, I hears a chap at the window, an' fa sud this be but Eppie 'ersel', peer creatur. I pat my tartan shawl aboot my heid immedantly, an' aifter tellin' the littleans to keep weel ootbye fae the fire, an' biddin' their sister pit them to their beds shortly, I crap my wa's roun' as fest 's aw cud. Jock was nae lang come hame fae 's day's wark, an' was sittin' i' the neuk at 's bit sipper. 'He's jist makin' ready to gae for Mrs. Slorach,' says she. 'Awat I was rael ill-pay't for 'im, peer stock, tir't aneuch nae doot, jist aff o' a sair day's wark. It was a freely immas[24] nicht, wi' byous coorse ploiterie[25] road; an' it's three mile gweed, but I can asseer ye Jock hed gane weel, for it wasna muckle passin' twa oors fan he's back an' Mrs. Slorach wi' 'im.'

'Weel, weel, Jock'll get 's nain o' 't lickly, honest man. It'll be a won'er an' they hinna the tsil'[26] to fesh up.'

'Ou weel-a-wat that's true aneuch; but there's never a hicht but there's a howe at the boddom o' 't, as I said to Eppie fan she first taul' me o' Baubie's misfortune; an' there's never a mou' sen' but the maet's sen' wi' 't.'

'Div they ken yet fa's the fader o' the creatur?'

'Weel, she hed been unco stubborn aboot it no; but aw'm thinkin' she hed taul' 'er mither at the lang len'th. At a roch guess, a body with gae farrer agley, aw daursay, nor licken 't to ane o' yon chiels 't was aboot the toon wi' 'er at Briggies'—yon skyeow-fittet[27] breet.'

The foregoing brief extract from the conversation of a couple of those kindly gossips who had all along taken a special interest in her case will indicate with sufficient distinctness the facts surrounding the birth of Baubie Huie's Geet.

[21] struggle   [22] attractive   [23] comely   [24] gloomy, dull   [25] muddy

[26] child   [27] skew footed

The reputed father of the geet was a sort of nondescript chap, whose habit it was to figure at one time as an indifferent second or third 'horseman,' and next time as an 'orra man';[28] a bullet-headed bumpkin, with big unshapely feet, spreading considerably outward as he walked; a decided taste for smoking tobacco; of somewhat more than average capability in talking bucolic slang of a gross sort; yet possessing withal a comfortable estimate of his own graces of person and manner in the eyes of the fair sex. Such was the–sweetheart, shall we say?–of Baubie Huie.

How one might best define the precise relationship existing between the nondescript chiel and Baubie, it would not be easy to say. It was believed that on the feeing market night he had taken Baubie home to Briggles', he being not greatly the worse of drink, and that on the term night he had accompanied her part of the way toward her father's house. There was also a sort of vague impression that he had since then come once or twice to visit Baubie, keeping as well out of sight and ken of Jock Huie and his wife as might be. Be that as it may, now that the child was born, Jock, who was very much of a practical man, desired to know articulately from the man himself whether he was to 'tak wi' 't an' pay for't.' The idea of asking whether the fellow had any intention of doing the one thing which a man with a shred of honour about him would have felt bound to do in the circumstances–viz., marrying his daughter–had really not occurred to Jock Huie. And so it came to pass, that after a certain amount of rather irritating discussion between himself and the female members of his family, and as the nondescript took very good care not to come to him, Jock 'took road' to hunt up the nondescript, who, as he discovered after some trouble, was now serving on a farm some five or six miles off. He found him as third horseman at the plough in a field of 'neep-reet,'[29] along with his two fellow ploughmen. The nondescript had a sufficient aspect of embarrassment when Jock Huie caught him up at the end rig, where he had been waiting till the ploughs should come out, to indicate that he would not have been disappointed had the visit been omitted; and it seemed not improbable that his two companions might thereafter offer one or two interrogatory remarks on the subject, which would not be a great deal more welcome. At anyrate, Jock Huie had the satisfaction of finding that the nondescript 'wasna seekin' to deny't'; nay, that he did not refuse to 'pay for't', any backwardness on his part in that respect up to the date of

---

[28] odd-job man   [29] growing turnips

visit, being readily accounted for by the fact that it was the middle of the half-year, when a man was naturally run of cash. Threats about ''reestin' waages,' therefore, were perfectly uncalled-for; and, indeed, a sort of unjust aspersion on the general character of the nondescript. It was right that Jock Huie should know that.

'Ye sud hae the civeelity to lat fowk ken faur ye are than; an' ye think ony ill o' that. Bonnie story to haud me traillin' here, lossin' half a day seekin' ye,' retorted Jock with some roughness of tone.

Between the date of Jock Huie's visit just mentioned and the term of Whitsunday, the father of Baubie Huie's geet visited the abode of the Huies once at anyrate; and in course of the conference that ensued, it so happened that the subject of getting the geet christened came up–the needful preliminary to that being, as Jock explained, to appear and give satisfaction to that grave Church Court, the Kirk-Session. This was a point which both the paternal and maternal Huie were a good deal more eager to discuss and settle about than either of the immediate parents of the geet. Indeed, the nondescript seemed penetrated with a sort of feeling that that was a part of the business hardly in his line. Not that he objected on principle to the geet being christened; far from it; for when Eppie Huie had stated the necessity of getting themselves 'clear't,' and having that rite performed, and Jock Huie had vigorously backed up her statement, the nondescript assented with a perfectly explicit 'Ou ay'; only he showed a decided tendency always to let the matter drop again. This did not suit Jock Huie's book in the least, however, and he manifested a determination to have the business followed out that was not at all comfortable to the nondescript.

When the nondescript had pondered over the situation for a few days, and all along with the feeling that something must really be done, for he did not in the least relish the idea of further calls from Jock Huie, the happy thought occurred to him of calling on his old master, Briggies, who was one of the elders of the Kirk, and, being after all a humane man, would no doubt be prevailed upon to pave the way for him and Baubie making penitential appearance before the session, and receiving censure and 'absolution.' So he called on Briggies, and was rather drily told that, neither Baubie nor he being 'commeenicants,' apart from the censure of the session, which had to be encountered in the first place, he, at anyrate, 'as the engaging parent' (and perhaps

Baubie too), would have to undergo an examination, at the hands of the minister, as to his knowledge of the cardinal doctrines of the Christian faith, and the significance of the rite of baptism in particular.

'Fat wye cud ye expeck to win throw itherweese, min?' Briggies felt bound to speak as an elder in this case–'Gin fowk winna leern to behave themsel's they maun jist stan' the consequences. The vera Kirk-Session itsel' cudna relieve ye, man, upo' nae ither precunnance.'[30]

The nondescript returned much pondering on this disheartening information, which he got opportunity, by and bye, of communicating to Baubie. In private conference, the two agreed that 'a scaulin' fae the session,' by itself–a thing they had been both accustomed to hear spoken of with extreme jocularity, not less than they had seen those who had undergone the same, regarded as possessing something of the heroism that is rather to be envied–a scaulin' fae the session might well be borne; but to stand a formal examination before the minister in cold blood was another affair. The dilemma having occurred, the two horns were presented to Jock Huie, who was so relentlessly forcing them on to impalement, in the hope of softening his heart, or at anyrate awakening his sympathy; but Jock was just as determined as ever that they must go forward in the performance of their Christian duty, and his one reply was, 'Ou, deil care; ye maun jist haud at the Catechis.'

IV

THE GEET'S STATUS, ECCLESIASTICAL AND SOCIAL, DEFINED

'Aw'm sayin', 'oman, that geet maun be kirsen't some wye or anither; we canna lat the creatur grow up like a haethen.'

The speaker in this case was Jock Huie, and the person addressed his wife Eppie. It was a fine Saturday evening toward the latter end of June, and Jock, who had got home from his work at the close of the week, was now in a deliberative mood.

'Weel, man, ye'll need to see fat wye 't's to be manag't,' was Eppie's reply.

'They'll jist need 'o tak' her 'er leen; that's a' that I can say aboot it,' said Jock.

---

[30] understanding

'Ah-wa, man; wa won'er to her ye speak.'

'Weel fat else can ye dee? Aw tell ye the littlean 'll be made a moniment[31] o' i' the kwintra side.'

'Ou, weel, ye maun jist gae to the minaister yersel', man, an' tell 'im fat gate her an' huz tee 's been guidet; he's a rael sympatheesin person, an' there's nae doot he'll owreleuk onything as far's he can.'

'Sorra set 'im, weel-a-wat!' said Jock Huie emphatically, as he knocked the half-burnt 'dottal' of tobacco out of his pipe into the palm of his hand, with a sort of savage thump.

Whether Jock Huie's portentous objurgation on the subject of the Catechism had much or anything to do with the result it would perhaps be difficult to say, but it was a simple matter of fact that after it had been uttered, the father of Baubie's geet exhibited even more than previously a disposition to fight shy of the path of duty on which Jock sought to impel him. The Whitsunday term was drawing on; the Whitsunday term had arrived and the geet still unchristened. Then it was found that the father of the geet had deemed it an expedient thing to seek an appreciable change of air by 'flittin'' entirely beyond 'kent bounds.' True it was, that on the very eve of his departure he had by the hands of a third party transmitted to Baubie for the maintenance of her geet a 'paper note' of the value of one pound, and along with it a verbal message to the effect that he was 'gyaun to the pairis' o' Birse'; but as it had been a not infrequent practice among the witty to mention the parish named as a sort of mythical region to which one might be condemned to go, for whom no other sublunary use was apparent, Baubie herself was far from assured that the literal Birse was meant; and we may add was equally at a loss as to whether she had further remittances to look for, or if the note was a once and single payment, in full discharge of the non-descript's obligations in respect to the present maintenance, and prospective upbringing of his son–the Bastard Geet.

Baubie Huie's Bastard Geet had now reached the age of fully four months; no wonder if the grand-paternal anxieties should be aroused as to the danger of the 'peer innocent' merging into heathenism and becoming a bye-word to the parish. And as Jock Huie had expressed his sense of the importance of kirsenin' as a preventative, so after all, it fell to Jock's lot to take the responsible part in getting the rite performed. The name was a matter of difficulty; had there been an available father, it

[31] spectacle

would have been his duty to confer with the mother on the point, and be fully instructed what name to bestow on the infant; and in the case of his own children, the male part of them at anyrate, Jock Huie had never been much at a loss about the names. Among his sons, Tam, Sawney, and Jock, came in, in orderly succession; but, ponder as he would, the naming of Baubie's geet puzzled him long. Its reputed father bore the name of Samuel–cut down to Samie–Caie, and Jock rejected promptly and with scorn the suggestion, coming from its mother, to inflict upon the bairn any such name, which he, in strong language, declared to be nauseous enough to serve as an emetic to a dog. Indeed, Jock's honest hatred of the nondescript had now reached a pitch that made him resolutely decline to pronounce his name at all; a practice in which, as a rule, he was tacitly imitated by his wife and daughter. Partly from this cause, and partly by reason of the still further delay that occurred in getting the christening over, it came to pass that the poor youngster began to have attached to it, with a sort of permanency, the title of Baubie Huie's Bastard Geet; and when at last the parson had done the official duty in question, and Jock Huie, with a just sense of his position in the matter, had boldly named the bairn after himself, it only led to the idle youth of the neighbourhood ringing the changes on the geet in this fashion–

Aul' Jock, an' young Jock, an' Jock comin' tee;
There'll never be a gweed Jock till aul' Jock dee.

But notwithstanding of all these things the geet throve and grew as only a sturdy scion of humanity could be expected to do.

To say that Baubie Huie was passionately attached to her child, would perhaps be rather an over-statement, yet was she pleased to nurse the poor geet with a fair amount of kindness; and physically the geet seemed to make no ungrateful return. It was edifying to note the bearing of the different members of the family towards the geet. The practical interest taken in its spiritual welfare by old Jock Huie has been mentioned; and despite the trouble it had caused him, Jock was equally prepared now to let the geet have the first and tenderest 'bite' from his hard-won daily crust to meet its temporal wants; a measure of self-denial such as many a philanthropist of higher station and greater pretensions has never set before himself. The nature of Eppie Huie's feelings toward the geet was sufficiently indicated by the skilled and careful nursing she would expend upon it at those times when Baubie, tired of her charge, with an unceremonious–'Hae, tak' 'im a file, mither'–would hand over the geet 'body bulk' to the charge of its grannie. When any of Jock Huie's grown-up sons happened to visit home, their cue was simply to ignore the geet altogether. Even when it squalled the loudest they would endeavour to retain the appearance of stolid obliviousness of its presence; just as they did when the hapless geet crowed and 'walloped' its small limbs in the superabundance of its joy at being allowed the novel pleasure of gazing at them. The members of the family who were Baubie's juniors, did not profess indifference; only their feeling toward the geet, when it came under their notice on these temporary visits home, was in the main the reverse of amicable. Her younger sister, indeed, in Baubie's hearing, designated the unoffending geet a 'nasty brat,' whereat Baubie flared up hotly and reminded her that it was not so very long since she, the sister, was an equally 'nasty brat,' to say the very least of it; as she, Baubie, could very well testify from ample experience of the degrading office of nurse to her. 'Fat ever 't be, ye may haud yer chat ony wye,' said Baubie, and the sister stood rebuked.

When harvest came, the geet being now six months old, was 'spean't,'[32] and Baubie 'took a hairst.' Handed over to the exclusive custody of its grannie for the time being, the geet was destined thenceforth to share both bed and board, literally, with Eppie and Jock her husband. The tail of the speaning process when the geet got 'fretty,' and especially overnight, brought back to Jock Huie a lively remembrance of by-gone experiences of a like nature; and he once or twice rather strongly protested against the conduct of 'that ablich'[33] in 'brakin' 's nicht's rest' with its outcries. But, on the whole, Jock bore with the geet wonderfully.

When her hairst was finished, it was Baubie's luck to get continuous employment from the same master till Martinmas. When that period had arrived, Baubie, of her own free will and choice, again stood the feeing market, and found what she deemed a suitable engagement at a large farm several miles off, whither she went in due time; and where, as was to be expected, she found the domestic supervision of the male and female servants less stringent on the whole than it had been at the elder's at Brigfit. In so far as her very moderate wages allowed, after meeting her own needs in the matter of dress, Baubie Huie was not altogether disinclined to contribute toward the support of her bastard geet.

[32] weaned   [33] dwarf

As a matter of course, nothing further was heard of or from the nonde-script father of the geet. He had moved sufficiently far off to be well out of sight at anyrate, and Jock Huie had no means of finding him out and pressing the claim against him in respect of the child's maintenance, except by means of the Poor Law Inspector; and Jock, being a man of independent spirit, had not yet thought of calling in the services of the 'Boord.' As time went on, Baubie's maternal care did not manifest itself in an increasing measure in this particular of furnishing the means to support the geet more than it did in any other respect affecting her offspring.

After one or two more flittings from one situation to another, it became known that Baubie Huie was about to be married. At another Martinmas term–there had been an interval of two years–Baubie once more returned home; but this time frankly to announce to Jock and Eppie Huie that she was 'gyaun to be mairriet' to one Peter Ga', who had been a fellow-servant with her during a recent half-year. From considerate regard for the convenience of her parents, and other causes, the happy day would not be delayed beyond a fortnight; and there would be no extensive 'splore' on the occasion, to disturb materially the domestic arrangements of the Huies.

On this latter point certain of the neighbours were keenly disap-pointed. Because there were no marriage rejoicings to speak of, they missed an invitation to join in the same, and they spoke in this wise:–

'An' there's to be nae marriage ava, ye was sayin'?'

'Hoot–fat wye cud there? The bridegreen an aul' widow man 't mith be 'er fader, wi' three-four o' a family.'

'Na, sirs; a bonny bargaine she'll be to the like o' 'im–three or four o' a family, ye say?'

'So aw b'lieve; an' aw doot it winna be lang ere Baubie gi'e 'im ane mair to haud it haill wi'.'

'Wee, weel! Only fat ither cud ye expeck; but the man maun hae been sair misguidet 't loot 's een see the like o' 'er.'

'An' ye may say 't.'

'Fat siclike o' a creatur is he, ken ye?'

'Ou weel, he's a byous quate man it wud appear, an' a gweed aneuch servan', but sair haud'n doon naitrally. Only the peer stock maun be willin' to dee the richt gate in a menner, or he wud a never propos't mairryin Baubie.'

'Gweed pit 'im wi' the like o' 'er, weel-a-wat–senseless cuttie.'

Naturally, and by right, when Baubie had got a home of her own, she ought to have resumed the custody of her Bastard Geet, now a 'gangrel bairn' of fully two years; but on the one hand, it was evident that Mr. and Mrs. Ga' had the prospect of finding the available accommodation in a hut, whose dimensions afforded scope for only a very limited but and ben, sufficiently occupied by and bye without the geet; and on the other, Eppie Huie, though abundantly forfough'en for a woman of her years in keeping her house, attending to the wants of her husband, Jock, and meeting such demands as her own family made upon her exertions as general washerwoman, would have rather demurred to parting with the geet, to whom she had become, as far as the adverse circumstances of the case allowed, attached. And thus the geet was left in the undisputed possession of Jock and Eppie Huie, to be trained by them as they saw meet.

Unlucky geet, say you? Well, one is not altogether disposed to admit that without some qualification. Sure enough, Jock Huie, senior, would and did permit Baubie's geet to grow up an uncouth, unkempt, and, in the main, untaught bairn; yet was there from him, even, a sort of genuine, if somewhat rugged affection, flowing out toward little Jock Huie (as the geet was alternatively styled); as when he would dab the shaving brush playfully against the geet's unwhiskered cheek, while sternly refusing him a grip of the gleaming razor, as he lifted the instrument upward for service on his own face; or, at another time, would quench the geet's aspiration after the garments of adult life, manifested in its having managed to thrust its puny arms into a huge sleeved moleskin vest belonging to Jock himself, by dropping his big 'wyv'n[34] bonnet' over the toddling creature's head, and down to his shoulders. Bitter memories of Samie Caie had faded into indistinctness more or less. And when the neighbour wives, as they saw the geet with an old black 'cutty' in his hand, gravely attempting to set the contents of the same alight with a fiery sod in imitation of its grandfather, would exclaim, admiringly, 'Na, but that laddie is a bricht Huie, Jock, man,' Jock would feel a sort of positive pride in the youngster, who bade so fairly to do credit to his upbringing.

No; it might be that meagre fare–meagre even to pinching at times–was what the inmates of Jock Huie's cot had to expect; it might

[34] woven

be that in a moral and intellectual point of view the nourishment going was correspondingly scanty and insufficient, to say the least of it; but in being merely left to grow up under these negatively unfavourable conditions, a grotesque miniature copy of the old man at whose heels he had learnt to toddle about with such assiduity, I can by no means admit that, as compared with many and many a geet whose destiny it is to come into the world in the like irregular fashion, the lot of Baubie Huie's Bastard Geet could be justly termed unlucky.

J. LOGIE ROBERTSON (HUGH HALIBURTON)

⋮

James Logie Robertson (1846–1922) was born in Milnathort, educated at Orwell Parish School and Edinburgh University and, for almost forty years, taught at Edinburgh Ladies' College. He edited Burns, Ramsay, Scott and James Thomson collections and from 1881, as Hugh Haliburton, contributed a series of Kailyard idylls to *The Scotsman*. They became known as 'Hughies' and were pinned to factory walls, bothy doors and French trenches.

Robertson reprinted this piece, freshly titled 'Lament for the Language', in a collection of essays entitled *For Puir Auld Scotland's Sake*. It was dedicated to Robert Burns Begg, grandson of Burns, and published in 1887, two years after the Scottish Office was established in Edinburgh, one year after the founding of the first Scottish Home Rule Association and a year before Keir Hardie and Cunninghame Graham formed the Scottish Labour Party.

:ON THE DECADENCE OF THE SCOTS LANGUAGE, MANNERS AND CUSTOMS

They're wearin' by, the guid auld lives
O' leal an' thrifty men an' wives;
They're wearin' oot, the guid auld creeds
That met a simple people's needs;

The auld Scots character an' laws
That made oor kintra what it was–
Esteemed at hame, envied abroad,
Honoured o' man an' loved o' God;
Oor nationality, oor name,
Oor patriotic love for hame–
I 'maist could greet; I can but sigh–
They're wearin' oot, they're a' gaun by!

The gude auld honest mither tongue!
They kent nae ither, auld or young;
The cottar spak' it in his yaird,
An' on his rigs the gawcie[1] laird.
Weel could it a' oor wants express,
Weel could it ban, weel could it bless;
Wi' a' oor feelin's 'twas acquent,
Had words for pleasour an' complent.

[1] jovial

As wide could range the auld Scots tongue;
'Twas meet alike for auld an' young,
For jest an' earnest, joy an' wae,
For cursin' an' caressin' tae.
'Twas gentler at a hushaba
Than a wuid-muffled waterfa',
Or cushats wi' their downie croon
Heard through a gowden afternoon,
Or streams that rin wi' liquid lapse,
Or wun's among the pine-tree taps.
'Twas sweet at a' times i' the mooth
O' woman moved wi' meltin' ruth;
But oh! when first love was her care,
'Twas bonnie far beyond compare.
'Twas mair sonorous than the Latin,
Cam' heavier on the hide o' Satan,
When frae his Ebal o' a poopit
The minister grew hearse an' roopit,[2]
Bannin' wi' energetic jaw
The author o' the primal fa'.
But if the poopit's sacred clangour
Was something aw'some in its anger,
Gude keep my Southlan' freen's fra' hearin'
A rouch red-headed Scotsman swearin'!
But wha would hae audacity
To question its capacity?
The mither croon'd by cradle side,
Young Jockie woo'd his blushin' bride,
The bargain at the fair was driven
The solemn prayer was wing'd to heaven,
The deein' faither made his will,
In gude braid Scots:–a language still!

[2] shouted

It lives in freedom-Barbour's lines,
In bauld Dunbar it brichtly shines,
On Lyndsay's page in licht it streams,
In Border scraps it fitful gleams,
An' like the shimmerin' spunkie strays
By Ettrick banks an' Yarrow braes.
It lives for aye in Allan's play,
In Coila's sangs. the Shepherd's lay,
The bird-like lilts fra' Paisley side,
The Wizart's tales that flew sae wide,
Forbye the vast an' various lore
O' later ballants by the score:
The gude auld Scots!–a language still,
Let fortune vary as she will.
Though banish'd from oor College ha's,
It frames the siccar auld Scots laws;
Though from the lips, of speech the portal,
It lives in Literature immortal.

JAMES KENNEDY

First published in *Punch* in 1903, this poem was thought to be an affectionate tribute to Gavin Campbell, third Marquis of Breadalbane, whose estates stretched from Taymouth Castle to the Atlantic. The Ben More mentioned is in Mull rather than by Crianlarich, which also belonged to the marquis. The poem appeared in a number of publications, usually crediting James McTavish as the author, though when *In Famed Breadalbane* was published in 1938 it gave the author as J. L. Robertson; and when Sydney Goodsir Smith parodied the poem in *Carotid Cornucopius* he named the author as Jawbone Leakie Rabbitson.

James McTavish farmed near Doune. He reared sheep on the slopes of Uamh Mhor and never wrote a line of poetry in his life. *Punch* had credited and paid Robertson for the poem they published as 'In Braid Albyn: Lines From Ben Lawyers'. The real author was unearthed in a remarkable piece of detective work by Archie McKerracher and recounted in *Perthshire in History and Legend*.

The poem was written in 1840 as an attack on John Campbell, second Marquis of Breadalbane who, between 1834 and 1850, evicted thousands of tenants. The first Marquis had raised more than 1,500 men to fight in the Napoleonic Wars but, when his son tried to raise a fencible regiment in 1850, only 100 could be found and none of them volunteered. In Shakespeare, Perth County, Ontario in 1936, John Buchan, then Lord Tweedsmuir, Governor General of Canada, unveiled a memorial cairn to the pioneers 'who came from Perthshire, Scotland, from 1832–33 and 1841–45, principally from Glenquaich, Annatfauld, Shian, Aberfeldy, Amulree and Kenmore'. While living in Glen Quaich, Annie S. Swann wrote *Sheila*, based on the evictions.

The original poem was written in Gaelic by James Kennedy, a blacksmith and evicted crofter, who lived on the shores of Loch Tay and settled in Doune. James McTavish liked the poem and quoted it so often he was assumed to be the author. It is likely, says Archie McKerracher, that James Logie Robertson came upon the verses and adapted them for *Punch*.

The death of the second Marquis in 1862 started the decline of Breadalbane Estate, which was broken up shortly after the 1914–18 war.

:THE HIGHLAND CROFTER

Frae Kenmore tae Ben More
The land is a' the Marquis's;
The mossy howes, the heathery knowe
An' ilka bonnie park is his;
The bearded goats, the towsie[1] stots,[2]
An' a' the braxie[3] carcases;
Ilk crofter's rent, ilk tinkler's tent,
An ilka collie's bark is his;
The muir-cock's craw, the piper's blaw,
The ghillie's hard day's wark is his;
Frae Kenmore tae Ben More
The warld is a' the Marquis's.

The fish that swim, the birds that skim,
The fir, the ash, the birk is his;
The castle ha' sae big an' braw,
Yon diamond crusted dirk is his;
The roofless hame, a burning shame,
The factor's dirty wark is his;
The poor folk vexed, the lawyer's text,
Yon smirking legal shark is his;
Frae Kenmore tae Ben More
The warld is a' the Marquis's.

But near, mair near, God's voice we hear
The dawn as weel's the dark is his;
The poet's dream, the patriot's theme,
The fire that lights the mirk[4] is His.
They clearly show God's mills are slow
But sure, the handiwork is His;
And in His grace our hope we place,
Fair Freedom's sheltering ark is His;
The men that toil should own the soil,
A note as clear's the lark's is this;
Breadalbane's land – the fair, the grand –
Will no' be aye the Marquis's.

[1] dishevelled   [2] young bulls or oxen   [3] an internal inflamation of sheep   [4] dark

S. R. CROCKETT   :

Our regional voices are so strong it is often difficult to imagine the work of a Scottish writer being set in another part of the country. The local, often the parochial, has defined our national consciousness and locality lies at the heart of the Kailyard. The term literally means cabbage patch and was coined as an insult, though J. M. Barrie, Ian MacLaren, S. R. Crockett and Annie S. Swan wrote the most popular of all nineteenth-century Scottish fiction.

Their works were tailored to serve specific market demands and, although they often accurately depicted local places and rural voices, they effectively wrote the rural poor out of existence. This was rustic affairs for an urban audience and, while it could be said to belong to the Scottish tradition of domestic realism, it used the same setting as 'The Cottar's Saturday Night' and preached similar virtues of goodness and faithfulness, often filtered through Professor John Wilson's fondness for moral judgement and doleful consequences. Given the social upheavals that were happening throughout the country, it is scarcely surprising that these fictions were popular, even with those who knew the pictures were fake.

Though J. M. Barrie is the best known of the Kailyard writers, largely because of his long career and work for the theatre, it is Samuel Rutherford Crockett (1859–1914), a friend of R. L. Stevenson and author of historical romances such as *The Raiders*, who embodied most of the Kailyard virtues.

Like Ian MacLaren, Crockett was a Free Church minister; in common with the others, his work is set in a previous generation. He voices their values and concerns and though his charm can be beguiling, with strong dialogue and natural description, his picture of village life is fairly bleak.

: THE LAMMAS PREACHING

'And I further intimate,' said the minister, 'that I will preach this evening at Cauldshaws, and my text will be from the ninth chapter of the book of Ecclesiastes and the tenth verse, "Whatsoever thy hand findeth to do, do it with thy might."'

'Save us,' said Janet MacTaggart, 'he's clean forgotten "if it be the Lord's wull." Maybe he'll be for gaun whether it's His wull or no'–he's a sair masterfu' man, the minister; but he comes frae the Machars, an' kens little aboot the jealous God we hae amang the hills o' Gallowa'!'

The minister continued, in the same high, level tone in which he did his preaching, 'There are a number of sluggards who lay the weight of their own laziness on the Almighty, saying, "I am a worm and no man–how should I strive with my Maker?" whenever they are at strife with their own sluggishness. There will be a word for all such this evening at the farmtown of Cauldshaws, presently occupied by Gilbert M'Kissock–public worship to begin at seven o'clock.'

The congregation of Barnessock kirk tumbled amicably over its own heels with eagerness to get into the kirkyaird in order to settle the momentous question, 'Wha's back was he on the day?'

Robert Kirk, Carsethorn, had a packet of peppermint lozenges in the crown of his 'lum' hat–deponed to by Elizabeth Douglas or Barr, in Barnbogrie, whose husband, Weelum Barr, put on the hat of the aforesaid Robert Kirk by mistake for his own, whereupon the peppermints fell to the floor and rolled under the pews in most unseemly fashion. Elizabeth Kirk is of opinion that this should be brought to the notice of Session, she herself always taking her peppermint while genteelly wiping her mouth with the corner of her handkerchief. Robert Kirk, on being put to the question, admits the fact, but says that it was his wife put them there to be near her hand.

The minister, however, ready with his word, brought him to shame by saying, 'O Robert, Robert, that was just what Adam said, "The woman Thou gavest me, she gave me to eat!"' The aforesaid Robert Kirk thinks that it is meddling with the original Hebrew to apply this to peppermints, and also says that Elizabeth Kirk is an impident besom, and furthermore that, as all the country well knows–(Here the chronicler omits much matter actionable in the civil courts of the realm).

'Janet,' said the minister to his housekeeper, 'I am to preach tonight at Cauldshaws on the text, "Whatsoever thy hand findeth to do, do it with thy might."'

'I ken,' said Janet, 'I saw it on yer desk. I pat it ablow the clock for fear the wun's o' heeven micht blaw it awa' like chaff, an' you couldna do wantin' it!'

'Janet MacTaggart,' said the minister, tartly, 'bring in the denner, and do not meddle with what does not concern you.'

Janet could not abide read sermons; her natural woman rose against them. She knew, as she had said, that God was a jealous God, and, with regard to the minister, she looked upon herself as His vicegerent.

'He's young an' terrable ram-stam an' opeenionated–fu' o' buik-lear, but wi' little gracious experience. For a' that, the root o' the maitter's in 'im,' said Janet, not unhopefully.

'I'm gaun to preach at Cauldshaws, and my text's "Whatsoever thy hand findeth to do, do it with thy might,"' said the minister to the precentor that afternoon, on the manse doorstep.

'The Lord's no' in a' his thochts. I'll gang wi' the lad mysel',' said the precentor.

Now, Galloway is so much out of the world that the Almighty has not there lifted His hand from reward and punishment, from guiding and restraining, as He has done in big towns where everything goes by machinery. Man may say that there is no God when he only sees a hand-breadth of smoky heaven between the chimney-pots; but out on the fields of oats and bear, and up on the screes of the hillsides, where the mother granite sticks her bleaching ribs through the heather, men have reached great assurance on this and other matters.

The burns were running red with the mighty July rain when Douglas Maclellan started over the meadows and moors to preach his sermon at the farmtown of Cauldshaws. He had thanked the Lord that morning in his opening prayer for 'the bounteous rain wherewith He had seen meet to refresh His weary heritage.'

His congregation silently acquiesced, 'for what', said they, 'could a man from the Machars be expected to ken about meadow hay?'

When the minister and the precentor got to the foot of the manse loaning, they came upon the parish ne'er-do-weel, Ebie Kirgan, who kept himself in employment by constantly scratching his head, trying to think of something to do, and whose clothes were constructed on the latest sanitary principles of ventilation. The ruins of Ebie's hat were usually tipped over one eye for enlarged facilities of scratching in the rear.

'If it's yer wull, minister, I'll come to hear ye the nicht. It's drawing to mair rain, I'm thinkin'!' said the Scarecrow.

'I hope the discourse may be profitable to you, Ebenezer, for, as I intimated this morning, I am to preach from the text, "Whatsoever thy hand findeth to do, do it with thy might."'

'Ay, minister,' said Ebie, relieving his right hand, and tipping his hat over the other eye to give his left free play. So the three struck over the fields, making for the thorn tree at the corner, where Robert Kirk's dyke dipped into the standing water of the meadow.

'Do you think ye can manage it, Maister Maclellan?' said the precentor. 'Ye're wat half-way up the leg already.'

'An' there's sax feet o'black moss water in the Laneburn as sure as I'm a leevin' sowl,' added Ebie Kirgan.

'I'm to preach at Cauldshaws, and my text is, "Whatsoever thy hand findeth to do, do it with thy might!"' said the minister, stubbornly glooming from under the eaves of his eyebrows as the swarthy men from the Machars are wont to do. His companions said no more. They came to Camelon Lane, where usually Robert Kirk had a leaping pole on either bank to assist the traveller across, but both poles had gone down the water in the morning to look for Robert's meadow hay.

'Tak' care, Maister Maclellan, ye'll be in deep water afore ye ken. O man, ye had far better turn!'

The precentor stood up to his knees in water on what had once been the bank, and wrung his hands. But the minister pushed steadily ahead into the turbid and sluggish water.

'I canna come, oh, I canna come, for I'm a man that has a family.'

'It's no' your work; stay where ye are,' cried the minister, without looking over his shoulder; 'but as for me, I'm intimated to preach this night at Cauldshaws, and my text–'

Here he stepped into a deep hole, and his text was suddenly shut within him by the gurgle of moss water in his throat. His arms rose above the surface like the black spars of a windmill. But Ebie Kirgan sculled himself swiftly out, swimming with his shoeless feet, and pushed the minister before him to the further bank–the water gushing out of rents in his clothes as easily as out of the gills of a fish.

The minister stood with unshaken confidence on the bank. He ran peat water like a spout in a thunder plump, and black rivulets of dye were trickling from under his hat down his brow and dripping from the end of his nose.

'Then you'll not come any farther?' he called across to the precentor.

'I canna, oh, I canna; though I'm most awfu' wullin'. Kirsty wad never forgie me gin I was to droon.'

'Then I'll e'en have to raise the tune myself–though three times "Kilmarnock" is a pity,' said the minister, turning on his heel and strid- ing away through the shallow sea, splashing the water as high as his head with a kind of head-strong glee which seemed to the precentor a direct defiance of Providence. Ebie Kirgan followed half a dozen steps behind. The support of the precentor's lay semi-equality taken from him, he began to regret that he had come, and silently and ruefully plunged along after the minister through the waterlogged meadows. They came in time to the foot of Robert Kirk's march dyke, and skirted it a hundred yards upward to avoid the deep pool in which the Laneburn waters were swirling. The minister climbed silently up the seven-foot dyke, pausing a second on the top to balance himself for his leap to the other side. As he did so Ebie Kirgan saw that the dyke was swaying to the fall, having been weakened by the rush of water on the farther side. He ran instantly at the minister, and gave him a push with both hands which caused Mr. Maclellan to alight on his feet clear of the falling stones. The dyke did not so much fall outward as settle down on its own ruins. Ebie fell on his face among the stones with the impetus of his own eagerness. He arose, however, quickly–only limping slightly from what he called a 'bit chack' on the leg between two stones.

'That was a merciful Providence, Ebenezer,' said the minister, solemnly; 'I hope you are duly thankful!'

'Dod, I am that!' replied Ebie, scratching his head vigorously with his right hand and rubbing his leg with his left. 'Gin I hadna gi'en ye that dunch, ye micht hae preachen nane at Cauldshaws this nicht.'

They now crossed a fairly level clover field, dank and laid with wet. The scent of the clover rose to their nostrils with almost overpowering force. There was not a breath of air. The sky was blue and the sun shining. Only a sullen roar came over the hill, sounding in the silence like the rush of a train over a far-away viaduct.

'What is that?' queried the minister, stopping to listen.

Ebie took a brisk sidelong look at him.

'I'm some dootsome that'll be the Skyreburn coming doon aff o' Cairnsmuir!'

The minister tramped unconcernedly on. Ebie Kirgan stared at him.

'He canna ken what a "Skyreburn warnin'" is—he'll be thinkin' it's some bit Machars burn that the laddies set their whurlie mills in. But he'll turn richt eneuch when he sees Skyreburn roarin' reed in a Lammas flood, I'm thinkin'!'

They took their way over the shoulder of the hill in the beautiful evening, leaning eagerly forward to get the first glimpse of the cause of that deep and resonant roar. In a moment they saw below them a narrow rock-walled gully, ten or fifteen yards across, filled to the brim with rushing water. It was not black peat water like the Camelon Lane, but it ran red as keel, flecked now and then with a revolving white blur as one of the Cauldshaws sheep spun downward to the sea, with four black feet turned pitifully up to the blue sky.

Ebie looked at the minister. 'He'll turn noo if he's mortal,' he said. But the minister held on. He looked at the water up and down the roaring stream. On a hill above, the farmer of Cauldshaws, having driven all his remaining sheep together, sat down to watch. Seeing the minister, he stood up and excitedly waved him back. But Douglas Maclellan from the Machars never gave him a look, and his shouting was of less effect than if he had been crying to an untrained collie.

The minister looked long up the stream, and at a point – where the rocks came very close together, and many stunted pines were growing, he saw one which, having stood on the immediate brink, had been so much undercut that it leaned over the gully like a fishing-rod. With a keen glance along its length, the minister, jamming his dripping soft felt hat on the back of his head, was setting foot on the perilous slope of the uneven red-brown trunk, when Ebie Kirgan caught him sharply by the arm.

'It's no' for me to speak to a minister at ordinar' times,' he stammered, gathering courage in his desperation; 'but, oh, man, it's fair murder to try to gang ower that water!'

The minister wrenched himself free, and sprang along the trunk with wonderful agility.

'I'm intimated to preach at Cauldshaws this night, and my text is, "Whatsoever thy hand findeth to do, do it with thy might!"' he shouted.

He made his way up and up the slope of the fir-tree, which, having little grip of the rock, dipped and swayed under his tread. Ebie Kirgan fell on his knees and prayed aloud. He had not prayed since his step-mother boxed his ears for getting into bed without saying his prayers twenty years ago. This had set him against it. But he prayed now, and to infinitely more purpose than his minister had recently done. But when the climber had reached the branchy top, and was striving to get a few feet farther, in order to clear the surging linn before he made his spring, Ebie rose to his feet, leaving his prayer unfinished. He sent forth an almost animal shriek of terror. The tree roots cracked like breaking cables and slowly gave way, an avalanche of stones plumped into the whirl, and the top of the fir crashed downwards on the rocks of the opposite bank.

'Oh, man, call on the name of the Lord!' cried Ebie Kirgan, the ragged preacher, at the top of his voice.

Then he saw something detach itself from the tree as it rebounded, and for a moment rise and fall black against the sunset. Then Ebie the Outcast fell on his face like a dead man.

In the white coverleted 'room' of the farmtown of Cauldshaws, a white-faced lad lay with his eyes closed, and a wet cloth on his brow. A large-boned, red-cheeked, motherly woman stole to and fro with a foot as light as a fairy. The sleeper stirred and tried to lift an unavailing hand to his head. The mistress of Cauldshaws stole to his bedside as he opened his eyes. She laid a restraining hand on him as he strove to rise.

'Let me up,' said the minister, 'I must away, for I'm intimated to preach at Cauldshaws, and my text is, "Whatsoever thy hand findeth to do, do it with thy might."'

'My bonny man,' said the goodwife, tenderly, 'you'll preach best on the broad o' yer back this mony a day, an' when ye rise your best text will be, "He sent from above, He took me, and drew me out of many waters!"'

: *'He's young an' terrable ram-stam an' opeenionated—fu' o' buik-lear, but wi' little gracious experience.'*

ROBERT LOUIS STEVENSON :

Robert Louis Stevenson's (1850–94) first piece of longer fiction was *Treasure Island*, serialised in 1882 and published as a book the following year. His first popular success came four years later with *Kidnapped* while *The Strange Case of Dr Jekyll and Mr Hyde*, published the same year, made his reputation on both sides of the Atlantic.

In 1890 Stevenson settled for health reasons in Vailima, on the island of Upolu in Samoa, with his family. The South Pacific gave him new themes and for the first time he wrote about contemporary issues, comparing the erosion of island traditions to Highland culture and criticising the exploitative impact of Europeans and Americans.

His short stories and fiction such as *The Master of Ballantrae* (1888) show a continuing interest in the effects of Scottish history and it was in Samoa that Stevenson wrote *Catriona* (1893), a sequel to *Kidnapped*. He was working on *Weir of Hermiston* the day he died and bequeathed his birthday, 13 November, to a girl who had been born on Christmas Day.

'Sair wark he had to get the siller; but he was weel freended, and at last he got the haill scraped thegether–a thousand merks. The maist of it was from a neighbor they caa'd Laurie Lapraik–a sly tod.' The quotation is from Scott's 'Wandering Willie's Tale' and, like Wandering Willie, 'Tod Lapraik' forms the chapter of a novel. 'Black Andie's Tale of Tod Lapraik' is the fifteenth chapter of *Catriona*.

Written in Samoa in February, 1892, the story is told to David Balfour by the Prefect of the Bass Rock, Black Andie Dale, while David is kept prisoner. 'Dale is 'a long-headed, sensible man, and a good Whig and Presbyterian [who] read daily in a pocket Bible and [was] both able and eager to converse seriously on religion, leaning more than a little towards the Cameronian extremes.'

And Stevenson was pleased with his work. 'He who can't read Scots can never enjoy *Tod Lapraik*,' he wrote to his friend Sydney Colvin in 1893. '*Tod Lapraik* is a piece of living Scots; if I had never writ anything but that and *Thrawn Janet*, still I'd have been a writer.'

: THE TALE OF TOD LAPRAIK

My faither, Tam Dale, peace to his banes, was a wild, sploring lad in his young days, wi' little wisdom and less grace. He was fond of a lass and fond of a glass, and fond of a ran-dan; but I could never hear tell that he was muckle use for honest employment. Frae ae thing to anither, he listed at last for a sodger and was in the garrison of this fort, which was the first way that ony of the Dales cam to set foot upon the Bass. Sorrow upon that service! The governor brewed his ain ale; it seems it was the warst conceivable. The rock was proveesioned frae the shore with vivers, the thing was ill-guided, and there were whiles when they but to fish and shoot solans for their diet. To crown a', thir was the Days of the Persecution. The perishin' cauld chalmers were all occupeed wi' sants and martyrs, the saut of the yearth, of which it wasnae worthy. And though Tam Dale carried a firelock there, a single sodger, and liked a lass and a glass, as I was sayin', the mind of the man was mair just than set with his position. He had glints of the glory of the kirk; there were whiles when his dander rase to see the Lord's sants misguided, and shame covered him that he should be haulding a can'le (or carrying a firelock) in so black a business. There were nights of it when he was here on sentry, the place a' wheesht, the frosts o' winter maybe riving in the wa's, and he would hear ane o' the prisoners strike up a psalm, and the rest join in, and the blessed sounds rising from the different chalmers – or dungeons, I would raither say – so that this auld craig in the sea was like a pairt of Heev'n. Black shame was on his saul; his sins hove up before him muckle as the Bass, and above a', that chief sin, that he should have a hand in hagging and hashing at Christ's Kirk. But the truth is that he resisted the spirit. Day cam, there were the rousing compainions, and his guid resolves depairtit.

In thir days, dwalled upon the Bass a man of God, Peden the Prophet was his name. Ye'll have heard tell of Prophet Peden. There was never the wale of him sinsyne, and it's a question wi' mony if there ever was his like afore. He was wild's a peat-hag fearsome to look at, fearsome to hear, his face like the day of judgment. The voice of him was like a solan's and dinnle'd folks' lugs, and the words of him like coals of fire.

Now there was a lass on the rock, and I think she had little to do, for it was nae place far dacent weemen; but it seems she was bonny, and her and Tam Dale were very well agreed. It befell that Peden was in the gairden his lane at the praying when Tam and the lass cam by; and what should the lassie do but mock with laughter at the sant's devotions? He rose and lookit at the twa o them, and Tam's knees knoitered thegether at the look of him. But when he spak, it was mair in sorrow than in anger. 'Poor thing, poor thing!' says he, and it was the lass he lookit at. 'I hear you skirl and laugh,' he says, 'but the Lord has a deid shot prepared for you, and at that surprising judgment ye shall skirl but the ae time!' Shortly thereafter she was daundering on the craigs wi' twa-three sodgers, and it was a blawy day. There cam a gwost of wind, claught her by the coats, and awa' wi' her bag an baggage. And it was remarked by the sodgers that she gied but the ae skirl.

Nae doubt this judgment had some weicht upon Tam Dale; but it passed again and him none the better. Ae day he was flyting wi' anither sodger-lad. 'Deil hae me!' quo' Tam, for he was a profane swearer. And there was Peden glowering at him gash an' waefu'; Peden wi' his lang chafts an' luntin' een, the maud happed about his kist, and the hand of him held out wi' the black nails upon the finger-nebs – for he had nae care of the body. 'Fy, fy, poor man!' cries he, 'the poor fool man! *Deil hae me*, quo' he; an' I see the deil at his oxter.' The conviction of guilt and grace cam in on Tam like the deep sea; he flang doun the pike that was in his hands – 'I will nae mair lift arms against the cause o' Christ says he, and was as gude's word. There was a sair fyke in the beginning, but the governor, seeing him resolved, gied him his dischairge, and he went and dwallt and married in North Berwick, and had aye a gude name with honest folk frae that day on.

It was in the year seeventeen hunner and sax that the Bass cam in the hands o' the Da'rymples, and there was twa men soucht the chairge of it. Baith were weel qualified, for they had baith been sodgers in the garrison, and kent the gate to handle solans and the seasons and values of them. Forby that they were baith – or they baith seemed – earnest professors and men of comely conversation. The first of them was just Tam Dale, my faither. The second was ane Lapraik, whom the folk ca'd Tod Lapraik maistly, but whether for his name or his nature I could never hear tell. Weel, Tam gaed to see Lapraik upon this business, and took me, that was a toddlin' laddie, by the hand. Tod had his dwallin' in the lang loan benorth the kirkyaird. It's a dark uncanny loan, forby that the kirk has aye had an ill name since the days o' James the Saxt and the deevil's cantrips played therein when the Queen was on the seas; and as for Tod's house, it was in the mirkest end, and was little liked by some that kenned the best. The door was on the sneck that day, and me and my faither gaed straucht in. Tod was a wabster to his trade; his loom stood in the but. There he sat, a muckle fat, white hash of a man like creish, wi' a kind of a holy smile that gart me scunner. The hand of him aye cawed the shuttle, but his een was steeked. We cried to him by his name, we skirled in the deid lug of him, we shook him by the shou'ther. Nae mainner o' service! There he sat on his dowp, an' cawed the shuttle and smiled like creish.

'God be guid to us,' says Tam Dale, 'this is no canny!'

He had jimp said the word, when Tod Lapraik cam to himsel'.

'Is this you, Tam?' says he. 'Haith, man! I'm blythe to see ye. I whiles fa' into a bit dwam like this,' he says; 'it's frae the stamach.'

Weel, they began to crack about the Bass and which of them twa was to get the warding o't, and by little and little cam to very ill words, and twined in anger. I mind weel, that as my faither and me gaed hame again, he cam ower and ower the same expression, how little he likit Tod Lapraik and his dwams.

'Dwam!' says he. 'I think folk hae brunt far dwams like yon.'

Aweel, my faither got the Bass and Tod had to go wantin'. It was remembered sinsyne what way he had ta'en the thing. 'Tam,' says he, 'ye hae gotten the better o' me aince mair, and I hope,' says he, 'ye'll find at least a' that ye expeckit at the Bass.' Which have since been thought remarkable expressions. At last the time came for Tam Dale to take young solans. This was a business he was weel used wi', he had been a craigsman frae a laddie, and trustit nane but himsel'. So there was he hingin' by a line an' speldering on the craig face, whaur it's hieest and steighest. Fower tenty lads were on the tap, hauldin' the line and mindin' for his signals. But whaur Tam hung there was naething but the craig, and the sea belaw, and the solans skirling and flying. It was a braw spring morn, and Tam whustled as he claught in the young geese. Mony's the time I heard him tell of this experience, and aye the swat ran upon the man.

It chanced, ye see, that Tam keeked up, and he was awaur of a muckle solan, and the solan pyking at the line. He thocht this by-ordinar and outside the creature's habits. He minded that ropes was unco saft things, and the solan's neb and the Bass Rock unco hard, and that twa hunner feet were raither mair than he would care to fa'.

'Shoo!' says Tam. 'Awa', bird! Shoo, awa' wi' ye!' says he.

The solan keekit daun into Tam's face, and there was something unco in the creature's ee. Just the ae keek it gied, and back to the rope. But now it wroucht and warstl't like a thing dementit. There never was the solan made that wroucht as that solan wroucht; and it seemed to understand it's employ brawly, birzing the saft rope between the neb of it and a crunkled jag o' stane.

There gaed a cauld stend o' fear into Tam's heart.

'This thing is nae bird,' thinks he. His een turnt backward in his heid and the day gaed black about him.

'If I get a dwam here,' he thoucht, 'it's by wi' Tam Dale.' And he signalled for the lads to pu' him up.

And it seemed the solan understood about signals. For nae sooner was the signal made than he let be the rope, spried his wings, squawked out loud, took a turn flying, and dashed straucht at Tam Dale's een. Tam had a knife, he gart the cauld steel glitter. And it seemed the solan understood about knives, for nae suner did the steel glint in the sun than he gied the ae squawk, but laigher, like a body disappointit, and flegged aff about the roundness of the craig, and Tam saw him nae mair. And as sune as that thing was gane, Tam's heid drapt upon his shouther, and they pu'd him up like a deid corp, dadding on the craig.

A dram of brandy (which he went never without) broucht him to his mind, or what was left of it. Up he sat.

'Rin, Geordie, rin to the boat, mak' sure of the boat, man – rin!' he cries, 'or yon solan 'll have it awa',' says he.

The fower lads stared at ither, an' tried to whilly-wha him to be quiet. But naething would satisfy Tam Dale, till ane o' them had startit on aheid to stand sentry on the boat. The ithers askit if he was for down again.

'Na,' says he, 'and neither you nor me,' says he, 'and as sune as I can win to stand on my twa feet we'll be aff frae this craig o' Sawtan.'

Sure eneuch, nae time was lost, and that was ower muckle; for before they won to North Berwick Tam was in a crying fever. He lay a' the simmer; and wha was sae kind as come speiring for him, but Tod Lapraik! Folk thocht afterwards that ilka time Tod cam near the house the fever had worsened. I kenna for that; but what I ken the best, that was the end of it.

It was about this time o' the year; my grandfaither was out at the white fishing; and like a bairn, I but to gang wi' him. We had a grand take, I mind, and the way that the fish lay broucht us near in by the Bass, whaur we forgaithered wi' anither boat that belanged to a man Sandie Fletcher in Castleton. He's no lang deid neither, or ye could speir at himsel'. Weel, Sandie hailed.

'What's yon on the Bass?' says he.

'On the Bass?' says grandfaither.

'Ay,' says Sandie, 'on the green side o't.'

'Whatten kind of a thing?' says grandfaither. 'There cannae be naething on the Bass but just the sheep.'

'It looks unco like a body,' quo' Sandie, who was nearer in.

'A body!' says we, and we nane of us likit that. For there was nae boat that could have broucht a man, and the key o' the prison yett hung ower my faither's heid at hame in the press bed.

We keept the twa boats closs for company, and crap in nearer hand. Grandfaither had a gless, for he had been a sailor, and the captain of a smack, and had lost her on the sands of Tay. And when we took the gless to it, sure eneuch there was a man. He was in a crunkle o' green brae, a wee below the chaipel, a' by his lee lane, and lowped and flang and danced like a daft quean at a waddin'.

'It's Tod,' says grandfaither, and passed the gless to Sandie.

'Ay, it's him,' says Sandie.

'Or ane in the likeness o' him,' says grandfaither.

'Sma' is the differ,' quo' Sandie. 'De'il or warlock, I'll try the gun at him,' quo' he, and broucht up a fowling-piece that he aye carried, for Sandie was a notable famous shot in all that country.

'Haud your hand, Sandie,' says grandfaither; 'we maun see clearer first,' says he, 'or this may be a dear day's wark to the baith of us.'

'Hout!' says Sandie, 'this is the Lord's judgments surely, and be damned to it!' says he.

'Maybe ay, and maybe no,' says my grandfaither, worthy man. 'But have you a mind of the Procurator Fiscal, that I think we'll have forgaithered wi' before,' says he.

This was ower true, and Sandie was a wee thing set ajee. 'Aweel, Edie,' says he, 'and what would be your way of it?'

'Ou, just this,' says grandfaither. 'Let me that has the fastest boat gang back to North Berwick, and let you bide here and keep an eye on Thon. If I cannae find Lapraik, I'll join ye and the twa of us'll have a crack wi' him. But if Lapraik's at hame, I'll rin up the flag at the harbour, and ye can try Thon Thing wi' the gun.'

Aweel, so it was agreed between them twa. I was just a bairn, an' clum in Sandie's boat, whaur I thoucht I would see the best of the employ. My grandsire gied Sandie a siller tester to pit in his gun wi' the leid draps, bein' mair deidly again bogles. And then the ae boat set aff for North Berwick, an' the tither lay whaur it was and watched the wanchancy thing on the brae-side.

A' the time we lay there it lowped and flang and capered and span like a teetotum, and whiles we could hear it skelloch as it span. I hae seen lassies, the daft queans, that would lowp and dance a winter's nicht, and still be lowping and dancing when the winter's day cam in. But there would be folk there to hauld them company, and the lads to egg them on; and this thing was its lee-lane. And there would be a fiddler diddling his elbock in the chimney-side; and this thing had nae music but the skirling of the solans. And the lassies were bits o' young things wi' the reid life dinnling and stending in their members; and this was a muckle, fat, crieshy man, and him fa'n in the vale o' years. Say what ye like, I maun say what I believe. It was joy was in the creature's heart; the joy o' hell, I daursay: joy whatever. Mony a time I have askit mysel', why witches and warlocks should sell their sauls (whilk are their maist dear possessions) and be auld, duddy, wrunkl't wives or auld, feckless, doddered men; and then I mind upon Tod Lapraik dancing a' they hours by his lane in the black glory of his heart. Nae doubt they burn for it in muckle hell, but they have a grand time here of it, whatever! – and the Lord forgie us!

Weel, at the hinder end, we saw the wee flag yirk up to the mastheid upon the harbour rocks. That was a' Sandie waited for. He up wi' the gun, took a deleeberate aim, an' pu'd the trigger. There cam' a bang and then ae waefu' skirl frae the Bass. And there were we rubbin' our een and lookin' at ither like daft folk. For wi' the bang and the skirl the thing had clean disappeared. The sun glintit, the wund blew, and there was the bare yaird whaur the Wonder had been lowping and flinging but ae second syne.

The hale way hame I roared and grat wi' the terror of that dispensa-

tion. The grawn folk were nane sae muckle better; there was little said in
Sandie's boat but just the name of God; and when we won in by the pier,
the harbour rocks were fair black wi' the folk waitin' us. It seems they
had fund Lapraik in ane of his dwams, cawing the shuttle and smiling.
Ae lad they sent to hoist the flag, and the rest abode there in the wabster's house. You may be sure they liked it little; but it was a means of
grace to severals that stood there praying in to themsel's (for nane cared
to pray out loud) and looking on thon awesome thing as it cawed the
shuttle. Syne, upon a suddenty, and wi' the ae dreidfu' skelloch, Tod
sprang up frae his hinderlands and fell forrit on the wab, a bluidy corp.

When the corp was examined the leid draps hadnae played buff
upon the warlock's body; sorrow a leid drap was to be fund; but there
was grandfaither's siller tester in the puddock's heart of him.

GEORGE BRUCE THOMSON   :

Gavin Greig was related to Edvard Grieg and Robert Burns. He edited a collection of airs for his friend J. Scott Skinner. He wrote four novels for serial publication in the *Buchan Observer* and one, *Logie o' Buchan*, was published as a book.

A schoolmaster and parish organist at Whitehill, New Deer, his poetry appeared in anthologies, his play *Mains's Wooin'* was widely performed, he wrote an operetta on Bonnie Prince Charlie and had a lifelong interest in folk song.

When he was asked to prepare a collection of traditional music for publication he immediately asked the Rev. James Bruce Duncan to collaborate. 'None of my correspondents seem to understand the subject as you do,' he wrote. 'Your aid and advice will be invaluable.'

Duncan was the United Free Church minister at Lynturk, near Alford, and was born a mile or so from the school he attended, where Greig became headmaster. Duncan had also been interested in folk song all his life and roughly half his collection of something over a thousand songs came from his family.

They worked together for almost ten years and communicated mostly by correspondence, addressing each other as Mr Greig and Mr Duncan to the end.

Between December 1907 and June 1911, Greig stimulated interest by writing for the *Buchan Observer*. 'Pirn-Tae't Jockie' appears in article no. 144: 'Through the continued courtesy of Mr G. Bruce Thomson, New Deer, I am enabled to print another of his original songs,' wrote Greig. 'Like the specimens of Mr Thomson's muse we have already given, "Pirn tae't Jockie" is full of the surprises of a fresh and quite unconventional kind of humour; while through all its whimsicalities runs a philosophy of life that reads many a useful lesson.' The verse is sung to 'The Girl I Left Behind Me' and the tune of the chorus is 'The White Cockade.'

'Scottish folk song is something materially different from the Scottish songs that mostly fill the books,' wrote Duncan. And Greig was in no doubt about folk song's importance. 'The vocabulary and

idiom of local speech, braced and quickened for its lyric task, may be
studied to good and fruitful purpose,' he wrote. 'Nor is all this a
detached and isolated field of investigation. It connects at every point
with the world beyond . . . our folk song like our language has endless
affinities and together they become twin handmaidens of ethnology.'

The project ended with Greig's death in August, 1914. They had
gathered more than 3,500 texts and 3,300 tunes. A selection was
published in 1925 as *Last Leaves of Traditional Ballads and Ballad Airs*,
edited by Alexander Keith. Their complete collection fills eight
volumes. 'Pirn-Tae't Jockie' is in vol. 6, song no. 1220. Its author is
better known for 'Macfarlan o the Sprotts'.

....

: PIRN-TAED JOCKIE

Fin I wis a little wee pirn-tae't loonie,[1]
I wis aye ca'd silly little Jockie;
Ae day I wis sittin' on my granny's window sill
Eatin' sweeties fae a broon paper pyockie;[2]
By cam' a lassie an' she offer't me a kiss,
An offer I wid never think o' scornin';
But she boltit wi' my sweeties, dang my heid throu' the window,
An' my granny tell't me this neist mornin'. –
   Ye shid never tie a kettle tull a big dog's tail,
   Nor tak' a drink o' water fae a bucket or a pail
   An' it's plain tae un'erstan'in as a bawbee for a bap,[3]
   That the reedest cheekit aipples aye are gotten on the tap
   A laddie aince pat snuff in his aul' grannie's tay
   Bit he drank it up 'imsel, afore he notice't, so they say;
   An' I'll wager tippence happeny tho' it's a' I ca' my ain,
   That the nickum[4] never tigget[5] wi' her sneeshin mull[6] again.

---

[1] pigeon-toed boy   [2] bag   [3] bun   [4] rogue   [5] tampered   [6] snuffbox

It's a sair thing love when it hits ye on the weskit,[7]
Tho' ye aften think ye're gettin' on sae fine, man;
Bit och hon-a-rie, tae fin' oot that ye've been coortin'
Anidder lad's lassie a' the time, man.
Oh, love's like a jujube[8] sprinkl't ower wi' sugar
Bit anidder chap changes this tae sooricks[9] a' thegidder;
Fin it's a' on ae side like the han'le o' a jug,
It's caul' kail early in the mornin'.

> *Fin a man gets a smack fae Cupid's little arra,*
> *It's like hurlin' in a prambulator doon the hill o' Barra;*
> *But suppose she winna hae ye, it's like lyin' on the rack,*
> *Wi' a thoosan maggie-mony-feets[10] crawlin' doon yer back*
> *Oh, it's aye the very biggest sheep that's smort[11] amo' the sna'*
> *Fin ye're fishin' it's the best troot that aye wons awa';*
> *If there's ae particler lassie that ye think ye'd like tae pet,*
> *That's jist the very ane ye may be sure ye winna get.*

I aince gaed tull a ball at the aul' toon o' Ribble
An' I never saw sae mony bonnie dawties;
Hooch! up tae the e'en amon marmalid an' tricle,
An' as happy as a craw amo' the taties.
There wis big lassies, small lassies, short lassies, tall lassies
A' kin' o' lassies fit tae blind me;
Bit the flo'er o' the ball wis little Polly Procter,
The lassie I was forc't to leave behind me.

---

[7] waistcoat   [8] jelly sweet   [9] sorrel, i.e. sourness   [10] centipedes
[11] smothered

I aince gaed tae my auntie's wi' a bag an' yellow haddicks,
Bit the idder loonies laiddert[12] me an' full't the bag wi' poddicks[13]
It wis sair sair tae thole,[14] I can say withoot a doot
Bit this time I thocht that I wid greet heech[15] oot;
For Polly said she'd mairry me an' nae anidder body,
An' fin I kiss't Polly she ne'er gaed a cheep;
Bit Polly ran awa wi' a lantern chaftit sodger,
Wi' a face that wis as yalla as a bilt swaddish neep.[16]

Oh ye never saw a rikkle[17] like my aul' horse Dobbin
Ye could hing up yer jacket on his hurdies;[18]
He wis broken in the win' an' fin he begood tae rin
He rais't a racket like a dizzen hurdy-gurdies.
I took 'im tae the market, an' swappit fair ower
Wi' a Balaklava chairger fae the sooth, man;
An' I didna wyte the blockin-ale[19] tho' I wis unca dry,
For fear they wid be finin' oot the truth, man.

I thocht that I hid fairly deen a smairt trick noo;
But sic a coupin' ower the tail[20] I never did expeck,
Fae a fraisy[21] aul' mannie wi' a roly-poly facie
Like a ginge-breed[22] rabbit, wi' a cloot roon's neck.
For I gaed tae the market, an' swappit, d'ye see,
My ain aul' Dobbin that wis blin' on an e'e;
But I cam fae the market as drouthy as a saith,[23]
Wi' a fiddle-heedit jigger[24] that was blin' upo' them baith.

---

[12] beat   [13] frogs   [14] endure   [15] right out   [16] boiled swede
[17] emaciated creature   [18] haunches   [19] wait for the drink to seal the bargain
[20] overturning   [21] gushing   [22] gingerbread   [23] coalfish
[24] long-headed oddity

NEIL MUNRO   :

Neil Munro (1863–1930) is best known as the inventor of Para Handy, who first appeared in the 'Looker On' column of the *Glasgow Evening News* in 1905 – where Erchie MacPherson, the beadle and waiter, and Jimmy Swan, the big-hearted commercial traveller, also materialised under the name of Hugh Foulis.

Munro's novels are mostly connected with the aftermath of the 1745 Jacobite Rebellion. The first, *John Splendid*, was published in 1898; his best and most accomplished, *The New Road*, appeared in 1914.

Munro maintained his connection with journalism and became editor of the *Glasgow Evening News* in 1918, having visited the First World War front four times as a war correspondent. A war poem, 'The Only Son', is a lament for his son Hugh who was killed at Loos in 1915.

The swagger of his earlier poem was reduced when soldiers sang verses of their own:

Hey, Jock, are ye glad ye 'listed?
Hey, Jock, is yer belly fu?
Hey, Jock, are ye aff tae Flanders?
Whit dae ye think o the Gordons noo?

: HEY, JOCK, ARE YE GLAD YE 'LISTED?

Hey, Jock, are ye glad ye 'listed?
    O Jock, but ye're far frae hame!
What d'ye think o' the fields o' Flanders?
    Jockey lad, are ye glad ye came?
Wet rigs we wrought in the land o' Lennox,
    When Hielan' hills were smeared wi' snaw;
Deer we chased through the seepin' heather,
    But the glaur o' Flanders dings them a'!

This is no' Fair o' Balloch,
    Sunday claes and a penny reel;
It's no' for dancin' at a bridal
    Willie Lawrie's bagpipes squeal.
Men are to kill in the morn's mornin';
    Here we're back to your daddy's trade;
Naething for't but to cock the bonnet,
    Buckle on graith[1] and kiss the maid.

The Cornal's yonder deid in tartan,
    Sinclair's sheuched in Neuve Eglise;
Slipped awa wi' the sodger's fever,
    Kinder than ony auld man's disease.
Scotland! Scotland! little we're due ye',
    Poor employ and skim-milk board.
But youth's a cream that maun be paid for,
    We got it reamin', so here's the sword!

Come awa, Jock, and cock your bonnet,
    Swing your kilt as best ye can;
Auld Dumbarton's Drums are dirlin',
    Come awa, Jock, and kill your man!
Far's the cry to Leven Water
    Where your fore-folks went to war,
They would swap wi' us to-morrow,
    Even in the Flanders glaur!

[1] get your equipment ready

MARION ANGUS

Violet Jacob (1863–1946), Marion Angus (1866–1946) and Helen B. Cruickshank (1886–1975) share more than a geographic accident of birth. In many ways their work anticipates MacDiarmid, especially in their use of a lyric Scots that is rooted in the Angus countryside and in the ways they have drawn inspiration from the ballads and songs of the area. More importantly, they share the concerns and experiences of women in Scottish society.

Violet Jacob was born Violet Kennedy-Erskine at the House of Dun, near Montrose. She often uses the elements of the countryside and its labours to yield surprising conclusions and draws on ballad and folk song. A number of her poems, such as 'Rohallion', 'The Wild Geese' and 'Hallowe'en' have been set to music by Jim Reid and, like his setting of Helen Cruickshank's 'Shy Geordie', have entered the folk tradition.

In her *Octobiography*, Helen Cruickshank recalls that 'a Dun resident' was asked how Mrs Jacob, a member of a 'county' family, the Kennedy-Erskines of Dun, knew the farm folk's language so well. Her reply was that 'as a bairn I was aye in an oot amo' the ploomen's feet at the Mains o' Dun'.

Born near Montrose, Helen Cruickshank was a suffragette who, on the death of her father, was forced to 'say goodbye to her hopes of being able to wed a penniless artist'. She worked as a civil servant in Edinburgh and nursed her elderly mother for forty years. As secretary of Scottish PEN she was supportive of MacDiarmid and his family during the 1930s, when she was also friendly with William Soutar and Lewis Grassic Gibbon.

Marion Angus was brought up in Arbroath where her father was a minister. When he died she moved to Aberdeen and, like her friend Helen Cruickshank, nursed a sister and their invalid mother.

Despite not starting to write poetry seriously till she was in her fifties, Marion Angus is often considered the most accomplished of the Angus women poets, though she lacks Violet Jacob's variety. She is also strongly influenced by the place and its voice and the influence of folk song and ballads are especially obvious in the way she imbues the best of her work with a sad, eerie quality. Her most anthologised piece, 'Alas! Poor Queen', is in English but Scots poems like 'The Lilt', 'The Can'el' and 'Ann Gilchrist' have an abrupt, unsettling quality which is also evident in 'The Blue Jacket', where the Scots voice gives the piece its power and appeal.

: THE BLUE JACKET

When there comes a flower to the stingless nettle,
    To the hazel bushes, bees,
I think I can see my little sister
    Rocking herself by the hazel trees.

Rocking her arms for very pleasure
    That every leaf so sweet can smell,
And that she has on her the warm blue jacket
    Of mine, she liked so well.

Oh to win near you, little sister!
    To hear your soft lips say –
'I'll never tak' up wi' lads or lovers,
    But a baby I maun hae.

A baby in a cradle rocking,
    Like a nut, in a hazel shell,
And a new blue jacket, like this o' Annie's,
    It sets me aye sae well.'

HUGH MACDIARMID

However valid or contradictory the innumerable judgements may be, the man who was both Hugh MacDiarmid and Christopher Murray Grieve (1892–1978) – poet and polemicist, journalist and essayist, nationalist and communist – still fascinates and eludes us.

Perhaps this is because we seek to contain or maybe even understand him. For he shares a simple feature with Robert Burns – that, just as we think we are coming to terms with one or another aspect of his character, personality, work and beliefs, up pops another to contradict or confound us. He continues to occupy a place where extremes merge rather than meet, where contradictions abound, though it may well be that he provided the key to an easy under-standing, that we should accept his contradictions and get on with it.

Which would be all very well were it not for the poetry, which can be as challenging as its makar. Hamish Henderson reckoned the man he called the Langholm Byspale wrote some of the best poetry Scotland has seen and some of the worst. This somehow humanises him – not that it's possible to separate the man from his extraordinary achievement, especially in the mid 1920s, when two volumes of super-lative lyrics and *A Drunk Man Looks at the Thistle* were published in two successive years.

The extent of MacDiarmid's achievements is not always obvious, neither in their range nor complexity. For, as well as trying to be a poet, he was also attempting to forge the Scottish nation or, at least, to revitalise us into accepting our own possibilities. And, while the preposterous aspects of his personality can easily be used against him, especially given some of his ill-conceived, daft ideas, the initial problem seems to have little or nothing to do with his work or political beliefs but is a matter of personality.

The man whom Norman MacCaig considered 'as mild as milk' perpetuated trivial disputes, often gratuitously wounding those with whom he disagreed, and he never overcame the national inferiority complex within himself, continually using self-aggrandisement as a literary and political weapon, decrying our national icons, especially Burns and Scott, while assiduously campaigning for the job himself. And, for all that he would have hated the comparison, the irony is that the writer with whom he can most easily be compared is Scott for, like him, his work is in danger of being drowned in the swell of its author's political opinions and he is recognised as much for his attempts to establish and shape our national identity as for anything he wrote.

....

: WHEESHT, WHEESHT

Wheesht, wheesht, my foolish hert,
For weel ye ken
I widna ha'e ye stert
Auld ploys again.

It's guid to see her lie
Sae snod an' cool,
A' lust o' lovin' by–
Wheesht, wheesht, ye fule!

WILLIAM LAUGHTON LORIMER

William Lorimer's (1885–1967) intention was at least as ambitious as either Burns or MacDiarmid. He sought to restore the lost traditions of Scots prose and to refurbish the language's range and vitality; though his wonderful translation of the New Testament arrived too late to have the impact he hoped.

He disregarded the familiarity of the story and gave fresh life to the book itself. Other translators had laboured with the fact that Scots is primarily a spoken medium. Some speakers use English to discuss religious matters, especially when quoting from the Bible. Peter Hately Waddell, for example, used Burns and to a lesser degree Scott as exemplars and turned to the language of a previous generation.

Lorimer exploited what many saw as Scots' main defect and this became his translation's strength. Not only is the language fresh and free from bureaucratic or commercial associations, the dialogues mirror and in some cases seem to replicate conversations between living people. The arguments have zest and Christ's language especially is vivid, direct and anything but affected, grandiose or pompous. Lorimer even reflected stylistic differences between writers of the separate books.

: JOHN 2: 1-9

Twa days efterhin there wis a waddin at Câna in Galilee. Jesus' mither wis there, an Jesus an his disciples wis amang the fríends bidden til it.

Efter a while the wine wis aa dune, an his mither said til him, 'They hae nae mair wine.'

'Ye can lae that tae me,' said Jesus; 'my hour isna come.'

Syne his mither said til the servans, 'Dae oniething he bids ye.'

Conform tae the Jewish rules anent syndin the haunds, there wis sittin there sax stane watter-crocks, haudin a seiven gallon the píece. 'Fu thae crocks wi watter,' Jesus said tae the servans; an whan they hed fu'd them tae the lip, he gaed on, 'Draw some aff nou an tak it tae the stewart'; an they did as he baud them.

Whan the stewart pree'd[1] the watter turned intil wine, onkennin whaur it cam frae, tho the servans at hed drawn it kent, he turned tae the bridegroom an said, 'Aabodie pits doun his guid wine first an keeps back his puirer wine till fowk is fu, but ye hae hained your guid wine till nou!'

This at Jesus did at Câna in Galilee wis the first o the signs he wrocht. Bi it he kythed his glorie an wan the faith o his disciples.

Efter this he gaed doun tae Capernaüm wi his mither, brithers, an disciples, but they badena there monie days. Whan the Jewish Passowre wis comin on, Jesus gaed doun tae Jerusalem. Finndin i the Temple the cowpers o nowt,[2] sheep, an doos, an the money-cheyngers sittin at their tables, he made a whang o lingels an drave them out o the Temple, sheep, nowt, an aa; skailed the money-cheyngers' siller on the grund an kiltit owre their tables; an than said tae the doo-sellers, 'Out o here wi aa that! Nae mair o this makkin my Faither's houss a place o troke[3] an tredd!' His disciples mindit on the word o Scriptur, '*Zeal for thy houss will cowe me.*'

Here the Jews tuik speech in haund an said til him, 'What sign can ye shaw us in pruif o your richt tae dae this?'

'Ding doun the Temple here,' said he, 'an I will raise it up again in three days.'

'This Temple,' the Jews answert, 'tuik fortie-sax year tae bigg, an ye will raise it up again in three days, na?'

But the Temple he wis ettlin at wis his bodie.

Efter he had risen frae the deid, his disciples mindit on his sayin this, an it gae them faith in Scriptur an the wurds at Jesus hed spokken.

[1] tasted   [2] cattle   [3] exchange

LEWIS GRASSIC GIBBON   :

James Leslie Mitchell (1901–35) was born at Hillhead of Segget in the parish of Auchterless, Aberdeenshire and spent his boyhood in Aberdeenshire's Howe of the Mearns – a landscape he was to make famous in his great trilogy, *A Scots Quair* (*Sunset Song* [1932], *Cloud Howe* [1933] and *Grey Granite* [1934]). He left school early, dabbled in journalism and joined the armed forces to survive in the Depression.

Mitchell believed the Depression was the natural product of a corrupt system. The Scotland he had known was destroyed by the First World War, the Mearns had changed beyond recognition and, as a result, he believed the native, inherent decency, honesty, kindness and abilities were lost.

His work commemorates this lost Scotland, notably in *Sunset Song*, where a thinly disguised self, recast as Chris Guthrie, watches the dying age and celebrates its harsh beauty. Here and in the stories and essays he wrote for *Scottish Scene*, where he collaborated with Hugh MacDiarmid to criticise and cajole their country, he resists any romantic temptations and faces the consequences of change. This simple act of personal defiance against the current trends of his time has given many Scottish writers the confidence to believe that their own voice and experience was good enough.

Part of Gibbon's success lies in the innovative use of language. Gibbon listened to the sound of his own voice and tried to replicate it on the page. He did so not by looking back to what other writers had done, nor by imitating what others were doing, but by looking forward and absorbing what was current in world literature in innovators like William Faulkner, James Joyce and so on.

One of Gibbon's great achievements is that the author's voice merges with the community, yet he never loses sight of the fact that it is a communal voice he is using. This is extremely important in an area where the way words are spoken – as opposed to the way words are written – is extremely relevant. Gibbon's language on the page presents no great difficulty but, when read aloud, it demands to be heard in the local accent. This is an extraordinary achievement and one which no other Scottish writer has successfully emulated.

: SMEDDUM

She'd had nine of a family in her time, Mistress Menzies, and brought the nine of them up, forbye—some near by the scruff of the neck, you would say. They were sniftering and weakly, two-three of the bairns, sniftering in their cradles to get into their coffins; but she'd shake them to life, and dose them with salts and feed them up till they couldn't but live. And she'd plonk one down—finishing the wiping of the creature's neb or the unco dosing of an ill bit stomach or the binding of a broken head—with a look on her face as much as to say *Die on me now and see what you'll get!*

Big-boned she was by her fortieth year, like a big roan mare, and *If ever she was bonny 'twas in Noah's time,* Jock Menzies, her eldest son would say. She'd reddish hair and a high, skeugh[1] nose, and a hand that skelped her way through life; and if ever a soul had seen her at rest when the dark was done and the day was come he'd died of the shock and never let on.

For from morn till night she was at it, work, work, on that ill bit croft that sloped to the sea. When there wasn't a mist on the cold, stone parks there was more than likely the wheep of the rain, wheeling and dripping in from the sea that soughed and plashed by the land's stiff edge. Kinneff lay north, and at night in the south, if the sky was clear on the gloaming's edge, you'd see in that sky the Bervie lights come suddenly lit, far and away, with the quiet about you as you stood and looked, nothing to hear but a sea-bird's cry.

But feint the much time to look or to listen had Margaret Menzies of Tocherty toun. Day blinked and Meg did the same, and was out, up out of her bed, and about the house, making the porridge and rousting the bairns, and out to the byre to milk the three kye, the morning growing out in the east and a wind like a hail of knives from the hills. Syne back to the kitchen again she would be, and catch Jock, her eldest, a clour in the lug that he hadn't roused up his sisters and brothers; and rouse them herself, and feed them and scold, pull up their breeks and straighten their frocks, and polish their shoes and set their caps straight. *Off you get and see you're not late,* she would cry, *and see you behave*

[1] skewed, distorted

yourselves at the school. And tell the Dominie I'll be down the night to ask him what the mischief he meant by leathering Jeannie and her not well.

They'd cry *Ay, Mother,* and go trotting away, a fair flock of the creatures, their faces red-scoured. Her own as red, like a meikle roan mare's, Meg'd turn at the door and go prancing in; and then at last, by the closet-bed, lean over and shake her man half-awake. *Come on, then, Willie, it's time you were up.*

And he'd groan and say *Is't?* and crawl out at last, a little bit thing like a weasel, Will Menzies, though some said that weasels were decent beside him. He was drinking himself into the grave, folk said, as coarse a little brute as you'd meet, bone-lazy forbye, and as sly as sin. Rampageous and ill with her tongue though she was, you couldn't but pity a woman like Meg tied up for life to a thing like *that.* But she'd more than a soft side still to the creature, she'd half-skelp the backside from any of the bairns she found in the telling of a small bit lie; but when Menzies would come paiching in of a noon and groan that he fair was tashed with his work, he'd mended all the ley fence that day and he doubted he'd need to be off to his bed—when he'd told her that and had ta'en to the blankets, and maybe in less than the space of an hour she'd hold out for the kye and see that he'd lied, the fence neither mended nor letten a-be, she'd just purse up her meikle wide mouth and say nothing, her eyes with a glint as though she half-laughed. And when he came drunken home from a mart she'd shoo the children out of the room, and take off his clothes and put him to bed, with an extra nip to keep off a chill.

She did half his work in the Tocherty parks, she'd yoke up the horse and the sholtie together, and kilt up her skirts till you'd see her great legs, and cry *Wissh!* like a man and turn a fair drill, the sea-gulls cawing in a cloud behind, the wind in her hair and the sea beyond. And Menzies with his sly-like eyes would be off on some drunken ploy to Kinneff or Stone-hive. Man, you couldn't but think as you saw that steer it was well that there was a thing like marriage, folk held together and couldn't get apart; else a black look-out it well would be for the fusionless creature of Tocherty toun.

Well, he drank himself to his grave at last, less smell on the earth if maybe more in it. But she broke down and wept, it was awful to see, Meg Menzies weeping like a stricken horse, her eyes on the dead, quiet face of her man. And she ran from the house, she was gone all that night, though the bairns cried and cried her name up and down the parks in the sound of the sea. But next morning they found her back in their midst, brisk as ever, like a great-boned mare, ordering here and directing there, and a fine feed set the next day for the folk that came to the funeral of her orra man.

She'd four of the bairns at home when he died, the rest were in kitchen-service or fee'd, she'd seen to the settling of the queans herself; and twice when two of them had come home, complaining-like of their mistresses' ways, she'd thrashen the queans and taken them back–near scared the life from the doctor's wife, her that was mistress to young Jean Menzies. *I've skelped the lassie and brought you her back. But don't you ill-use her, or I'll skelp you as well.*

There was a fair speak about that at the time, Meg Menzies and the vulgar words she had used, folk told that she'd even said what was the place where she'd skelp the bit doctor's wife. And faith! that fair must have been a sore shock to the doctor's wife that was that genteel she'd never believed she'd a place like that.

Be that as it might, her man new dead, Meg wouldn't hear of leaving the toun. It was harvest then and she drove the reaper up and down the long, clanging clay rigs by the sea, she'd jump down smart at the head of a bout and go gathering and binding swift as the wind, syne wheel in the horse to the cutting again. She led the stooks with her bairns to help, you'd see them at night a drowsing cluster under the moon on the harvesting cart.

And through that year and into the next and so till the speak died down in the Howe Meg Menzies worked the Tocherty toun; and faith, her crops came none so ill. She rode to the mart at Stonehive when she must, on the old boxcart, the old horse in the shafts, the cart behind with a sheep for sale or a birn of old hens that had finished with laying. And a butcher once tried to make a bit joke. *That's a sheep like yourself, fell long in the tooth.* And Meg answered up, neighing like a horse, and all heard: *Faith, then, if you've got a spite against teeth I've a clucking hen in the cart outbye. It's as toothless and senseless as you are, near.*

Then word got about of her eldest son, Jock Menzies that was fee'd up Allardyce way. The creature of a loon had had fair a conceit since he'd won a prize at a ploughing match–not for his ploughing, but for good looks; and the queans about were as daft as himself, he'd only to nod and they came to his heel; and the stories told they came further than that. Well, Meg'd heard the stories and paid no heed, till the last one came, she was fell quick then.

Soon's she heard it she hove out the old bit bike that her daughter Kathie had bought for herself, and got on the thing and went cycling away down through the Bervie braes in that Spring, the sun was out and the land lay green with a blink of mist that was blue on the hills, as she came to the toun where Jock was fee'd she saw him out in a park by the road, ploughing, the black loam smooth like a ribbon turning and wheeling at the tail of the plough. Another billy came ploughing behind, Meg Menzies watched till they reached the rig-end, her great chest heaving like a meikle roan's, her eyes on the shape of the furrows they made. And they drew to the end and drew the horse out, and Jock cried *Ay*, and she answered back *Ay*, and looked at the drill, and gave a bit snort, *If your looks win prizes, your ploughing never will.*

Jock laughed, *Fegs, then, I'll not greet for that*, and chirked to his horses and turned them about. But she cried him. *Just bide a minute, my lad. What's this I hear about you and Ag Grant?*

He drew up short then, and turned right red, the other childe as well, and they both gave a laugh, as plough-childes do when you mention a quean they've known overwell in more ways than one. And Meg snapped *It's an answer I want, not a cockerel's cackle: I can hear that at home on my own dunghill. What are you to do about Ag and her pleiter?*[2]

And Jock said *Nothing*, impudent as you like, and next minute Meg was in over the dyke and had hold of his lug and shook him and it till the other childe ran and caught at her nieve.[3] *Faith, mistress, you'll have his lug off!* he cried. But Meg Menzies turned like a mare on new grass, *Keep off or I'll have yours off as well!*

So he kept off and watched, fair a story he'd to tell when he rode out that night to go courting his quean. For Meg held to the lug till it near came off and Jock swore that he'd put things right with Ag Grant. She let go the lug then and looked at him grim: *See that you do and get married right quick, you're the like that needs loaded with a birn*[4] *of bairns–to keep you out of the jail, I jaloose.*[5] *It needs smeddum*[6] *to be either right coarse or right kind.*

They were wed before the month was well out, Meg found them a cottar house to settle and gave them a bed and a press she had, and two-three more sticks from Tocherty toun. And she herself led the wedding dance, the minister in her arms, a small bit childe; and 'twas then as she

---

[2] complaint   [3] fist   [4] burden   [5] suspect   [6] mettle, spirit

whirled him about the room, he looked like a rat in the teeth of a tyke, that he thanked her for seeing Ag out of her soss,[7] *There's nothing like a marriage for redding things up.* And Meg Menzies said *EH?* and then she said *Ay*, but queer-like, he supposed she'd no thought of the thing. Syne she slipped off to sprinkle thorns in the bed and to hang below it the great hand-bell that the bothybillies took them to every bit marriage.

Well, that was Jock married and at last off her hands. But she'd plenty left still, Dod, Kathleen and Jim that were still at school, Kathie a limmer[8] that alone tongued her mother, Jeannie that next led trouble to her door. She'd been found at her place, the doctor's it was, stealing some money and they sent her home. Syne news of the thing got into Stonehive, the police came out and tormented her sore, she swore she never had stolen a meck, and Meg swore with her, she was black with rage. And folk laughed right hearty, fegs! that was a clour for meikle Meg Menzies, her daughter a thief!

But it didn't last long, it was only three days when folk saw the doctor drive up in his car. And out he jumped and went striding through the close and met face to face with Meg at the door. And he cried *Well, mistress, I've come over for Jeannie.* And she glared at him over her high, skeugh nose, *Ay, have you so then? And why, may I speir?*

So he told her why, the money they'd missed had been found at last in a press by the door; somebody or other had left it there, when paying a grocer or such at the door. And Jeannie—he'd come over to take Jean back.

But Meg glared *Ay, well, you've made another mistake. Out of this, you and your thieving suspicions together!* The doctor turned red, *You're making a miserable error*—and Meg said *I'll make you mince-meat in a minute.*

So he didn't wait that, she didn't watch him go, but went ben to the kitchen where Jeannie was sitting, her face chalk-white as she'd heard them speak. And what happened then a story went round, Jim carried it to school, and it soon spread out, Meg sank in a chair, they thought she was greeting; syne she raised up her head and they saw she was laughing, near as fearsome the one as the other, they thought. *Have you any cigarettes?* she snapped sudden at Jean, and Jean quavered *No*, and Meg glowered at her cold. *Don't sit there and lie. Gang bring them to me.* And Jean brought them, her mother took the pack in her hand. *Give's hold of a match till I light up the thing. Maybe smoke'll do good for the crow that I got in the throat last night by the doctor's house.*

---

[7] muddle   [8] a rascally girl

Well, in less than a month she'd got rid of Jean—packed off to Brechin the quean was, and soon got married to a creature there—some clerk that would have left her sore in the lurch but that Meg went down to the place on her bike, and there, so the story went, kicked the childe so that he couldn't sit down for a fortnight, near. No doubt that was just a bit lie that they told, but faith! Meg Menzies had herself to blame, the reputation she'd gotten in the Howe, folk said, *She'll meet with a sore heart yet.* But devil a sore was there to be seen, Jeannie was married and was fair genteel.

Kathleen was next to leave home at the term. She was tall, like Meg, and with red hair as well, but a thin fine face, long eyes blue-grey like the hills on a hot day, and a mouth with lips you thought over thick. And she cried *Ah well, I'm off then, mother.* And Meg cried *See you behave yourself.* And Kathleen cried *Maybe; I'm not at school now.*

Meg stood and stared after the slip of a quean, you'd have thought her half-angry, half near to laughing, as she watched that figure, so slender and trig, with its shoulders square-set, slide down the hill on the wheeling bike, swallows were dipping and flying by Kinneff, she looked light and free as a swallow herself, the quean, as she biked away from her home, she turned at the bend and waved and whistled, she whistled like a loon and as loud, did Kath.

Jim was the next to leave from the school, he bided at home and he took no fee, a quiet-like loon, and he worked the toun, and, wonder of wonders, Meg took a rest. Folk said that age was telling a bit on even Meg Menzies at last. The grocer made hints at that one night, and Meg answered up smart as ever of old: *Damn the age! But I've finished the trauchle of the bairns at last, the most of them married or still over young. I'm as swack as ever I was, my lad. But I've just got the notion to be a bit sweir.*

Well, she'd hardly begun on that notion when faith! ill the news that came up to the place from Segget. Kathleen her quean that was fee'd down there, she'd ta'en up with some coarse old childe in a bank, he'd left his wife, they were off together, and she but a bare sixteen years old.

And that proved the truth of what folk were saying, Meg Menzies she hardly paid heed to the news, just gave a bit laugh like a neighing horse and went on with the work of park and byre, cool as you please—ay, getting fell old.

No more was heard of the quean or the man till a two years or more had passed and then word came up to the Tocherty someone had seen her—and where do you think? Out on a boat that was coming from

Australia. She was working as stewardess on that bit boat, and the childe that saw her was young John Robb, an emigrant back from his uncle's farm, near starved to death he had been down there. She hadn't met in with him near till the end, the boat close to Southampton the evening they met. And she'd known him at once, thought he not her, she'd cried *John Robb?* and he'd answered back *Ay?* and looked at her canny in case it might be the creature was looking for a tip from him. Syne she'd laughed *Don't you know me, then, you gowk?*[9] *I'm Kathie Menzies you knew long syne—it was me ran off with the banker from Segget!*

He was clean dumbfounded, young Robb, and he gaped, and then they shook hands and she spoke some more, though she hadn't much time, they were serving up dinner for the first-class folk, aye dirt that are ready to eat and to drink. *If ever you get near to Tocherty toun tell Meg I'll get home and see her sometime. Ta-ta!* And then she was off with a smile, young Robb he stood and he stared where she'd been, he thought her the bonniest thing that he'd seen all the weary weeks that he'd been from home.

And this was the tale that he brought to Tocherty, Meg sat and listened and smoked like a tink, forbye herself there was young Jim there, and Jock and his wife and their three bit bairns, he'd fair changed with marriage, had young Jock Menzies. For no sooner had he taken Ag Grant to his bed than he'd started to save, grown mean as dirt, in a three-four years he'd finished with feeing, now he rented a fell big farm himself, well stocked it was, and he fee'd two men. Jock himself had grown thin in a way, like his father but worse his bothy childes said, old Menzies at least could take a bit dram and get lost to the world but the son was that mean he might drink rat-poison and take no harm, 'twould feel at home in a stomach like his.

Well, that was Jock, and he sat and heard the story of Kath and her stay on the boat. *Ay, still a coarse bitch, I have not a doubt. Well if she never comes back to the Mearns, in Segget you cannot but redden with shame when a body will ask 'Was Kath Menzies your sister?'*

And Ag, she'd grown a great sumph of a woman, she nodded to that, it was only too true, a sore thing it was on decent bit folks that they should have any relations like Kath.

But Meg just sat there and smoked and said never a word, as though she thought nothing worth a yea or a nay. Young Robb had fair ta'en a fancy to Kath and he near boiled up when he heard Jock speak, him and the wife that he'd married from her shame. So he left them short and went raging home, and wished for one that Kath would come back, a Summer noon as he cycled home, snipe were calling in the Auchindreich moor where the cattle stood with their tails a-switch, the Grampians rising far and behind, Kinraddie spread like a map for show, its ledges veiled in a mist from the sun. You felt on that day a wild, daft unease, man, beast and bird: as though something were missing and lost from the world, and Kath was the thing that John Robb missed, she'd something in her that minded a man of a house that was builded upon a hill.

Folk thought that maybe the last they would hear of young Kath Menzies and her ill-gettèd ways. So fair stammy-gastered they were with the news she'd come back to the Mearns, she was down in Stonehive, in a grocer's shop, as calm as could be, selling out tea and cheese and such-like with no blush of shame on her face at all, to decent women that were properly wed and had never looked on men but their own, and only on them with their braces buttoned.

It just showed you the way that the world was going to allow an ill quean like that in a shop, some folk protested to the creature that owned it, but he just shook his head. *Ah well, she works fine; and what else she does is no business of mine.* So you well might guess there was more than business between the man and Kath Menzies, like.

And Meg heard the news and went into Stonehive, driving her sholtie,[10] and stopped at the shop. And some in the shop knew who she was and minded the things she had done long syne to other bit bairns of hers that went wrong; and they waited with their breaths held up with delight. But all that Meg did was to nod to Kath *Ay, well, then, it's you—Ay, mother, just that—Two pounds of syrup and see that it's good.*

And not another word passed between them, Meg Menzies that once would have ta'en such a quean and skelped her to rights before you could wink. Going home from Stonehive she stopped by the farm where young Robb was fee'd, he was out in the hayfield coling the hay, and she nodded to him grim, with her high horse face. *What's this that I hear about you and Kath Menzies?*

He turned right red, but he wasn't ashamed. *I've no idea—though I hope it's the worse—. It fell near is—. Then I wish it was true, she might marry me, then, as I've prigged her to do.*

Oh, have you so, then? said Meg, and drove home, as though the whole matter was a nothing to her.

[10] pony

But next Tuesday the postman brought a bit note, from Kathie it was to her mother at Tocherty. *Dear mother, John Robb's going out to Canada and wants me to marry him and go with him. I've told him instead I'll go with him and see what he's like as a man—and then marry him at leisure, if I feel in the mood. But he's hardly any money, and we want to borrow some, so he and I are coming over on Sunday. I hope that you'll have dumpling for tea. Your own daughter, Kath.*

Well, Meg passed that letter over to Jim, he glowered at it dour, I know—near all the Howe's heard. *What are you going to do, now, mother?*

But Meg just lighted a cigarette and said nothing, she'd smoked like a tink since that steer with Jean. There was promise of strange on-goings at Tocherty by the time that the Sabbath day was come. For Jock came there on a visit as well, him and his wife, and besides him was Jeannie, her that had married the clerk down in Brechin, and she brought the bit creature, he fair was a toff; and he stepped like a cat through the sharn in the close; and when he had heard the story of Kath, her and her plan and John Robb and all, he was shocked near to death, and so was his wife. And Jock Menzies gaped and gave a mean laugh. *Ay, coarse to the bone, ill-gettèd I'd say if it wasn't that we came of the same bit stock. Ah well, she'll fair have to tramp to Canada, eh mother?—if she's looking for money from you.*

And Meg answered quiet *No, I wouldn't say that. I've the money all ready for them when they come.*

You could hear the sea plashing down soft on the rocks, there was such a dead silence in Tocherty house. And then Jock habbered like a cock with fits *What, give silver to one who does as she likes, and won't marry as you made the rest of us marry? Give silver to one who's no more than a—.*

And he called his sister an ill name enough, and Meg sat and smoked looking over the parks. *Ay, just that. You see, she takes after myself.*

And Jeannie squeaked *How?* and Meg answered her quiet: *She's fit to be free and to make her own choice the same as myself and the same kind of choice. There was none of the rest of you fit to do that, you'd to marry or burn, so I married you quick. But Kath and me could afford to find out. It all depends if you've smeddum or not.*

She stood up then and put her cigarette out, and looked at the gaping gowks she had mothered. *I never married your father, you see. I could never make up my mind about Will. But maybe our Kath will find something surer...Here's her and her man coming up the road.*

ANON.   :

This piece comes from Douglas Young's *Scottish Verse 1851–1951*, where it appeared in print for the second time. 'I owe this admirable piece, like much else,' he notes, 'to Miss Helen Cruickshank, who found it in *The People's Friend* of 2 April, 1917.'

: THE STATION-MASTER'S DOCHTER

(Otherwise, 'The Lament of Tammas Claiker, Bill-Sticker')

O wae's me for the station-master's dochter!
She doesna care a preen for me, tho I wad fain hae socht her.
She cocks a purple tammie on a stook o yalla hair:
A jersey haps her shouthers, but she keeps her thrapple bare,
in a what-d'ye-caa-'t–invitin ye tae tak a second luik–
a chemie, caad a blouse, wi a snippit gushet-neuk.
    Snippit, rippit, snippit,
    Rippit, snippit, rippit,
a chemie, caad a blouse, wi a snippit gushet-neuk.

Ay, see the stuck-up stockie standan there afore the wicket.
she kens she has a dainty hand for takin up your ticket.
But in the train at fowks like me she winna fling a word,
she's aye in sic a hurry nippin tickets in the third.
But I wad like to tell her–I wad tell her gin I durst–
she's an unco time in nippin wi the billies in the first!
    Nippin, clippin, nippin,
    Clippin, nippin, clippin,
she's an unco time in nippin wi the billies in the first.

Aince, at the Coperative Ball, I thocht I'd hae a dance wi her,
but–set her up, the besom !–I could never get a chance wi her,
sae I had juist tae skutch about the slippy flure and watch her
trippin here and trippin there and skippin round and round,
whiles slippin intae corners wi the gentry frae the toun.
    Trippin, skippin, slippin,
    Slippin, skippin, trippin,
slippin intae corners wi the gentry frae the toun.

O wae's me for the station-master's dochter!
She winna gie a luik at me—she's no the lass I thocht her.
An honest man's a worthy man, whatever be his trade;
the lass that lichtlies him for that deserves tae dee a maid.
Ye getna muckle guid, but ye get the fewer ills
in pickin up a livin, rinnin round and stickin bills.
    Pickin, stickin, pickin,
    Stickin, pickin, stickin,
in pickin up a livin rinnin round and stickin bills.

: Nippin, clippin, nippin,
Clippin, nippin, clippin

WILLIAM SOUTAR

William Soutar (1898–1943) is one of the greatest Scottish poets of the twentieth century and one of our finest diarists. MacDairmid considered his work a sufficient threat to omit sizeable chunks from the *Collected Poems* he edited, where the introductory essay is scarcely flattering, casting Soutar in a tragic if heroic role, as a bedridden invalid struggling against infirmity to produce minor poetry, escapist fantasy or bairnsangs (for children). This has tended to be the picture that survived.

Yet MacDiarmid's early lyrics were Soutar's constant inspiration; and he followed MacDiarmid's imprecation, going back not only to Dunbar, but to Henryson, and, most especially, to the ballads. In common with many poets of the time, once removed from MacDiarmid's shadow, Soutar is seen as a unique representative of an entire tradition. More than any other poet, he shows how layers of tradition can be synthesised into a personal achievement, producing poetry that places him, uniquely, between the world of fantasy, dream and illusion and a world of vision, commitment and the pursuit of ideal beauty. A host of subordinate tensions and oppositions exists in the world of Soutar's self but this dualism dominates and is ultimately realised in his greatest tension of all – the nature of self.

: THE HALTED MOMENT

Wha hasna turn'd inby a sunny street
And fund alang its length nae folk were there:
And heard his step fa' steadily and clear
Nor wauken[1] ocht[2] but schedows at his feet.
Shüther[3] to shüther in the reemlin[4] heat
The houses seem'd to hearken and to stare;
But a' were doverin[5] whaur they stüde and were
Like wa's ayont[6] the echo o' time's beat.
Wha hasna thocht whan atween stanes sae still,
That had been biggit up for busyness,
He has come wanderin into a place
Lost, and forgotten, and unchangeable:
And thocht the far-off traffic sounds to be
The weary waters o' mortality.

[1] waken   [2] anything   [3] shoulder   [4] trembling, shimmering   [5] dozing
[6] beyond

ROBERT MCLELLAN

Robert McLellan (1907–85) was born at Linmill Farm near Lanark in the Clyde Valley and spent childhood holidays on his grandparents' farm. The place is now spelt Linnmill but McLellan insisted it was named after a mill for dressing flax rather than the Falls of Clyde.

Best known for his plays, written between 1933 and 1967, McLellan wrote in a Scots that was firmly based on his native Lanarkshire tongue and emphasised that he was using a spoken language.

The *Linmill Stories* were written for radio and broadcast between 1960 and 1965. Six were published as a booklet in 1977, thirteen appeared in *Lallans* magazine and J. K. Annand edited the edition of twenty-four stories which appeared in 1990 – although the most anthologised story, 'The Cat', is not included. McLellan, he said, was the twentieth century's greatest writer of Scots prose.

These stories give a remarkably detailed picture of rural Scotland in the early years of the twentieth century. The bothy system is still in place, the farm work is labour intensive and casual labour involves schoolchildren and married women, though low-paid labour was imported from Ireland and men and women with learning difficulties were exploited in a system that was cheap and convenient for both the local authority and the farmer.

: THE RINGLETS

In the closs at Linmill, no faur frae the hoose back door and richt aneth the stable winnock, there was a muckle lump o stane used as a sait, though it was gey cauld on the dowp gin the sun hadna been on it for a while first to warm it.

That was whaur I sat the first day I had my heid cowed, and what a day that was.

As faur as I can mind ye had to be aboot fower-year-auld in thae days afore they wad let ye aff weirin petticoats and pit ye into breeks, and till ye were into breeks ye had to weir yer hair lang, like a lassie.

It didna fash ye, mind ye, till ye began to loss yer freinds, and loss them ye did as sune as they had growen into breeks and haen their heids cowed. Then they seemed aa at ance to see something aboot ye they had missed afore, and ran awa and left ye to play by yersell, or fin new freinds amang the younger bairns. They werena gaun to be seen wi ye ony langer. Ye were juist like a lassie.

It was fashious whan it happened, but as I say, there was a lang time whan ye juist took it for grantit that, lassie or laddie, ye wore lang hair and petticoats, and, to tell ye the truith, there was a time, though it seems hard to believe, whan I was prood o my hair, for I had glossie reid ringlets that my minnie spent hours on, twirlin her kaim through them ane efter the ither like she did her ain, then, whan they were aa ticht, tyin them into a bunch on the croun o my heid wi a silk ribbon.

My curls won me a lot o attention, for my maiks[1] aa had hair like towe,[2] moussie and straucht, and mony a sweetie I was gien, or cake or biscuit if the baker's van had caaed, by the lassies frae Kirkfieldbank or Donegal that cam aboot the ferm to pou the strawberries. In fact, some o them made ower muckle o my hair, and wad try to lift me up and kiss me. Black Aggie managed it ance, and I can mind the smell o her braith to this day. She was nearly aye fou, was Black Aggie, and drew awa aa day on a cuttie cley pipe. Sae ye can weill imagine.

But there it was. I had a heid o hair like naebody in the place, and it won me a lot o attention, and mony a titbit, and for a while I was prood

[1] equals   [2] flax or hemp

o it. As for my minnie, she fair dotit, and whan folk praised it to her face, and said there was nae dout whaur I had gotten it, for her ain hair was juist as curlie, and glossie tae, she wad purr like a cat wi pleisure.

The day cam, though, whan I began to want into breeks, and hae my hair cut short like ither laddies. I had gane wi my cuisin Jockie and young Tam Baxter o the Falls, baith aulder nor mysell, to the fute o the made walk abune Stanebyres Linn, whaur there was a sait for the folk that peyed sixpence up at the Falls hoose to Tam's mither Martha and cam doun the made walk to see the view.

It was gey awesome at that sait, for ye lookit straucht ower an airn railin into the face o the Linn, a muckle sheet o watter roarin doun into space. Gin ye had the nerve to lean on the railin and look doun, and it took some nerve, I can tell ye, because the stanchions o the railin were driven into the very lip o the rock, and didna hae muckle grip: but if ye did hae the nerve and lookit doun ye could see naething, for the force o the watter whan it hit the pule ablow filled the air wi spray. It wat ye, tae, and wi that, and the trummlin o the grun aneth yer feet, ye werena inclined to linger, though if the aulder laddies had taen ye there ye tried yer best to look gallus.

Nou, this day, Jockie and young Tam Baxter had heard frae Tam's aulder brither that there was a wey doun frae the made walk to the pule ablow the Linn. The Saumon Hole, the pule was caaed, though there had been nae saumon in Clyde for years, Tam's faither said, wi the watter sae dirty frae Hamilton doun, for the saumon had to come frae the sea. But the Saumon Hole it was caaed, for the saumon had ance been held there by the Linn, and couldna win faurer up the watter, and it had a queer fascination, for ye couldna see it frae the bank abune, as I hae said, for the spray, and ye couldna see it frae faurer doun the watter, for at the tail o it the watter took a turn, and left it oot o sicht in a neuk.

Weill, this day Jockie and young Tam Baxter were determined to win doun to the Saumon Hole, and though they didna invite me to gang alang wi them, they alloued me to follow them the length o the Falls sait.

Then they stertit to look for the wey doun. Jacob's Lether, it was caaed, said young Tam, and telt us a story he said was oot o the Bible, but Jockie said he didna see hou it could be the same lether, for Jacob bade in the Holy land; and that was somewhaur no near Clyde, and different athegither.

It wasna lang afore they fand the stert o the wey doun, at a bit near the sait whaur a wee dribble o a burn oot o Tam Baxter's orchard gaed through ablow the made walk in a cley drain, and then ran doun a nerra gully in the steep bank abune the watter. The pad they had been lookin for gaed doun the bank asides this bit spoot, and at first it didna look bye-ordinar steep, yet for aa that whan they had sclimmed the railin and were ready to stert aff on their wey doun to the watter they telt me to gang hame.

'I want to come wi ye, Jockie,' I said.

'Awa hame. Ye're ower wee.'

'I want to come wi ye.'

'Awa hame whan ye're telt,' said young Tam Baxter.

'Ay,' said Jockie, 'ye couldna sclim doun here in thae petticoats. And yer ringlets wad taigle in the briers. We'll tak ye doun some day whan ye hae short hair and breeks. But we canna tak ye like that.'

'Ay,' said young Tam Baxter, 'this is nae place for bairns.'

'I'll follow ye,' I said.

'Ye'll stick,' said Jockie.

'And we'll no wait for ye,' said young Tam Baxter. 'Come on Jockie.'

And wi that they set aff doun the pad.

I sclimmed the railin and gaed efter them, and Jockie saw me.

'If ye tummle ye'll faa on to the rocks and get killed,' he said.

'I want to come wi ye,' I said.

'If ye dinna gang back hame I'll pelt ye wi divots.'[3]

He tore a divot oot o the bank and lat flee at me, no hard, but some dirt cam aff it whan it was gaun past my heid and gaed into my een. I had to staun for a while blinkin to wark the dirt oot, and by the time I could see again Jockie and Young Tam Baxter were doun roun a bend and oot o sicht.

I stertit to sclim doun efter them.

At first the pad gaed doun amang a lot o plants wi lang peyntit leaves that tore in yer haunds gin ye tried to tak a grip o them, and smelt juist like ingans. But it wasna bye-ordinar steep, and I sune passed the wild ingans, if that's what they were, and cam to a shelf o rock whaur the spoot o watter gethert into a wee pule, and then disappeared ower the edge: The pad left the spoot at this peynt and gaed roun to the richt alang a shelf o rock aneth the rutes o a big ash tree growin oot o the bank, and syne doun a wat slide whaur the shelf o rock endit, on to a

---

[3] clods of earth

grassie ledge. On the wey doun the wat slide there was a lang thick ash rute that ye could haud on to like a railin, but what wad happen efter ye cam to the gressie ledge ye juist couldna tell. Aa ye could see frae the tap o the slide was the ledge and syne space.

Jockie and young Tam Baxter maun hae gane that wey, though, sae I grippit the ash rute ticht and stertit to sclim doun the slide. My feet couldna grip it sae I juist sat on my dowp, and gat my petticoats wat. But the ash rute held firm and I lat mysell doun haund ower haund, and afore alang I had won to the gressie ledge.

It led back to the left aneth the shelf o rock, and syne ahint the watter o the spoot, and ahint the spoot the grun was saft wi watter, and I could see Jockie and young Tam Baxter's futemarks.

Sae I kent that was the wey, and made efter them.

In ahint the spoot the watter dribblet ower my heid, and ran doun my neck and in aneth my claes, but that wasna aa that fasht me.

It was the saft wat grun. For juist whan I was aboot three quarters o the wey across it, and near the firm grun on the ither side, it stertit to slip, and there was naething to haud on to. I wastit nae time thinkin. I juist glued my een to the firm grun and ran, and though I slippit a wee at ilka step, I won the ither side afore I had slippit to the lip o the slope. Gin I had dune that, I dout, I wad hae been ower wi the spoot into space.

Ance on the firm grun I sat doun, and for a while I couldna gar mysel look roun. I juist glued my een to the grush atween my knees and waitit for my heid to stop birlin.

Syne I had a keek at whaur the pad gaed neist, and afore lang my heid was on the birl again, for it gaed on oot o sicht alang the fute o a steep rock, and juist on the peynt o gaun oot o sicht it grew sae nerra it was frichtsome.

I waitit for my heid to stop birlin again, and lookit to mak shair there was nae ither wey Jockie and young Tam Baxter could hae gane, but there was nane. The pad gaed alang that ledge, there was nae dout.

I kent I juist couldna face it, and that I wad hae to gang back, and I could hae grutten wi spite.

Then I thocht o the slippery wat grun aneth the spoot, and I kent I couldna face that again aither, and, though I tried my best no to, I grat in the end.

Syne I began to see that I couldna bide there aa day, for Jockie and young Tam Baxter wad likely gang doun the watter whan they had won the fute o the bank, and mak thir wey back to the made walk doun aboot Carlin, and maybe wadna fin oot that I was stuck till it was ower daurk to come to my help, and wad hae to tell my grandfaither, and maybe fetch oot the polis, wi lanterns. At the thocht o it I roared like a bull.

And whan I realised that naebody could hear me abune the roar o the Linn I cried oot lood for my minnie, and my grannie, and my grand-faither, and ein my cuisin Jockie himsell, till I hadna a braith left in my breist.

Syne in fair desperation I telt mysell that gin it had been possible to come doun it maun be possible to gang back, and I made mysell tak anither look at the saft wat slope ahint the spoot.

There was hinnie-suckle growin frae the rock at the heid o it, and the main brainch was thicker nor a finger. Shairly it wad be strang eneugh to haud me.

I made my wey ower to it and tried. At the first pou it cam richt awa frae the rock, and I gey nearly fell ower backwards. Syne the very rute itsell stertit to pou oot o the grun. I lowsed my grip as if I had haen my fingers brunt, and sat doun again, back on the firm grun.

In the end I made up my mind that the ae wey back ower that saft wat slope was the wey I had come, at a rin, sae I stude up and faced it, gluein my een hard to the firm grun on the ither side, and tryin no to look at the fullyery awa doun on the ither side o Clyde, and the tuim space atween.

Aa at aince I ran for it, and was across afore I kent I had stertit.

I could haurdly believe it. I was sae pleased wi mysell I gaed the length o thinkin o gaun back again, and tryin the ledge alang the fute o the steep rock, to see what happened whan it gaed oot o sicht, and I declare I wad hae tried it, gin I hadna thocht first o tryin to see if I could look doun at the faur awa fullyery withoot my heid birlin. It birlt, aa richt, and I had to sit for a while lookin at the gress atween my knees again afore I could force mysell juist to gang back hame the wey I had come.

I managed it, though whan I was pouin mysell up the wat slide by the ash rute I gat my knees cut, and anither soakin as weill, and by the time I had won back ower the wild ingans and on to the made walk I was a gey tousie sicht.

But I was fair pleased wi mysell, aa the same, for winnin back across that saft wat slope efter bein feart o it, and I began to tell mysell that if

Jockie and young Tam Baxter had been there to daur me on I wad hae won doun to the Saumon Hole wi nae bother.

Sae efter I had won back hame and haen a row frae my minnie for makin sic a sicht o mysell, and teirin my guid claes, and cuttin my knees, I stertit to prig at her for breeks and short hair.

'Ye shairly dinna want to loss yer braw ringlets,' she said.

'I want short hair and breeks, like a laddie.'

'Ye're no big eneugh yet for short hair and breeks.'

'I'm juist as big as Jockie.'

'Ye're no sae auld.'

'I'm juist as big.'

'But ye dinna want to loss yer braw ringlets.'

'I hate my ringlets.'

'I like yer ringlets, son.'

'I hate them.'

'Ah weill, we'll see.'

I keepit on at her ilka day efter that, and ilka time I brocht the maitter up she tried to mak oot she had forgotten, but the day cam at last whan she gied in, and bocht me a pair o breeks frae Willie Mitchell the packman, and gat my grandfaither to hae a word wi Tam Finlay up at Nether Affleck. Tam had been a shepherd, and they said he could cowe a heid o hair wi a pair o sheep shears as weill as Sandy Morrison the Lanark barber could dae it wi hair shears and clippers.

Tam Finlay cam doun frae Nether Affleck ae Setterday efternune, and my minnie pat me into my new breeks and took me oot to the stane sait aneth the stable winnock.

'No ower short, Tam,' she said, 'and dinna speyl the ringlets. I wad like to keep them.'

'Aa richt, Lizzie,' said Tam, and laid haud o me.

'Sit still, Rab,' he said.

I sat as still as daith, though it was hard, wi the hair frae the shears gaun doun my neck atween my claes and my skin, and ticklin me. But I tholed it like a Trojan, thinkin hou I wad sune be able to follow Jockie and young Tam Baxter aboot withoot aye bein telt to gang hame.

'There ye are, ye can staun up nou,' said Tam Finlay, whan he had feenished.

'Oh Rab,' said my minnie, and stertit to greit.

My grannie was lookin on, and she grat tae, but my grandfaither didna.

'Ye made a guid job of that, Tam,' he said. 'Come on inbye and hae a dram.'

'Thank ye,' said Tam.

'Can I rin awa and play nou?' I askit.

'Na na,' said my minnie, 'ye'll hae to come inbye and let me see if I can gar it lie doun wi a brush and kaim and some cauld watter.

She took me inbye and wat my heid and syne kaimed it, and brushed it, and syne kaimed and brushed it again, and aye wi the tears rowin doun her face as if her hairt was brekin, till I was smittlet,[4] and stertit to snivel mysell.

'What's wrang, hinnie,' she askit, 'are ye sorry efter aa?'

'Na,' I said. 'I want oot to play.'

'Awa wi ye, then,' she said, no very pleased.

I ran aa ower the ferm lookin for Jockie, and fand him i the end wi anither cuisin frae Linnville, inside the hedge o the front gairden, talkin in whispers.

I gaed up to them, fair preenin mysell, like a peacock.

'Oh Jockie,' I said, 'can we gang doun to the Saumon Hole efter tea-time?'

'It's auntie Lizzie's Rab,' said Jockie.

'Guid God,' said big Tam Hannah frae Linnville, 'I wadna hae kent him. What hae they dune to him?'

'He's lost his ringlets,' said Jockie.

'Look at his lugs,' said Tam Hannah. 'They're like saucers. And I wadna hae thocht his neb was sae lang.'

'He's no very stoot aboot the legs, aither,' said Jockie. 'Ye'll hae to sup mair parritch, Rab, nou that ye're into breeks.'

'Thae buttoned shune dinna help ony,' said Tam Hannah. 'God, he's a sicht.'

I could haurdly believe my ears, and I didna bide to hear ony mair. I ran back to the hoose as hard as I could, and slippit in at the front door and up the stair to my minnie's bedroom. There was a gless there abune a kist o drawers, that ye could turn on its middle, and first I tried to turn it sae that it was facin doun at me, but I couldna get it to bide still lang eneuch to let me see mysell, sae I sclimmed up on a chair and brocht it

---

[4] infected

doun on to the flair, and stude it against the kist o drawers whaur it had to bide the wey I wantit it, and syne had a look.

I juist couldna thole it. I wadna hae kent it was me. Gin I had met the laddie in that gless ootbye I wad hae peetied him. I slank oot o the hoose again by the front door and syne roun to the stable, and sclimmed up a travis into the hey laft, and lay doun and grat.

My grandfaither fand me there whan he cam lookin for me at tea-time.

'What's wrang wi ye?' he askit.

I telt him.

'Man,' he said, 'ye suldna fash yersell. Aabody looks like a skint rabbit the day they hae their heid cowed. Hae ye neir seen me?'

'Na.'

'Weill, juist you hae a look at me the neist time I come hame frae Sandy Morrison's. I can haurdly thole to be seen.'

'But my legs are sae skinny.'

'They juist look it the nou. It's because yer breeks are a wee thing shorter nor yer auld petticoats, and ye're showin white abune the knees. Wait till the sun wins at ye, and ye'll look fine.'

'Are ye shair?'

'Ay, come on in for yer tea.'

I kent ein at the time that he was leein, juist to please me, but in the end I got uised to mysell, and the ithers seemed to get uised to me tae.

: 'He's no very stoot aboot the legs, aither,' said Jockie. 'Ye'll hae to sup mair parritch, Rab, nou that ye're into breeks.'

ROBERT GARIOCH

Robert Garioch Sutherland (1909–81) served in the North African campaign and was a prisoner of war in Italy and Germany. His single prose work, *Two Men and a Blanket: Memoirs of Captivity*, published in 1975, is a vividly moving account of his experiences as a prisoner of war, reworking the chilling vision of his poem 'The Wire':

> The dugs loup on him, reivan flesh,
> crunchan the bane as they were wud;
> swith they come and swith are gane,
> syne nocht is left but pools of bluid.

Along with William Soutar and Sydney Goodsir Smith, Garioch was part of the generation of poets who followed Hugh MacDiarmid. His first poetry in Scots was written at Edinburgh University and he published his first piece in 1933. In 1941, with the Gaelic poet Somhairle MacGill-Eain (Sorley MacLean), whom he had met while a student, he published *Seventeen Poems for 6d*. This was followed in 1949 by *Chuckies on the Cairn*, Garioch's first pamphlet of eight poems, price one shilling. He typeset and printed these himself and, in the old chapman tradition, sold them by hand.

Introducing Garioch's *Selected Poems* in 1966, which he welcomed 'with shouts of joy and reverent hiccups', Sydney Goodsir Smith said Garioch sits easily in the company of Ramsay, Fergusson and Burns. Garioch felt an affinity with Fergusson. And though he translated Apollinaire, Pindar, Hesiod and George Buchanan, including the verse dramas *Jephthah* and *The Baptist*, his main translations were more than 120 sonnets of another kindred spirit, Guiseppe Belli, the nineteenth-century Roman poet.

Born in Wellington, New Zealand, Sydney Goodsir Smith (1915–75) came to Edinburgh – where his father was professor of forensic medicine – as a student. His adopted Scots was influenced by Dunbar, Henryson, Gavin Douglas, Fergusson and Burns but he fused this with his own voice to create a romantic, bawdy, compassionate tone which often pokes fun at himself. His best work, *Under the Eildon Tree*, was preceded in 1947 by his only novel, *Carotid Cornucopius*. It was, said MacDiarmid, 'as alive as an old tinker' and did for Edinburgh 'no less successfully what Joyce did for Dublin in *Ulysses*.'

: LESSON

I tuik it in ma heid to gae dounbye Leith Docks,
eftir hou monie years? I cannae mind,
binna[1] jist coming aff the ship frae Aiberdeen,
Saint Sunniva? Thae boats haena made that run for years.

I tuik the samyn gait that Stevenson[2] discryved.[3]

I yuistae like ships, but nou they're owre real for me.

The samyn gait as he's, binna five-hunner yairds
frae here to Heriot Row; his faither's lichthous tiles
are in his area yet, in some of his neibors' alsweill.

Leith wes a place for merchants, a century sinsyne,
wi weill-appyntit pubs whaur they cuid talk business,
carved wudden alcoves, tables, ye ken the kind of thing,
and I mind the time whan they still had that character about them,
whisky and port and buirdly[4] men wi confident heids.
Leith crined[5] in Embro's grup; Scotland in England's;
Britain in . . . ? Aweill, Leith's maistly rubble nou.

Stevenson likit ships, he says, while yet a bairn,
and he likit the walk to Leith, past yon stationer's shop,
aye thair yet and whiles wi a theatre in its windae.
While a bairn masel I didnae heed whit ma faither said about ships;
breakwaters and lichthouses wadnae be aa that real to Stevenson.

---

[1] except
[2] Robert Louis Stevenson's father was a harbour engineer and lighthouse builder, like
  his father before him.
[3] described   [4] sturdy   [5] shrunk

The Forth Brig is riveted wi plates like a ship yuistae be.
It isnae real to me, even to this day.
The side of a ship in a dry dock is a flegsom[6] thing.
Hou can a man spend his day near eneuch it to touch?
It wes the bottoms of ships that scunnert[7] ma faither as a laddie,
sae he wad aften tell me, the raws of rivet-heids
to be pentit wi red-leid, nae holidays oniewhaur,
the edges of plates hammert ticht wi the caulking-airn,
water ablow his plank, weit waas baith sides of him,
and the ship's bottom abuin his heid, *le rouge et le noir*.[8]
He wes learning nicht-schuil French and takkin an art-schuil cless.
He wad tell me aa this in the Twenties, on a Sunday fresh-air walk
to the end of the West Pier, as guid as a sail, cost naethin.

Sae here I wes, last week, aince mair at the famous corner,
wi Burns's statue, lately Moved On at enormous expense,
Constitution Street, Bernard Street, wi Commercial Street ayont the
brig,
braw, confident names, like the muckle heids of the merchants
snod in their carved alcoves, c.i.f. and f.o.b.,[9]
and Baltic Street aye thair, but whaur's the Baltic tred?
Whaur the Leith merchants? Whaur the tables and cushions?
This is the place aa richt; has memory gane wrang?
Nae sawdust on the flair, tho, jist guid Leith stour.

It's yin of thae near-island pubs, whaur ye glowre at the folk fornenst
ye owre a neutral space of sinks and glesses and pourin and splairgin.[10]
I tilt ma pint and a heavy swell rises throu the freith.

---

[6] frightening   [7] disgusted

[8] *The Red and the Black*: the title of a novel by Stendhal, referring to the military and the
   Church. Also the colours of anarchism

[9] Cost/insurance/freight | free/on/board   [10] splashing

Stevenson's faither, he tells us, suffered ae major defeat;
He cuidnae mak Wick Hairbour siccar. This ae failure
is a meisure of the sea's virr[11] he owrecam aawhair else,
Stevenson felt this, maybe later in life,
haean walit by that time words insteid of stanes.
They were trying a new idea, the last time I saw Wick,
piling concrete calthrops[12] in the newest hole in the waa.
Meantime I hadnae noticed something byordnar gaun on,
aabody luikan ae airt, at naething that I cuid see.
A scrauchin and duntin and yowlin, full blast, wi nae warning,
stertit up at the end of the room, frae a lit-up gless case
switched on, it wad seem, by a lassie in a see-throu pink gounie,
yin of thae go-go girls that I hae heard tell about.
Aweil, she wes nae gret dancer, but bonnie and clean,
and her taes gaed neatly eneuch owre yon dirt-coloured flair,
the same that we strampit about on, in shoon or working-buitts.
But this wee dance wes just whit ye micht cry an eye-opener.
She disappeart ahint the Gents, til some cubby-hole of her ain,
syne cam back in a kinna bathing-suit, aa ticht and trig,
and danced maist eydently up and doun, clawing the air,
perfectly douce and assured, as tho she cuid dae it aa nicht,
like Tchaikowsky whan stumpt for ideas, makkan-dae wi passage-wark.
Syne, for a bit of a cheenge, she gaed roun the har's peninsula
by whit passage-wey there wes, neatly wan throu.
The folk lookit on calmly, wi interest, respect and pleisor,
tho wi the faces of men, had luikit aa day at the side of a ship,
as yon lassie's clean taes acceptit the ordinary stourie flair.

Guillaume Apollinaire, wad ye hae gliskit here
a phantom of Leith haar? Duis it still glimmer thair?

---

[11] energy
[12] angular blocks; lit: star-shaped iron spikes to be scattered against medieval cavalry.

JEANNIE ROBERTSON

Travellers speak of the Mysie. For them it is the mark of authenticity. Voice, performance and style are secondary, they're looking for the feeling and for an expression of that feeling, for the hairs to rise on the back of the neck.

Anyone who heard Jeannie Robertson (1908–78) sing this version of the ballad 'Edward' knew about the Mysie. No matter how often she sang it or how often one heard her sing it, she brought a sense of occasion to every performance, which made it both moving and direct.

This is not a complete version. Others have an incest motif, where the elder brother kills the younger because of their sister's love, which goes some way to explaining the comprehensive expulsion in this version, something not usual in murder ballads. The ballads often treat murder as justified or at least as an inevitable consequence. Here the sense of banishment is complete, even though the sister has been airbrushed out of the ballad.

Versions of ballads collected in the field are rarely as full as the printed sources. This obviously has to do with memory but also with the singer's personal requirements and the way he/she views the song.

Jeannie Robertson MBE was a traveller, first recorded by the American folklorist Alan Lomax. He came to Scotland in 1951, returning in 1953 and 1957, and with the assistance of Hamish Henderson, Calum and Sorley MacLean and William Montgomerie, recorded dozens of hours of ballads, work songs, children's songs and contemporary folk songs from performers such as John Burgess, John Strachan, Jimmy MacBeath, Davy Stewart, Flora MacNeill, Isla Cameron and Ewan MacColl.

: SON DAVID

'Oh, what's the blood 'it's on your sword,
    My son David, ho, son David?
What's that blood 'it's on your sword?
    Come, promise, tell me true.'

'Oh, that's the blood of my grey meer,[1]
    Hey, lady Mother, ho, lady Mother,
That's the blood of my grey meer,
    Because it wadnae rule by me.'

'Oh, that blood it is owre clear,
    My son David, ho, son David,
That blood it is owre clear,
    Come, promise, tell me true.'

'Oh, that's the blood of my greyhound,
    Hey, lady Mother, ho, lady Mother,
That's the blood of my greyhound,
    Because it wadnae rule by me.'

'Oh, that blood it is owre clear,
    My son David, ho, son David,
That blood it is owre clear,
    Come, promise, tell me true.'

'Oh, that's the blood of my huntin hawk,
    Hey, lady Mother, ho, lady Mother,
That's the blood of my huntin hawk,
    Because it wadnae rule by me.'

[1] mare

'Oh, that blood it is owre clear,
    My son David, ho, son David,
That blood it is owre clear,
    Come, promise, tell me true.'

'For that's the blood of my brother John,
    Hey, lady Mother, ho, lady Mother,
That's the blood of my brother John,
    Because he wadnae rule by me.'

'Oh, I'm gaun awa in a bottomless boat,
    In a bottomless boat, in a bottomless boat,
For I'm gaun awa in a bottomless boat,
    An I'll never return again.'

'Oh, whan will you come back again,
    My son David, ho, son David?
Whan will you come back again?
    Come, promise, tell me true.'

'When the sun an the moon meet in yon glen,
    Hey, lady Mother, ho, lady Mother,
When the sun an the moon meet in you glen,
    For I'll return again.'

: *'Oh, what's the blood 'it's on your sword,*
My son David, ho, son David?'

HAMISH HENDERSON

Hamish Henderson (1919–2002) was born in Blairgowrie. After his death, it emerged he was the illegitimate son of the Duke of Atholl's cousin, and a direct descendant of Robert Bruce. Educated at Dulwich College and Cambridge University, to anyone in the Scottish folk scene the name Hamish was enough to identify him.

His war experiences, in the Desert campaign in Sicily and Italy, inspired *Elegies for the Dead in Cyrenaica*, an outstanding, clear and compassionate view of war, published in 1948. He had already started song writing and as a collector later gathered versions of his work, such as 'The Ballad of the D-Day Dodgers', 'The 51st Highland Division's Farewell to Sicily' and 'The John MacLean March'.

Following his time collecting with Alan Lomax in Aberdeenshire in 1951, he became a 'temporary honorary research fellow' at the new School of Scottish Studies at Edinburgh University and in 1954 he was offered a permanent post. The man whom Sorley MacLean called Comrade Captain lived for months at a time with the travellers, collecting songs, ballads and stories, gathering an oral tradition that had been overlooked or ignored by previous collectors. He was a prime mover in the Edinburgh People's Festival Ceilidhs, a forerunner of the Edinburgh Festival Fringe and the first public platforms shared by traditional and revivalist singers.

Songs like 'The Flyting o' Life and Daith' and 'The Ballad o the Speakin Heart' brought a literary aspect to Scottish folk song; however, Hamish was embarrassed when 'The Freedom Come-All-Ye' was suggested as a National Anthem, pointing out that internationalism, rather than nationalism, is at its heart.

He publicly turned down an OBE in 1983 in protest to the Thatcher government's nuclear arms policy and was, as a result, voted Scot of the Year by listeners to Radio Scotland. 'OBE failed,' said Norman MacCaig.

: THE FREEDOM COME-ALL-YE

Roch the wind in the clear day's dawin
    Blaws the cloods heelster-gowdie ow'r the bay,
But there's mair nor a roch wind blawin
    Through the great glen o' the warld the day.
It's a thocht that will gar oor rottans
    – A' they rogues that gang gallus, fresh and gay –
Tak the road, and seek ither loanins
    For their ill ploys, tae sport and play

Nae mair will the bonnie callants
    Mairch tae war when oor braggarts crousely craw,
Nor wee weans frae pit-heid and clachan
    Mourn the ships sailin' doon the Broomielaw.
Broken faimlies in lands we've herriet,
    Will curse Scotland the Brave nae mair, nae mair;
Black and white, ane til ither mairriet,
    Mak the vile barracks o' their maisters bare.

So come all ye at hame wi' Freedom,
    Never heed whit the hoodies croak for doom.
In your hoose a' the bairns o' Adam
    Can find bried, barley-bree and painted room.
When MacLean meets wi's freens in Springburn
    A' the roses and geans will turn tae bloom,
And a black boy frae yont Nyanga
    Dings the fell gallows o' the burghers doon.

JOHN STEWART   :

Tinkers were traditionally regarded as entertainers as well as craftsmen and the discovery of their oral traditions by twentieth-century collectors provided an audience rather than turned them into public entertainers. Because they lived on the fringes of society, they acquired little in the way of sophistication and therefore kept their stories, songs and language alive.

John Stewart's father was a piper to Lord Ward of Dudley at Dunkeld House before the First World War. John was born in Aldour, Pitlochry, in 1910; and, as Sheila Douglas, who recorded John, his brother Alec and sister-in-law Belle Stewart (better known as the Stewarts of Blair) notes, the image of the Perthshire landscape is ever present. 'John Stewart's memory is a repository of old story motifs, which he understands perfectly and which he shakes like pieces in a kaleidoscope into new patterns, sometimes making new stories that are just as traditional in their motifs as the old ones he tells.'

'The King o' the Black Art' is listed in the Aarne Thomson index of tale-types as no. 325, 'The Magician and his Pupil'. The Grimm Brothers knew it well and spoken or sung versions have popped up across Europe.

: THE KING O THE BLACK ART

Once upon a time, not in my time, nor in your time, but in somebody's time, there was an auld fisherman and his wife stayed at the side o this sea loch. He fished every day and they were lonely because they had nae family. One day he was doon mendin his nets and lookin at his boat an he saw this thing floatin into the side o the water. He never bothered aboot it for a while, then curiosity got the better o him and he went to look at it and it was a basket, lined so that the water couldnae get in, and there was an infant in the basket. He carried the wean up tae his wife in the wee fisher cottage and he says, 'Look what I've got for you doon at the side o the water.'

'Aw,' she says, 'a wee laddie! Gie me it here an I'll gie it milk. It's maybe stervin o hunger.' She gets the wean an she warms it at the fire an heats milk for it an feeds it wi a wee horn spoon.

The wean thrived and they reared him an reared him. When he came to about fourteen he would be doon wi the auld fisherman helpin him wi his nets helpin him tae fish. One bright early mornin, the auld fisherman an laddie were doon at the waterside daein somethin wi the boat, when they saw this ship. It lowered a boat and the auld man looked. 'Oh,' he says, 'that's somebody of importance. I can see jewels an a crown upon his head. He's some kind o king fae a foreign land!'

So they looked again an saw the man standin in the bow o the boat, an he was throwin three golden balls wi spikes up in the air an catchin them again. Then the boat came ashore and this king stepped oot o the boat ontae the beach an he comes up tae the auld man an he says, 'Good-morning, old man.'

'Oh,' he says, 'good mornin, your honour, your highness.'

'What do you do here?'

'Well I just fish and do one thing and another like that.'

'There'll not be much livelihood in that?'

'No,' he says, 'there's not.'

Then the king says, 'That's a nice boy you've got there. What age is he?'

'Fourteen,' he says.

'He's a strappin fellow. He'll be a fine man yet, that boy. Has he nothin to do?'

'Well,' he says, 'he helps me with the nets and the fishin and he's handy aboot the hoose for splittin sticks an goin for wood to the auld wife when she's cookin. We'd miss him if he wisnae there.'

The king says, 'I'll tell ye what I'll do. If you lend him to me for a year, let ye see a man made o him.'

'Oh,' says the auld man, 'I couldna dae that. My wife would kill me. I'd be feart, in fact, tae go an ask her.'

'You go an ask her,' he says, 'and see what she says. Or let me have a talk wi her. I'll make your boy worth his weight in gold.'

The auld man says, 'I'll ask her.' So he went up an explained it tae the auld wife but oh she wouldnae! No! No! 'But look,' he says, 'the laddie's daein nothin here, anyway, he's only wastin his time. That man is willin tae tak him an learn him some kind o a trade. We're as well lettin him go for the sake o a year when it's benefitin him.'

After a lot o argy-bargying the auld wife consents tae let him go for a year, so the laddie takes his bits o things wi him, cuddles his auld mither, shakes hands wi his faither, jumps on the boat an is away out tae the ship.

The auld man and the auld woman come up tae the hoose an she's sittin an she's greetin an she's sayin tae him, 'It wis you that made me pit the laddie away.' As the weeks went in, she was waitin then for the year an a day comin up. The auld man's away fishin and workin here an there an the year an a day was a long time in draggin by.

But at last the year an a day was by an the auld man's up bright an early an he's down on the beach and here the boat comes right roon an up tae the shore. An his son's standin on deck throwin three poison balls wi spikes in them up above his heid, golden poison balls wi spikes in them, an catchin them wi his feet. The auld man says, 'Oh my goodness! What that laddie can do now!'

So the laddie came ashore an cuddlet his faither an mither and gave them what money he had an telt them aboot the great castle he was in miles away.

The king says, 'Ye think that's good, what he's doin now, but if ye lend him tae me anither year an a day, I'll make him twice as good.' He gave them two or three gold pieces an the auld wife consented tae let her son go for another year an a day. The laddie shakes hands wi them again and says, 'It'll no be lang in passin, mither, it'll be nae time.'

'Ah,' she says, 'it's aa right for you, away in strange places, wi things tae look at. But we're in the wilderness here an it's a lang time o passin.'

But anyway the laddie goes away an the boat turns an hoochs away intae the horizon out o sight. The auld man keeps on fishin an mendin his nets. Eventually time drags on and drags on till the year an a day was up again. He couldnae sleep that night. He couldnae sleep a week before the boat would come. But he's down on the beach waitin an here the boat comes again. His son's standin wi a shimmerin kin o gold suit on him an he's firin seven poison balls in the air, golden balls wi jags on them like horse chestnuts. Oh the faither was well-pleased wi him, so was his mither. He gies his father an mither handfu's o money an they give the king refreshment.

'Now,' says the king, 'this'll be his last year. If ye let him go for anither year an a day, I'll let you see that your son *is* a man!'

So they consented again and the laddie goes away wi the king in the boat. Time's slow o passin an it's makin the auld woman argue wi her husband, when the laddie's no there and her sittin aboot the hoose thinkin. But time creeps by till the year an a day was up again. The auld man's doon on the beach lookin an lookin an lookin. He stood aa day–but there was no boat! When he comes back tae the hoose, his wife's lookin wi her hand up tae her eyes tae see better an when she sees the laddie's no there, she takes a stick an she's layin intae the auld man. 'You'll pack up tomorrow mornin,' she says, 'an you'll go an search for my laddie.'

Next day she gies him some barley bannocks an his pipe an tabaccy an he says fareweel tae her. 'I'll get him,' he says, 'wadnae matter if it were the ends the earth I'll find him.'

So he's on an on an on, owre sheep's parks, bullocks' parks an aa the parks o Yarrow an through wuds an down glens an up hills. In those days the hooses was very scarce in the forest an hills an if ye did come tae a bare bit o grun, it was a moor. An he comes owre this place an down intae a great dell, where the trees were sae high it was as dark as a dungeon. An he comes tae a wee hoose in the wud made wi sticks an bits o trees and an auld man came oot. 'Aha,' he says, 'I've been expectin ye.'

'I dinna ken whaur I'm gaun,' he says. 'I'm lookin for my son.' An he tells, the auld man what happened. He says, 'I know where your son is. He's only aboot three days march fae here. But ye'll need tae watch what you're doin for that's the King o the Black Art. Ye'll have tae be very, very careful. Rest the night here and when ye go away in the mornin, I'll tell ye whit tae dae.'

So the auld fisherman stayed in the hut aa night an in the mornin he got a taste o meat. The auld man says tae him, 'I'll tell ye, keep due north, straight as a die. Ye can't miss the castle after three days' march. When ye go tae it, go straight up to the front door. Don't go down any back ways. Go straight to the big front door and pull the bell. He'll send a but-ler out. Tell him you don't want to see the butler. Ye want tae see the king himself, or ye'll make the highest stone in the castle the lowest in five minutes. And he'll come. When ye ask aboot your son he'll start arguin wi ye that he's no there, but keep persevering and he'll go in and come oot again wi twelve pigeons strung on his arm. He'll say tae ye tae pick your son oot o that an he'll throw the pigeons up in the air. Now, there'll be one wee plucky feathert cratur among them, flyin half sideweys. You would think it wis in the moult, and aa gutters. Tell him ye'll tak that one.'

So the auld fisherman spits on his stick, thanks the auld man an he's off through the forest, marchin an marchin, drink o water here, drink o water here. On the dawnin o the third day, he looks doon on this valley an there's this great castle. He couldnae get doon tae it quickly enough, he's faain an stumblin owre bushes an roots. He goes right up tae the front door an pulls the big bell. Out comes this uniformed butler an says, 'What do you want? You know this is the king's palace that you're at?'

He says, 'Go an tell the king I want to see him immediately or I'm gaun tae mak the highest stone in his castle the lowest in five minutes.'

So he goes in and a while after that, out comes the king. Oh he knew him right away when he saw him. 'I've come,' says the fisherman, 'tae see where ma son is.'

'Oh,' he says 'I don't know where your son is.'

'Now,' he says 'don't come that. You got my son away for a year and a day an he come back. Ye got him for another year an a day an he come back. But the third time ye took him away, he never come back. Now I want him back.'

'Well,' he says, 'wait here and I'll go in an see if I can get him.'

So the king went in an in aboot quarter o an oor he comes out an he has twelve pigeons on his airm. 'There ye are,' he says, 'pick your son oot o that.' An he throws the pigeons up in the air. So the auld man looks at aa these lovely pigeons flyin aboot. This wee one is flutter, flutter, fluttering at the side, wi dirty skittery-lookin feathers on it. He says, 'I think I'll chance takin that wee one at the bottom, that bad-looking one.'

'Well,' he says, 'take him an be damned tae ye. May the Devil take away your learnin-master.' He claps his hands an just like that the boy was standin at his side.

So the faither says, 'Come on then, we'll get oot o here.' So the faither and son walks oot crackin away an he asks his son what happened.

'Oh,' he says, 'he's an enchanter, King o the Black Art, but I've learned that much o him that I can dae nearly everything that he can dae. Noo when we go back yon road, we'll come tae a congregation o hooses, a wee village place, where there'll be a fair. When we go there, I'll turn masel intae a greyhound dog, wi a lovely big brass-studded, buckled collar an lead on ma neck. They're great men roon this airt for good dogs, an they'll be at ye for tae sell the dog. Ask a thousand gold pieces for me an ye'll get it, but when ye give me away, don't part wi the collar an leash.'

So they come tae this fair an there were stalls an men drinkin an women an lassies an weans squealin an runnin up an doon. As one man passes he asks, 'How much for the dog?'

'I'll take a thousand gold bits for it,' he says.

'Well I don't know about that. I'll give ye five hundred.'

'Naw, naw, naw.'

But eventually he sells it for the thousand gold pieces. 'There's your dog,' he says, 'but I wouldnae take ten thousand for the collar that's on its neck. It's a keepsake.' So he lowsed the belt and put a string on the dog's neck and handed it tae the man, who went away with it.

In just about five minutes his son was standin at his fit. He says, 'Well done father. When we get home tae ma auld mither, we'll have some money.'

So they goes on again, on again. 'Now,' says the son, 'at the next place we come to, there'll be a horse fair. I'll turn masel intae a lovely black stallion. Ye can sell me for a lot o money, but don't sell the bridle, the halter that's on ma heid.'

So the father says, 'All right then. Fine.'

On they comes tae this toon an the ither fair. There's horses an cattle an goats an everythin like that. But the king o the Black Art had turned hissel intae a man that was lookin for a horse, an he wisnae far off. The boy turned hissel intae this black stallion an he's kickin his heels, he's jumpin an he's even clearin some o the stalls. So the King o the Black Art comes up tae him an says, 'Hello! Wad ye sell yer horse?'

'Oh,' he says, 'that's what I'm here for.'

'Well,' he says, 'how much dae ye want for him?'

'I'll take five thousand.'

'Oh I wouldnae give ye that,' says the King. 'I could buy a good horse for less than that.'

'Oh but ye'll no buy one like this.' An the horse is buck-leppin an skirlin up in the air.

'Well, I don't know how good he is. If I could get a ride on his back—'

'Oh I'm afraid I canny do that. I wouldnae let ye ride him.'

'He wouldnae be much good tae me unless I got a try on him.'

'No', says the fisherman, 'I wouldnae like tae dae that.'

'I tell ye what,' says the King. 'Come here.' An he opened the door o this shed. 'See that heap o gold there? I'll gie ye that heap o gold if ye let me test him tae the end o the village an back.'

'Very temptin,' says the old man, lookin at the gold. So he gives the King the halter and he jumped on its back and away! Off!

The old man's tearin his hair, now. He doesnae know what to do. An the heap o gold was just a pile o dung. The King o the Black Art takes the horse back to the castle. He tells his grooms tae tie him up. 'Never take the bridle off his heid and don't give him anything but a bucket o salt beef a day. No water! I'm warnin youse!'

So the horse was in the stall an, efter a week o this, his tongue is swollen up an cracked for lack o water. The stable door looked oot on a lovely wee stream runnin doon. When the groom came in wi the bucket o salt beef, he says 'Look, wad ye no gie me a drink o water?'

'I can't,' he says. 'It wad be more than my life's worth tae gie ye one spot o water, because *he* would know right away.'

The next day passed an the next. An he asked the groom again. 'Look, dinny take the water intae me. Lead me oot tae that wee stream till I get wettin ma tongue at it. Oh if I could just get wan dip o the water!'

'Well,' says the groom, 'I'll take ye oot by the halter an I'll pit your nose in it. But never say I've done this, or my heid'll be on the poisoned spears afore sunset.'

So the groom lowses the rope, leads the horse oot tae the water an the horse is snuffin and snuffin. 'Look, groom,' he says, 'I canny get right doon. The rope's too short. Could ye no slacken the halter so that I can get a right drink?'

The groom says, 'You'll be the daith o me,' and he lowses the halter and the boy dives in the burn as a salmon an he's off!

Aa the bells in the castle started tae ring and the King o the Black Art was oot on the hill wi his two sons wild boar huntin, an they heard the bells. 'That horse has escaped!' he says. So in two or three minutes they were doon an they changed themselves intae three otters an they're doon the burn an doon the burn, efter the salmon. An soon they're just aboot a table's length off him. An he changed hissel intae a swallow in the air. They changed intae three hawks an they're chasin this swallow an chasin it an chasin it. An it's divin an dippin and swervin an it comes across this hoose an there's a woman sittin in the gairden sewin. An he changes intae a ring on the wumman's finger. An the hawks is fleein aboot.

An the ring speaks tae the wumman an she looks aa roon aboot for the voice. 'It's me,' he says, 'I'm on your finger. Don't be frightened,' he says.

'Oh,' she says, 'where did that ring come from?'

'Look,' he says, 'there'll be three gold dealers come an they'll promise ye the world for it, but I'll tell ye whit tae dae. Go an build a big fire in your back yard an have it blazin because they'll be here before long. Walk by the fire when they're askin tae buy the ring off ye an before ye'll give it tae them, tell them ye'd rather fling it intae the fire. Then throw it straight intae the heart o the fire. Now be sure an do that. Give me your word.'

She says, 'All right, I'll do that.'

So she went and made a big fire and the fire was roastin the same as burnin brushwood. A while after that, roon comes these three men, tappin the doors, lookin for gold. It was the King o the Black Art an his two sons. 'Good mornin, ma'am,' he says, 'Have you any gold pieces or anything at all in the jewellery line tae buy off ye, this mornin?'

'No,' she says, 'I haven't a thing.'

'That's a nice ring ye've got there. Will ye not sell it tae me?'

'No,' she says, 'I wouldn't take any money for it.'

'I'll give ten thousand.'

'I wouldn't take anything for it. I wouldn't sell it at all.' An she's walkin back by the fire. 'In fact before I wad sell it, I'd rather do that!' An she flung it straight intae the heart o the ragin fire.

So the King o the Black Art an his two sons they turned theirsels intae three blacksmiths wi bellows an they blew the fire an blew the fire an blew the fire till there were just three or four wee red grains left. Then the boy changed hissel intae a seed o corn among the bags o barley the woman had for feedin her hens. They changed theirsels intae three cocks an they picked the barley an picked the barley an picked the barley, till they were that fu they could hardly move. Then he changed hissel intae a real savage fox and snapped the heids off the three cocks. An that was the end o the King o the Black Art.

: *An the ring speaks tae the wumman an she looks aa roon aboot for the voice. 'It's me,' he says, 'I'm on your finger. Don't be frightened,' he says.*

EDWIN MORGAN

Trying to summarise Edwin Morgan's poetry is difficult. He is continually inquisitive, open-minded, tender and humane, has translated a variety of European poets, experimented with the language of machines, Egyptian mummies and spacemen, created and abandoned his own techniques and devised everything from sonnets to concrete and sound poems. His work is modernist, inventive, energetic, firmly grounded in Scotland and exhilarating, though each new departure appears to outdate his capacity and unpredictable novelty.

On 21 December 1965 he constructed a recognisable map out of local names for our most common garden bird.

'It's always very hard to define something like Scottishness,' he said. 'I think in a certain context if it's felt to be important to try to establish identity then people will do this even although they won't always convince people outside.

'I'm a pretty strong anti-traditionalist. I really on the whole dislike history and tradition. I'm interested in what is happening. I'm interested in what will happen, more than I'm interested in what has happened.'

:THE CHAFFINCH MAP OF SCOTLAND

```
                    chaffinch
                chaffinchaffinch
            chaffinchaffinchaffinch
            chaffinchaffinchaffinch
                chaffinchaffinch
                    chaffinch
                    chaffie      chye      chaffiechaffie
                    chaffie      chye      chaffiechaffie
                                 chye  chaffie
                    chaffiechaffiechaffie
                    chaffiechaffiechaffie
                        chaffiechaffie
                        chaffiechaffie
                        chaffiechaffie
                        chaffiechaffie


                        shillyshelly
                shelfyshilfyshellyshilly
                    shelfyshillyshilly
                    shilfyshellyshelly
                shilfyshelfyshelly
                        shellyfaw
                    shielyshellyfaw

            shilfy
        shilfyshelfy shielyshiely
    shilfyshelfyshelfy            shielychaffie
        chaffiechaffie            chaffiechaffie
        chaffiechaffie
    shilfyshilfyshilfyshelfyshelfy
chaffieshilfyshilfyshelfyshelfyshelfyshelfy
chaffieshilfyshilfyshelfyshelfyshelfyshelfyshelfyshelfy
    shilfyshilfyshilfyshelfy            shelfyshelfy
    shilfy        shilfy
                  shilfy
                  shilfyshelfy
        brichtie
```

ADAM MCNAUGHTAN

His album *Words, Words, Words* offers an introduction of sorts: 'I, Adam McNaughtan, being of sound mind, write my own sleeve notes. I . . . sing my own and other people's songs without accompaniment. My detractors claim that I only break the monotony by pitching every third song too high.' And in *Last Stand at Mount Florida* he adds, 'The chief function of my singing is to cheer myself up.'

It goes without saying that the man who reduced Hamlet to three minutes is one of our best songwriters. His work is as diverse, inventive and exciting as any. He is a champion of popular music, from nineteenth-century broadsides and music halls to Matt McGinn, and his enormous range, learning and love of the subject is obvious in everything he does. He edited a volume of the Greig-Duncan manuscripts, is a fund of knowledge about Glasgow life and song, has a strong interest in things Scandinavian and spent a year or more cataloguing the Poet's Box, a collection of about 3,000 broadsides, dating from about 1850 to the First World War.

Many of us are waiting for Adam McNaughtan to produce an edition of his own songs, or the kids' songs he's gathered, or even to edit a selection of the material he sings. 'Where Is The Glasgow?' was quoted by Prince Charles at the opening of the Glasgow Garden Festival and 'The Jeely Piece Song' is the city's best-known anthem. 'The Yellow on the Broom' was inspired by Betsy Whyte's book and she used to sing Adam's song. 'Erchie Cathcairt' mocks healthy eating and 'Cholesterol' prompted the sleeve note, 'Glasgow is recognised as the heart disease capital of the universe. Glasgow doesnae care.'

His work sits best beside a Glasgow accent and perspective, an English which, he says, in common with us all, is uniquely individual, influenced by the Scots he absorbed as a reader, the language he heard as a child, and American film.

'The Scottish Song' is the second of four Shakespeare abbreviations and is sung to the tune 'Soldier's Joy'.

:THE SCOTTISH SONG

TUNE: 'Soldier's Joy' (AAB)

When the Scots had smashed the Norsemen, like steelies against
    jauries,
Oor Generals, Macbeth and Banquo, walked it back tae Forres,
They met three dames that did a kinna fortune-tellin' thing,
Who hailt Macbeth an' tellt him he'd be Cawdor, Glamis an' King.

Then Macbeth fell in a dwam but Banquo says, 'Haud on a wee!
'Ye've a loat tae say to him, huv ye got onythin' for me?'
The witches said, 'The good news first an' then the bad we'll tell:
'Ye'll faither loatsa kings but ye'll no' be wan yersel.'

When the King said, 'Ye're the hauder o' the title "Thane o'
    Cawdor"'.
Macbeth wis fair excitit an' ambitious tae get oan
But his jaw near hut the flair when he heard the King declare,
'Ma boay's the Prince o' Cumberland an' heir tae the throne.'

Macbeth, afore the rest, went rushin' hameward at full tilt,
Tae let his wife know she wid need tae air the king-size quilt.
She says, 'Ye're mad tae say it or else Duncan's aff his heid.
'Cause if he sleeps here the night he's gonnae waken up deid.

Then Macbeth convinced himsel' that his motives were the best:
That he widnae murder Duncan as his cousin, King an' guest.
'Ye're a coward, ye're a beast an' you don't love me!' says his wife,
'An' we'll blame it oan the guairds.' Says he, 'Juist ca' me "Mac the
    Knife!"'

So he killt Duncan and his lady smeart the drunken
Guairds wi' bluid an says, 'C'moan tae bed. It's easy as snuff.'
But Malcolm shot the craw, an' so did Donalbain an' a'
An' they didnae baffle Banquo an' they didnae fool Macduff.

Then Macbeth invitit Banquo to a feast as guest of honour,
Eftir hirin' three miscreants tae make sure he wis a goner.
An' at the feast he simpert aboot Banquo no' bein' there
But then he hud tae staun 'cause Banquo's ghost wis in his chair.

But what made him loass his marbles wis when wan o' the miscreants
Came an' said they'd malkied Banquo, but they'd missed the fleein'
        Fleance.
'Avaunt!' he starts, but Lady Mac says, 'Friends, the party's closed,
'An' ye must excuse ma husband, he's a wee bit indisposed.'

    Banquo's line upoan the throne juis' so obsessed his haill
        subconcious
    That he ordert them tae kill Macduff, wife, weans, cats, dugs, the
        loat.
    Lady Mac says, 'Ah must try, if anything that Ah can buy.
    Persil, Ariel, Daz or Flash'll shift this bluidy spot.

But Macduff wis aff tae England for tae fetch back Malkie,
An' the boay says, 'Ah'm nae use. Juist a randy greedy alkie.'
Cries Macduff, 'Ma hope ends here!' Malkie says, 'Ah'm only kiddin'
'Ah'll lead an army north an' cut doon trees tae keep it hidden.'

Macbeth meanwhile decidit the weird sisters tae get haud ae
An' he fund them bilin' soup wi' Tartars' lips tae gie it body.
They tellt him he could not be killt by man that's born o' wumman,
An' he didnae need tae fear till he saw Birnam wuid was comin.

    So Macbeth became quite gallus, he had nothin' left but malice;
    He couldnae show emotions like compassion, joy or sorra,
    When he heard his wife had died, he juist said, 'Ah wid've cried,
    'If it had been the morra an' the morra an' the morra.'

Though a' his pals had skied it, he was safe in Dunsinane,
An' he passed the time by pittin' armour oan an' aff again.
Then the news that Birnam wuid wis oan the mairch gied him a scare.
He says, 'We'll fight ootside, Ah don't want bluid a' ower ma flair.'

He wis swashin', he was bucklin', he talked Siward's boay tae death,
But his confidence wis shattert when Macduff shouts, 'Hey, Macbeth!'
'Against men o' weemen born,' he says, 'Ah've goat divine protection.'
Quips Macduff, 'Ah wis delivert by Caesarian section.'

Then Macduff cut aff his heid an' when he saw that he wis deid,
Malkie says, 'Yese a' are earls, come oan alang tae Scone.'
So noo the play is played an the best that can be said:
    It's juist hauf the length o' 'Hamlet' when the curtain comes doon.

TOM LEONARD

The poster for the Makars' Society advertises a

GRAN' MEETIN'
THE NICHT
TAE DECIDE THE
SPELLIN'
O' THIS POSTER

And the admission price is Thritty pee (a heid)

This wasn't the only anachronism in the language argument Tom Leonard spotted. On the publication of *Six Glasgow Poems* in 1969 he altered the argument and rules of engagement by introducing the urban voice and insisting it should be heard, transcribing living Glaswegian speech to prove that language is defined by class as much as by region or country and that working-class speech is as suitable a vehicle for poetry and serious thought as any other; an argument James Kelman and Irvine Welsh extended into prose.

His anthology *Radical Renfrew* reintroduced more than sixty writers and showed the people of the West of Scotland and, by implication, the rest of the country that working-class poetry, concerned with working-class issues, was at the heart of their culture. It also showed the extent to which the local, working-class voice had been devalued.

: THE VOYEUR

what's your favourite word dearie
is it wee
I hope it's wee
wee's such a nice wee word
like a wee hairy dog
with two wee eyes
such a nice wee word to play with dearie
you can say it quickly
with a wee smile
and a wee glance to the side
or you can say it slowly dearie
with your mouth a wee bit open
and a wee sigh dearie
a wee sigh
put your wee head on my shoulder dearie
oh my
a great wee word
and Scottish
it makes you proud

KATHLEEN JAMIE   ⋮

In 'Arraheids' and 'The Queen of Sheba' Kathleen Jamie asks, 'Whae dae ye think ye ur?'

It's a question loaded with disapproval, directed at the educated, the exotic and the feminine. It suggests suspicion of aspirations and dreams, of questioning too deeply for one's own good. In 'Arraheids' the museum pieces are 'a show of grannies' tongues', which is dismissive of their grand setting, though she puts the record straight with a tart 'Ye arenae here tae wonder'.

The *Queen of Sheba* collection, published in 1994, saw Kathleen Jamie confront her Scottishness and the conflicting emotions it aroused in her. But this is only part of her work. Jamie is no pedagogue and subscribes to no simplistic views. From the earliest poems, her work speaks for itself – it is not part of a clique but rather a tradition with which she often wrestles.

This realisation brings a tenderness which fits easily with her unflinching eye. Through the skill and beauty of her verse, she redeems the harsh realities of lives plainly lived and long forgotten. In 'Mr and Mrs Scotland Are Dead' she picks through a handful of meagre possessions and forms a connection between the university graduate and people who are confined by their narrow existences – one day, perhaps, her possessions will be sifted and discarded.

In 'Child with Pillar Box and Bin Bags' a young mother takes a picture of her child, watching the people

[on] the other side of the street to that she'd chosen
if she'd chosen or thought it possible to choose.

Yet something harks back to a different world and different times. In the poem 'Fountain', throwing a penny for luck is a subconsciously remembered tradition and, briefly, the modern plastic environment of the shopping mall is transcended:

Who says
we can't respond; don't still feel,
as it were, the dowser's twitch
up through the twin handles of the buggy.

In 'Den of the Old Men' she constructs a myth of freedom for the 'auld buggers' set in their ways, as seemingly being typical of the old Scotland just like the John Bull puncture-repair kits flung on the scrap heap of 'Mr and Mrs Scotland Are Dead'. Yet these are 'half dozen relics of strong men', with their dominoes, their arguments and wee brown dugs. The poet imagines them building their own means of escaping the confinements of their lives, using what the land provides and their ingenuity supplies. It is a poem full of hope and affirmation: 'this first spring day', the old men sailing off, back to the heart of the land that bore them,

> the lot of yez
> staring straight ahead
> like captains . . .

. . . .

:DEN OF THE OLD MEN

C'mon ye auld buggers, one by one
this first spring day, slowly down
the back braes with your walking sticks
and wee brown dugs, saying: *Aye, lass*
a snell wind yet but braw. Ye
half dozen relics of strong men
sat in kitchen chairs
behind the green gingham curtain
of yer den, where a wee dog grins
on last year's calendar – we hear ye
clacking dominoes the afternoon for pennies.
And if some wee tyke
puts a chuckie through the window
ye stuff yesterday's Courier
in the broken pane, saying
jail's too guid fur them, tellies in cells!

We can see your bunnets nod
and jaws move: what're ye up to
now you've your hut built,
now green hame-hammered benches
appear in the parish's secret soft-spots
like old men's spoor?
Is it carties? A tree-hoose?
Or will ye drag up driftwood;
and when she's busy with the bairns
remove your daughters' washing-lines
to lash a raft? Which,
if ye don't all fall out and argue
you can name the *Pride o' Tay* and launch
some bright blue morning on the ebb-tide
and sail away, the lot of yez,
staring straight ahead
               like captains
as you grow tiny
out on the wide Firth, tiny
as you drift past Ballinbriech, Balmurnie, Flisk
with your raincoats and bunnets,
               wee dugs and sticks.